Champions of Change

The Manager's Guide to Creating Sustainable
Business Process Improvements

Jeffrey A. Berk

ISBN 10: 1-932205-95-0 • ISBN 13: 978-1-932205-95-4
Library of Congress Control Number: 2004101039

Word Association Publishers
205 Fifth Avenue,
Tarentum, Pennsylvania 15084
www.wordassociation.com

Overview

This book is a teaching tool for all managers regardless of their industry or functional area. It educates managers on the concepts and tools needed in future leadership positions to make changes in the areas for which they have accountability. Specifically, a performance improvement methodology is presented along with constructive tools to apply the methodology. Application of the methodology to business processes is detailed in the book. The processes that will be examined through detailed case studies in the book are 1) Finance and Accounting, 2) Human Resources, 3) Supply Chain, 4) Customer Relationship Management, and 5) Information Resource Management. However, practitioners have found the book to be an excellent guide for any process or industry. It is a one-stop shop for any manager targeted for leadership potential.

Special features of this book that will benefit any manager include:

- a methodology of performance improvement in business processes
- a detailed background with case studies on key continuous improvement movements, including Six Sigma, ISO, and Baldrige
- a series of continuous improvement tools that can be applied to any project along with detailed examples and illustrations of each in practice
- a discussion of the use of historic data analysis and data mining principles
- the best practices for using focus groups, questionnaires and interviews
- a succinct checklist of the core attributes for achieving excellence in any business process
- a template and guidelines for creating useful action planning forms
- a discussion on how to implement knowledge management into business processes
- the major principles of change management to ensure successful implementation of process changes
- a process to measure the return on the investment in a process improvement initiative
- the project management principles needed to conduct a performance improvement initiative
- innovative and creative ways to communicate the results of a performance improvement initiative
- highly detailed case studies to illustrate examples for the business processes covered in the book
- numerous examples from world-class organizations that have successfully applied process improvements

Acknowledgements

This book would not have been completed were it not for the encouragement and support of several individuals. Hopefully this brief recognition will provide a small thank you for the immense gratitude I feel toward their efforts.

Susan Leandri, was instrumental in shaping my early thoughts around best practices and benchmarking. Sue has and will always be a 'best practice' inspiration. Lynn Matera, Stephanie Mantis and Joe Cothrel must also be thanked because they provided encouragement and taught me valuable research techniques I will never forget.

I would like to thank Kent Barnett who has been a wonderful role model, mentor and coach. Jack Phillips deserves my thanks as he provided credible advice and suggestions for improving the text.

Diana Caponigri, Rocco Caponigri, and Anna Marie Caponigri must be acknowledged as they were supportive in this process and urged me not to give up.

Arleen and Terry Berk deserve special recognition as they provided unwavering support, encouragement, advice, and feedback. They have done so all my life, not just with this book and I thank them for all they have taught me.

Finally, I must acknowledge my wife Carolyn who has stood by me from the beginning. She encouraged my attendance of graduate school and teaching. She makes me a better person each and every day.

Table of Contents

Preface: Overview of Performance Improvement

Why I wrote the book

So now that you have this book, why should you read it? Okay, that's a fair question. I think I'll answer it by telling you why I wrote this book.

While attending undergraduate school and then graduate school I was too busy taking classes on strategy, statistics, and accounting to even think about performance improvement. Yet every manager, especially the new one's are almost always asked to improve or fix a problem. If they're not asked to do it, at least the good one's who move on to middle management are smart enough to find the problems themselves without being handed a flashlight to show them the way.

So as I sat in those classes I envisioned a new type of class that would teach all the things that I was being asked to do as a new manager. I actually drafted a detailed syllabus before I finished graduate school hoping to someday take this to a willing university to become an adjunct professor and enlighten up and coming managers with this wisdom.

Within months of receiving my MBA I was hired by Loyola University in Chicago to teach an evening course on performance improvement in business processes. The class was about improving core business processes using common tools and techniques. Case studies, guest speakers, readings and lecture were the main delivery tools of the class. The first class I taught was as much a learning experience for me as it was for my students. But, I managed to do something right because the class ranked in the top quartile amongst classes in the department. The next time I taught the class, the class size had more than doubled in size.

Some students who were not even enrolled in the class approached me and asked to obtain my lecture notes to help prepare them for continuous improvement projects as new managers. Former students often email me requesting information and a refresher on concepts from class because they were suddenly thrown on a project strikingly similar to what we discussed in class.

It was after all of this that I decided I would right a book that mirrors my class. My passion is to share the knowledge and experiences I have had with as many new managers as I can. I was fortunate enough to have good support and mentors along the way even if I didn't have a book to show me how to do things. I hope this book helps provide you with some creative insight and useful tools to steer you in the right direction.

What we'll discuss

The book itself is composed of two parts. The first part represents the methodology and tools you need to conduct successful performance improvement projects within your organization. The second part is a series of case studies from the real world where the methodology and tools were used to improve various processes. Below is an overview of each chapter to lay the groundwork for what lies ahead.

The first chapter is the performance improvement methodology. It is a process that you can apply to most any business process problem. It begins with identifying the process then defining the 'as is' state which is really gaining an understanding of the process inputs, activities and outputs. Next you analyze the 'should be' state that represents what other organizations have done to be successful at the process. This is followed by a gap analysis where you compare your process to the others and figure out where the biggest improvement opportunities exist. From this point you adapt, not adopt the necessary steps to narrow the gaps. By adapting steps you customize and tailor them to fit your needs. Finally, you create a performance measurement system to help ensure the changes you implement keep your process on track for the long term.

We then move into the second chapter that discusses some famous improvement movements. Specifically we discuss the main features and benefits of three widely accepted improvement movements used in business today: ISO, Malcolm Baldrige, and Six Sigma. Each is also compared and contrasted against one another. Ultimately, the best approach for your organization may be a hybrid of the three. Nonetheless it is important for any manager to understand the major themes of each as you may be faced with the task of having to use one of these as your improvement approach. Each combined with the methodology of chapter one can make a powerful combination in fighting the war on performance problems in your business processes.

If you consider the improvement movements and the methodology like a toolbox, you would then realize you need the right tools to go into the toolbox to make those approaches work properly. This is precisely the focus of the remaining chapters leading up to the case study section of the book.

Chapter three specifically discusses some classical performance improvement tools that have long been used in the process improvement space. Several originated from Japanese business management and are a combination of data analysis tools and project management tools. Detailed explanations for each tool are represented with concise examples of several tools listed at the end of the chapter.

Chapter four continues the tool discussion but focuses on a type of tool called a Diagnostic Tool. This is sometimes referred to as a needs assessment and is the up front work done, at a higher level, to pinpoint problems before diving deeper into your analysis. Think of the diagnostic tool as the same work a doctor does when she first examines you. The doctor asks questions, takes blood pressure and temperature among other high level tasks. Once done, the more detailed tests can be ordered. In business, use of a high level tool to understand what the problem is and why you have it is critical before you can think about the solution. The Diagnostic Tool is the instrument you should use to help define the problem and understand needs. It helps point you in the right direction for more detailed analysis.

The fifth chapter provides a concise yet powerful discussion on the why and how you should leverage historical data in your performance improvement initiatives. In today's world of CRM's and ERP's your organization probably collects more data then it knows what to do with it. To this end, it makes sense to understand the existing data you have historically collected and leverage it in your analysis to spot trends, forecast future performance, and pinpoint past problems. It does not make sense to collect a new battery of data sets if you already have mountains of it. This chapter helps you think through this important type of analysis.

The sixth chapter gives you the tips and tools you need to gather data using questionnaires, interviews and focus groups. These data gathering mechanisms are commonly used but commonly used incorrectly or with limited effect because the administrator of these instruments does not understand the optimal ways to use them. Surely anyone can write a survey but if you do not take the time to understand the outputs you want to derive you will have missed a golden opportunity to gather great information. By understanding the fundamentals behind these tools you will quickly learn how to elicit the best information from respondents through these data collection vehicles.

The seventh chapter is one of my personal favorites. It represents a checklist of items that any business process owner should do in order to maintain excellence in their process. A few years ago, a director of an internal audit department, Manny Rosenfeld, spoke to my class with these useful tips. They greatly mirrored the tools of performance improvement. They take on a focus of business risk, process efficiency, teamwork, change management and many other general themes that comprise this book. If you can successfully check the box on each of the items in this chapter you are on your way to business process bliss.

The art of balancing process efficiency and effectiveness with business risk and internal controls is a delicate one. It goes without saying that increasing efficiency and effectiveness means letting go of certain constraints and controls. Chapter eight discusses business risk and internal controls. It helps point out the fact that even though most performance improvements are aimed at more efficient processes (faster, better, cheaper) one must never sacrifice internal controls that mitigate serious risk to do so. This is a must read chapter in today's world of accounting irregularities, ethics issues, and general lack of faith in business. Solid controls can help restore a process and a company to comfort stakeholder fears about lack of control and high risk.

Chapter nine is a necessary chapter to read because it discusses how you combine all of your research and analysis about the process into prioritized action steps that you can recommend to management for implementation. This is in essence your roadmap. It lets management know you thoroughly researched the problem and acceptable solutions and given various resources here is your list of recommendations. Templates are presented to help you articulate your action steps in the best possible light.

Because action plans and recommendations for the future result in organizational change, chapter ten focuses on how to properly manage change. This is often one of the most overlooked aspects of performance improvement initiatives. However, it is one of the most important elements because without consideration for change implementation of action plans can be very challenging. The chapter focuses on how to manage change and presents a sample change management survey to help understand the organizations attitude toward change.

A necessary element of any change will likely be training. Training is the focus of chapter eleven. Without appropriate training, performance improvement teams won't be as effective as they should and without proper training, those affected by your changes won't have a smooth implementation path to change. This important chapter looks at training as a necessary tool for performance improvement and change management.

Chapter twelve takes a brief look at knowledge management. It is critical for a manager conducting performance improvement initiatives to familiarize themselves with knowledge management. Part of a well-run process, especially in a large organization, is to ensure the effective creation, maintenance and dissemination of knowledge. This chapter helps the new manager think about how best to capture, store, and disseminate knowledge. A giant business risk is that turnover can erode knowledge capital and cause the business process to spiral out of control. Appropriate attention paid to knowledge management by the process improvement team can help mitigate this risk.

Chapter thirteen takes a look at how the performance improvement team should communicate the results of its efforts. Specifically, this chapter investigates the best way to analyze, plan, create, and present the results of your work to management. It is important not to take this step lightly. If you have spent considerable time and resources gathering information, this is where you pull it all together and present your findings and recommendations to your sponsors, stakeholders, and parties affected by change. This chapter presents multiple tips on how best to proceed here.

Management is often concerned with quantifiably measuring the return on investments it makes. Conducting performance improvement projects is no different. Management may come back to the leader of the effort and ask for a return on its investment. Chapter fourteen presents a detailed approach toward measuring return on investment for performance improvement projects. Hopefully you'll find that the financial benefits derived from your improvement efforts outweigh the costs of conducting the improvement initiative.

The final chapter prior to the case studies is a concluding chapter on project management. A performance improvement project is one giant set of multiple tasks and activities that need to be properly managed so that objectives are met on time and on budget. This chapter provides some best practices to help you control your performance improvement project through fundamental project management principles.

The remaining chapters present detailed, real life case studies. Each case uses the methodology presenting in the first chapter of this book along with other tools learned in proceeding chapters. The cases were specifically chose to cover multiple functional areas that are common to most organizations. These functions include: supply chain, customer relationship management, finance, human resources, and information technology. So, no matter what your functional discipline might be, hopefully you will find a case study that is of interest to you. I encourage reviewing all of the cases as each offers its own unique creative insights. Along with each of these cases is a brief overview about the functional area including various activities and performance measures you can use to monitor that function.

Let's Go!

Now that you have read about what you're going to read about we should get started. But before we do let me set expectations. I always tell my students this on the first day of class so I'll tell you the same thing. Continuous improvement techniques are not the answer to a problem. They are merely tools to help you make better decisions to hopefully solve a problem.

It is important to set this expectation not only with you but also with your superiors and subordinates that might be involved in a project you lead some day. You will get burned if you over promise and under deliver so don't do it. Set expectations. Let your stakeholders know that this process is going to help you uncover ideas and insights into helping solve a problem but it does not produce the answers.

Okay, let's begin!

Chapter One: Performance Improvement Methodology

Background

It would be challenging to teach a class or write a book without a framework that ties it all together. The purpose of this chapter is to present this framework in the form of a performance improvement methodology.

I guess I'll start by explaining the concept of a methodology. A methodology sets out a process that should be followed to ensure consistent, systematic delivery of results. Methodologies are like road maps. They help guide you through complex situations. And, just like a road map, you don't have to follow the exact route, but can wander off the beaten path based on your view of the situation and your propensity for risk.

The need to formalize and standardize procedures is very important as long as it does not stifle creativity and create administrative burdens. Allowing team members to follow the spirit of a methodology rather than the letter of it is a goal you should strive to achieve when using methodologies as a tool in your continuous improvement toolbox.

Organizations like Lucent Technologies regard the setting of clear agendas through solid problem solving methodologies to be critical to their success. In their Electronic Wire & Cable business group they successfully deployed an approach that defines the problem, identifies the root cause and then eliminates the root cause. Ultimately the Lucent team exceeded its goal to reduce defects by 25% within the first quarter of the change implementation.

Other organizations such as Campbell's Soup Company uses standardized tools to measure and manage performance in the area of product quality. They help the company pinpoint areas that need improvement before they get out of control.

When using methodologies and standards, remember to do so for the ultimate reason of creating a more empowered, knowledgeable learning organization. Organizational learning is the process of improving actions through better knowledge and understanding. Organizations like Xerox take a 6-step approach in their problem-solving methodology to help them learn to do processes better. Exhibit 1-1 illustrates their approach.

Exhibit 1-1. Xerox's Problem-Solving Process

Step	Question to be Answered	Expansion/ Divergence	Contraction/ Convergence	What's Needed to Go to the Next Step
1. Identify and select the problem	What do we want to change?	Lots of problems for consideration	One problem statement, one "desired state" agreed upon	Identification of the gap "Desired State" described in observable terms
2. Analyze problem	What's preventing us from reaching the "desired state"?	Lots of potential identified	Key cause(s) identified and verified	Key cause(s) determined and ranked
3. Generate potential solutions	How *could* we make the change?	Lots of ideas on how to solve the problem	Potential solutions clarified	Solution list
4. Select and plan the solution	What's the best way to do it?	Lots of criteria for evaluating potential solutions Lots of ideas on how to implement and evaluate the selected solution	Criteria to use for evaluating solution agreed upon Implementation and evaluation plans agreed upon	Plan for making and monitoring the change Measurement criteria to evaluate solution effectiveness
5. Implement the solution	Are we following the plan?	-	Implementation of agreed upon contingency plans if necessary	Solution in place
6. Evaluate the solution	How well did it work?	-	Effectiveness of solution agreed upon Continuing problems, if any identified	Verification that the problem is solved, or Agreement to address continuing problems

Design and Definitions

In attempting to shape your thoughts around performance improvement methodologies, it is important to understand some common designs in performance improvement methodologies and go through a few definitions. First, a lot can be learned by the work of prior thought leaders and project teams that were successful and have best practices to share or went through challenging times and have war stories to tell.

First, The American Society for Quality and the Institute for Healthcare Improvement worked on a joint collaborative in 1996 to focus on motor vehicle injury prevention. The broader conclusions reached by the collaborative brought forth some common lessons for any project team to strive to achieve as goals for their projects. The following summarizing the goals of this collaborative:

- Demonstrated improvements. The project team should show quantifiable improvement in its pre vs. post process changes.
- Tools of improvement. Tools like process mapping, site observations, data stratification, and flowcharting are some productive tools to have in your tool kit when improving processes.
- Replicable model. Use a model that can be used across a broad base of topics and processes.
- Good ideas equal change concepts. Change concepts ("a general notion …not specific enough to use directly") are a starting point for teams to then apply to specific situations.

Another groundbreaking effort came from The Electric Boat Division of General Dynamics Corporation who, in the early 1990's created a Process Improvement Road Atlas. The Atlas, like the collaborative mentioned above, offers creative insights for practitioners embarking on a process improvement methodology. Some of the more significant activities in the Atlas include the following:

- Identify the improvement opportunity
- Establish an owner or sponsor team
- Define boundaries
- Collect data to understand the process
- Analyze data and identify improvements
- Quantify the improvement's costs and benefits
- Prioritize the improvements
- Make recommendations
- Build the implementation team
- Define the implementation approach
- Plan implementation
- Perform scheduled implementation activities

Another interesting finding from movements since past, primarily TQM (Total Quality Management) and BPR (Business Process Reengineering) is to consider an approach to continuous improvement that will weather time. From this come some simple best practices offered up by Anne Webster, a consultant from Plymouth, UK whose short list below helps create more realistic expectations about process improvement:

- No "magic bullet." By this no methodology or approach can be copied and pasted into your problem it must tailored to fit the uniqueness of the situation.
- Focus. Understand the functional roles of the team and focus their attention accordingly. For example a staff employee whose daily focus is transactional detail should focus here in the improvement as well likewise a manager may focus on the broader process.

- Coordination. Ensure that those involved in a process improvement work together, not against each other. A key individual or group should guide the team.
- Training. Use training to build expertise, coach, mentor and build confidence and expand morale/manage change.
- Techniques. Tools like statistical process control, process mapping etc. not only help in the design of the improvement initiative but can be a tool used across groups as well as stimulate objectivity and fact within the rigor of the process instead of subjectivity and opinion.
- Completeness. Try and address structure, process and culture rather than just one and not the others.
- Change management. A very important part of the improvement initiative. Recognize there will be resistance to change and take steps to manage that as best you can.
- Compare. Select appropriate benchmarks to provide meaningful, credible and helpful information.
- Target. Set goals for performance improvements that are challenging yet achievable.
- Report. Celebrate success and recognize failure by regularly reporting on your improvement endeavors.
- Re-invigorate. Continue to motivate the team for change by celebrating success but reinforcing that the competition is succeeding to. Motivate by external example and press to incrementally improve.

Many of the above helpful hints will resurface throughout this book, even in the methodology that we will discuss in detail in a moment. Nonetheless it is helpful to complement the methodology design with some definitions. Below are some basic definitions you might have always wanted to know in the context of process improvement.

- Re-engineering. An approach to improvement where the goal is dramatic improvement in process of business performance characterized by redesign of processes, activities, and organizational structures.
- Business process. A series of logical steps that combine to form a business objective. A process has inputs, activities and outputs.
- Total Quality Management (TQM) a continuous improvement based approach aimed at changing the culture of the organization
- Business Process Reengineering (BPR). Improving the holistic business process through revolutionary and radical improvements.
- Business Process Improvement (BPI). Incremental improvements in business processes without radical change to the process or organizational structure.

Definitions like the above although helpful can be dangerous. You're improvement approach needs to be what fits your situation, no matter what you want to call it. Even if you name your tailored approach 'Aunt Merdle's Really Cool Approach to Change', it doesn't matter so much as long as it works. Nonetheless, I would be remiss if I did not at least offer up these definitions, so forgive me for digressing.

More on methodology

Before transitioning into the methodology that fuels this book and the case studies in the second half of this text, it is helpful to continue to discuss with you other methodologies that you can continue to consider in your approach to improvement and process design.

First, let's look at the SCOR model. SCOR stands for Supply Chain Operations Model. It is a tool used by the Supply Chain Council and their member supply chain practitioners. It is a great improvement methodology tailored for supply chain improvements. It involves five steps: Plan; Source; Make; Deliver; and Return.

There are three levels of process detail included in SCOR. The Top Level is defining the scope and content of the processes. This is where performance goals are set.

The second level is the Configuration Level. This is where process categories for implementing the strategy are outlined.

The third level is the Process Element Level. This is where the processes are decomposed and each process is broken down into a definition; inputs and outputs; performance metrics; best practices; system support for best practices; tools.

A fourth level, the Implementation Level is not within the scope of SCOR but would define the practices the company needs to achieve competitive advantage and adapt to changes in the business environment.

SCOR is a nice working model of an improvement methodology because it is a typical process reference model. A process reference model, per the Supply Chain Council, contains:

- Standard descriptions of management processes
- A framework of relationships among standard processes
- Standard metrics to measure process performance
- Management practices that produce best-in-class performance
- Standard alignment to features and functionality

IDEFO is another model for improvement. This is the Integrated Computer-Aided Manufacturing Definition Language that is comprised of a several re-engineering tools developed by the Air Force to facilitate manufacturing automation. It's an activity modeling method that provides a structured representation of the functions performed by an organization. The method collects the following data relative to activities:

- Inputs. Data or material used to produce an output of an activity.
- Controls. Data or material that regulates the activity and its transformation of inputs to outputs.
- Outputs. Data or material produced by or resulting from the activity. It must include the input data in some form.
- Mechanisms. Resources (peoples, machines, systems) that provide energy to, or perform, the activity.

Another model, the Business Process Model, was developed to demonstrate that TQM is a process of integrating customer values with business management principles. Its guiding principles include the following seven core components:

- Identification of customer requirements and expectations. This is the main step that the other 6 steps support. The premise is that you must understand the requirements of your customer before you can make improvements to what they require.
- Strategic planning. This is the long-term support process that aligns customer input with other business levers such as cash flow, inventory, efficiencies, defect reduction, cycle-time reduction, new products, automation etc. The strategic plan also shapes the organizational leadership.
- Manage business processes. Strategies are assigned a process owner in charge of executing the strategy.
- Cross-functional support. Use of cross-functional team to implement the strategy (if applicable)
- Process measurement. Metrics are established for each strategy to demonstrate improvement and achievement of the business objective.
- Management review. This is the continuous feedback loop to ensure the organization is proceeding with the appropriate rate of change and improvement.
- Business improvement system. The act of continuously improving the business model to ensure it is relevant in the current business environment.

When a phone company was faced with reducing operating expenses, they derived the following steps to process design that begin with defining the problem and end with hand-off to the implementation team.

- Create a relationship map. This is essentially a process map showing the components and relationships within the process as well as process stakeholders, inputs and outputs.
- Select the people to be trained. Picking the people affected by the changing process to lead the process improvement and undergo training to get it done.
- Train the teams. The basics of process analysis were taught to the teams.

- Select the process and the project team. Scoping the process to narrow it done to a "small" manageable project and then picking the specific smaller team to manage this scoped process.
- Plan the project. A schedule to accomplish the project.
- Create a specific process relationship map. Now that the process was narrowed down and scoped, a revised relationship map analyzed that processes procedures, inputs, and outputs.
- Build the IS map. A flowchart or map of the existing process and its sub-processes.
- Identify disconnects. Identify duplication of duties, unnecessary duties, delays, opportunities for automation etc.
- Decide to patch or redesign the process. Decide to 'reengineer' the process through complete redesign or simply fix the cracks in the process discovered through the mapping.
- Define SHOULD Map. List of desired features and attributes of the new process.
- Build SHOULD Map. The process map of the desired process, which is hopefully streamlined.
- Speed and Measures. List of the outputs from the process and the performance metrics to be put in place to track performance.
- Critique and revise. Present the proposed new process to the stakeholders to incorporate modifications and feedback.
- Formulate recommendations. The project teams final list of proposed process changes.
- Implement or not. Decide which and if the recommendations are implemented.

We have all heard of pride. Pride in one's work is important and that is a great acronym for the next performance improvement methodology nicknamed PRIDE (Process, Relevance, Interpretation, Design, and Execution.) This was the model developed by New York Presbyterian Hospital as they worked on moving inpatient facilities and encountered old ways clashing with new. As a result, a committee was formed to evaluate needs and brainstorm on ways to improve, PRIDE was born. Below is a brief description of PRIDE:

- Process. This is where the team stated its objectives and goals for the proposed improvement.
- Relevance. This is where the team used various tools like focus groups and surveys to gather relevant data about the process.
- Interpretation. This is where the team performed data analysis on the information they had collected.
- Design. This is where the team developed specific improvement strategies.
- Execution. This is where the team implemented the approved strategies.

Another model is the Business Process Improvement Methodology. It was formulated by analyzing other methodologies. The methodology is based upon research done by Short Bros. Plc an industrial employer in Northern Ireland in partnership with the Ulster Business School. In summary the major components of their model are the following 4 phases:

- Identify the critical process for improvement. This includes identifying a process owner, training the team, and documenting the Key Success Factors.
- Analyze the current process. In this stage the process is mapped and validated using a range of continuous improvement tools and techniques. Opportunities for improvement are identified.
- Improve the process. This could be anything from small changes to radical process redesign. Ownership over the changes is documented and benchmarking either generically, internally or externally is done. The result is a revised process map reflecting the transformed process.
- Implement improved process. Change management is addressed, planning and communications is addressed as well as regular review during the implementation itself.

Similar to the above example, Barry Pover, (IBM UK, Portsmith, Hampshire, UK) studied many BPI methodologies to sort out their shortcomings and create a new "best of breed" methodology. Mr. Pover reviewed the following 10 BPI methodologies in his analysis:

- The O&M Approach (Webster 1973)
- The soft systems methodology (SSM) (Checkland 1981)
- Generic model developed by Elzinga et al. (1995)
- International Benchmarking Clearinghouse Methodology (Zairi and Leonard 1994)
- POPI – the process of process improvement (Abbott, 1991)
- Davenport and Short (1990)
- Kaplan and Murdock (1991)
- IBM (1992)
- Hardaker and Ward (1987)
- TQMI (1994)

As a result of studying the above models, a new methodology was developed. This "best of breed" methodology blends the best approaches of the above models and adds to it a missing element of change management. The major improvements to the above methodologies incorporated here are the following:

- Top management (CEO) involvement from the beginning.
- Staff trained in process management and process improvement.
- Define the process (i.e. map the process including its inputs, activities and outputs)
- Test each proposed change to ensure it is culturally and technically feasible.

- Focus on continuous improvement and performance measurement once implemented.
- Benchmarking is emphasized.
- Consider human aspects of change are considered from the beginning.

As can be seen, by looking at the aforementioned methodologies and approaches, much has been done in the way of methodology. Hopefully, as you read the following pages that discuss the methodology utilized in this book and the supporting case studies you will see where these methodologies compliment the one we are about to examine.

Methodology Overview

So, now that we have discussed some background about methodology and how some organizations use it, I'd like to present our continuous improvement methodology that we'll refer back to throughout this book. Exhibit 1-2 provides a snapshot of the methodology.

Exhibit 1-2. Continuous Improvement Methodology

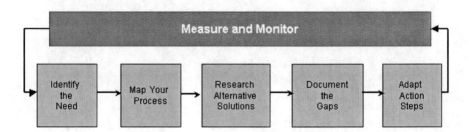

As you can see there are 5 core steps and one overlying step to our methodology. Before getting into the guts of it I want to take a second and explain that this methodology is NOT . . .

1. A silver bullet to improve your business processes.
2. A cookie cutter approach to continuous improvement.
3. A document on how to run your business.
4. A document on where you go for the answers.

If the methodology is not the above, then what is at? I addressed that on the aforementioned pages when I defined a methodology. But, I can now put it into context for you. You would want to use a continuous improvement methodology and commit yourself to continuous improvement programs because . . . .

1. Stimulates change.
2. Creates a sense of urgency.
3. Uncovers new ways of improving a process.
4. Motivates by external example.

5. Stimulates innovation.
6. Ensures process alignment with organizational objectives.
7. Provides a deeper understanding of your own processes.

As we begin to peel back the layers of this methodology and see it applied in practice through various case study examples it will be equally important to remember to avoid the following pitfalls when applying this methodology . . .

1. Not achieving buy-in and support from leadership, team members, or those affected by the change.
2. Failing to understand your own process before you implement changes or talk to other organizations about what they do.
3. Collecting data superficially.
4. Selecting inappropriate benchmark partners.
5. Collecting the wrong data.
6. Not being prepared (i.e. not doing your homework)
7. Insufficient analysis of results.
8. Believing and communicating to others that the continuous improvement project is "the answer."

Because I don't want to sound negative in the opening pages of this book and scare you away so soon, it is only fair for me to also tell you what I think the keys to a successful application of this methodology are . . .

1. Involve management early in the process.
2. Involve those affected by the potential changes from beginning to end.
3. Understand your own process before looking at others.
4. Train people on your project team.
5. Create and use data collection tools.
6. Devote adequate time to do analysis of your data.
7. Address cultural change (i.e. change management)
8. Always be prepared.

Okay, I'll get off of my soapbox and explain the methodology. Ready, set, go!

Step 1. Identify the Need

Focus on where the change is at

In many cases as a new manager you are often told what to improve and it is your job to do it. Several of the cases we'll examine fall into this scenario. However, it is always best to try and set the appropriate scope for a continuous improvement project. For example, it is one set of resource requirements to examine the entire supply chain compared to a subcomponent of it.

The best managers won't wait for someone to tell them to solve a problem. If you think about it that indicates they let a problem happen and have to clean it up. Instead, managers want a continuous improvement process that monitors changes in their environments to spot problems before they spiral out of control.

The most common question I am asked is how do you know what needs improvement until it is already a big problem? To me, there are two ways to do this. The first is a system of small, well-balanced performance measures with goals and historic baselines that are computed on a regular basis and serve as symptomatic signs of distress. In a later part of this book we'll discuss performance measures and how to use those to monitor results of an improvement effort.

In addition to performance measures, I always recommend a business intelligence system that helps you monitor surrounding factors. I don't necessary mean a billion dollar covert intelligence system. I am simply saying to routinely think about what could cause change because wherever there is change there is bound to be repercussions of that change resulting in a process that might be pulled off its routine track.

Think of it this way, when you get sick, there are likely changes that led to it. Perhaps you had been working long hours on a special project and have not got much sleep so your body gets run down and you end up with a nasty cold that turns into an infection. Your business is no different. You need to look for those warning signs and react to them.

To me, the changes that you should look for fall into 5 broad categories. If a major change takes place in any of these it might produce a business risk for the area you manage. If that happens you should analyze it to assess if a problem could exist.

The 5 categories of change that might prompt problems are as follows:

1. Strategic change
These are those high level visions handed down from senior management that might take a while to trickle down to your area but if you don't watch out you could be greatly impacted. For example, if your organization decides to initiate major cost cutting efforts to increase profitability your department is susceptible to change.

2. Process change
These are any changes in policy, procedure and workflow. If the team you manage was used to doing things one way and now does it different, there is risk that the change might not be implemented properly or that key tasks fall through the cracks.

3. Personnel change
This can be employee turnover within your group all the way up to the CEO of your company. Let's look at your team. If a key employee with a great deal of knowledge leaves and you don't have proper transition plans there could be a problem. Even if the CEO of your organization is replaced a new one with a much different philosophy can replace him or her so you want to be prepared to react to that change.

4. Technology change

This has become a big driver of continuous improvement projects in recent years. Technology often has dramatic changes on personnel and process factors too. If you implemented a new system you want to ensure that the functional requirements address business needs otherwise you may have a problem waiting to happen.

5. External shifts

As a new manager, keep your eyes on external factors. Monitor key supplier and customer relationships. Stay tuned into what your key competition is doing. In addition understand how the economy and industry factors influence the group you manage. Often times senior management will dictate projects and strategic shifts from external shifts so the more you are aware how these effect your area the better positioned you are to react to them.

Gather information about what needs improvement

Having said this, I would say that when determining what needs improvement, start by thinking through some of the above changes and how they might impact the critical components of the area you manage. In addition, there are other pro-active ways to gather information about what might need a high-level review. Below are some of the additional ways you can gather information about what needs improvement:

- Hold high-level focus groups with your team, your key customers and suppliers and ask them if they are aware of problems or potential issues. You'll be surprised how open people can be if you just ask them where you need improvement.
- Talk with management to understand their strategies and focus areas. As a new manager it is important to stay in the loop on key initiatives sweeping your organization. Even if these things might be perceived as "flavor of the month" initiatives, you want to make sure you understand what they are and how it might impact your neck of the woods.
- Review past performance. Later in the book we'll discuss historic data collection and how to use it to analyze a process. But, one of the first things you can do to get acquainted with a situation is understand what has happened in the past. Calculate some performance measures about your process and look at the trends over time. Are there any downward trends that need to be addressed?
- Perform a high level diagnostic. We'll discuss needs assessments later in the book and that is what we mean here. Self-assess or have key stakeholders assess your performance currently where you want to be or versus how important it is. This is a "gut check" to help you frame problems better. For example think about some key questions that might fall under each of the 5 categories we discussed above. Ask others and ask yourself how you rate given

those issues. If you are lacking in certain areas those represent gaps that need to be filled.

Once you have a good grasp of the issues through the above steps, you'll want to plan the next steps. This is where you want to define the scope to drive your improvement work. Depending upon your assessment of the situation or the importance to management you'll have an idea about the resources you're willing to put forth on this initiative. So you want to communicate a scope that adequately uses these limited resources. For example, don't communicate you're going to review the entire supply chain if you have a team of two and a week to do it, it just won't happen. Maybe you could look at a subcomponent of it that is particularly problematic. In any event it is important to communicate your scope to help manage the project and set appropriate expectations.

<u>Assemble the Team</u>

Another element of your planning for this project is to assemble the right team of people. Exhibit 1-3 illustrates the composition of a typical project team for a continuous improvement project:

Exhibit 1-3 Typical Continuous Improvement Team Compositions

Project Sponsor	Process Owner	Facilitator	Team Member
-Project initiator -Resource provider -Obstacle remover -Implementation driver	-Leader of process under review -Source of information -Leads process improvement effort	-Benchmarking expert -Trainer -Facilitator	-Provider of varying functional/process expertise -Provider of issues and insights -Field visits -Data gatherer
e.g. Managing Director, Quality Director (the project champion)	e.g. Billing Manager, Purchasing Director (the Process Owner)	e.g. Team Leader, External or Internal Consultant	e.g. Line Manager, Process Staff

The typical team will have a sponsor or champion that really drives it. This is typically a senior manager who really wants to drive this change. Next is the process owner that is likely to be you. As the manager you'll be responsible for leading this effort sometimes in a large organization there may be a middle level manager here and a new manager may play the role of facilitator. The facilitator is the coordinator and team leader that manages the project's day-to-day operations. In smaller organizations you will be both the process owner and facilitator. Then you have your staff, the team members. They help you carry out the steps that need to be taken to analyze the issues and come up with the suggestions for improvement. In large organizations or prominent projects the new manager may be here in smaller organizations you may be your own staff as well!

<u>Keys to Success</u>

The keys to successfully performing this step in the methodology are to:

- Try and remove any hidden agenda's from the project, or at least make them known up front. For example, perhaps the overall goal of reviewing the structure of your team is to merge it with another team. Difficult as it is, it is important to try and understand this up front to avoid problems later.
- Understand stakeholder expectations. That's why you ask before hand and you communicate a proper scope that people buy into. My motto is under promise and over deliver.
- Empower the project team. Give them the power; accountability and resources to really understand the issues and make some suggestions that have teeth.
- Ensure there is a problem to solve. Don't do things without a purpose. The key here is to make sure your stakeholders agree there is a problem and time should be spent addressing it otherwise you might get your resources pulled before you get to far.

Step 2. Map Your Process

<u>Steps to Process Mapping</u>

This is the step where you try and understand what is happening currently and historically. I can't tell you how often I have seen organizations start making changes without really knowing what they are changing. Likewise, I have had many executives come to me and say "I'd like to talk to GE or Motorola about what they do." My reaction is what do you do, can you explain that to me? Is it documented? Where are the issues? It is pointless to try and improve or speak to world-class organizations before you know more about what you do currently.

So how do you understand your own process? It starts with identifying the key inputs, activities and outputs of your process. Later on we'll discuss some continuous improvement tools like flowcharting, process mapping, and cause/effect diagrams. These tools are excellent ways to help you dissect your process. You'll be surprised how much you can learn and what needs to be improved just by drawing a simple flowchart of the process.

Another key aspect of understanding your own process is to find out what was done in the past to solve problems and why they did not work. The last thing you want to do is repeat the mistakes from the past. Use history to learn from the past. So use this step in the methodology to understand this. Was it political issues? Were resource limitations a problem? Was there lack of commitment? What happened?

Address the root causes. You may have uncovered some issues at their surface when you decided to take on this project. Now you need to ask not just "what" but "why" and "how" during this step. For example, historic data may have stated you're trending downward in the quality of your key deliverables. This is the step where you peel back the onion to understand why that is and how it all came about.

When addressing root cause try and look for redundancies, bottlenecks, manual tasks that need to be automated, key risk points that require more review, less risky points that need less manager intervention. Identify job skills not properly met with current resources, pinpoint areas where handoffs to other areas are mismanaged or where the information you receive to begin your process is inadequate or not timely.

Collect more data to baseline performance. Use these historic results and trends to truly understand where to investigate root cause in a deeper manner. Ensure you look at cost elements, quality elements, time elements, productivity elements, and customer service elements.

Keys to Success

The keys to a successful process mapping involve the following:

- Devote less attention to unimportant areas. Try not to get distracted. Certain individuals have their own agendas but stay focused.
- Understand your own process before researching what others are doing. As tempting as it is to immediately pick up the phone and talk to your buddy who does what you do at another company, you won't know what to ask him or her until you know enough about your own situation.
- Think about problem solving. You know you'll need to suggest ways to improve. Be thinking about where the bottlenecks exist. Probe into these issues with more rigor.
- The ultimate goal of the "As Is" step is to define your process and identify specific areas that are problematic and know why they are that way.

Step 3. Research Alternative Solutions

Primary and Secondary Research

Now that you have understood your own process, identified the problems and know why they occur, you have enough information to think about ways to improve those problems. This step explores how you can get insights for solving problems.

There are two primary tasks that you want to do during this step to get the creative juices flowing: primary and secondary research. Primary research is when you work directly within or outside your organization to gather first hand business intelligence about what others are doing who perform similar processes like the one's under investigation by your team. Secondary research is when you perform a more cursory review of the major thoughts and movements pertaining to your issue. The advantage to primary research is you can ask a lot of questions and gather direct information but it can be more time consuming and costly. Secondary research is less costly and time consuming but you can't interact with others.

First let's talk about secondary research. I suggest doing it before primary research even if you plan on doing primary research. Secondary research includes the following techniques:

- Review articles and publications that may have been written on your topic recently. This can help you to identify some best practice companies that may be used in your primary research too.
- Research books written by thought leaders on your topic. These may be by academics or those who have been there and done it before. Skimming through these can provide some insights.
- Surf the net. Specialized web sites are on the Internet for almost anything you can imagine. Spend time on the Internet looking around for ideas.
- Contact trade and industry associations. Most exist for major industries and processes. They offer a wealth of research, studies, training, and networking products and services. Many benchmark studies are sponsored by such organizations that you can use to quickly compare your process against.
- Online databases. Many subscription databases exist. Some are pay for use others are annual. These are extended knowledge bases that can provide great insights, job aides, and networking contacts. Just try and balance cost versus benefit with these.

Next is primary research. This is a direct interaction with a company who has been there and done that. Or it could be a direct interaction with a thought leader, subject matter expert, or academic that has a wealth of knowledge to assist you.

The first source of primary research I would look at is within your organization. I once did a project for a large multinational organization. It was part of a finance function reengineering effort. The average experience levels of most employees on the project were over 12 years. However, many of them had never spoken to each other. The first thing we did was identifying the process champions that others could talk to about specific issues and share knowledge and ideas.

The next source is external organizations that you have relationships. It is much easier to get a dialogue with people whom you have an existing relationship. That is why many managers will look to existing customers or suppliers or friends to try and speak to their organizations more intimately about a problem.

Next, use consultants and their network of contacts to try and hook you up with world-class organizations that might schedule a site visit with you to talk about process issues.

Data Collection Techniques

An important element of research gathering is to know how to collect the data. Certain circumstances call for different data collection techniques. Exhibit 1-4 walks you through certain techniques depending on your situation.

Exhibit 1-4 Data Collection Techniques

Method	When to Use It	When Not to Use It
Personal Interview	-sensitive issues -build relationships -convey importance -questionnaire follow-up	-issues requiring exhaustive research -the number of people to interview is numerous -the person to interview may not be the right person
Telephone interview	-lack number of people to interview -lack time and budget for personal interview -people with whom you had little contact	-important issues -complex issues -when an impersonal approach is inappropriate -with highly committed people -one-on-one benchmarking
Questionnaire	-more quantitative questions -essay type questions -obtain structured responses -needed preparation and research time -information is needed from many sources -a structured building block for follow-up	-lack of significant time or resources -risk of misinterpreted data without proper follow-up -overly complex issues may be misunderstood
Focus group	-to brainstorm ideas -to gain consensus -to foster innovation -to document multiple opinions -to do process mapping	-lack flexibility in time (it can be logistically difficult) -lack required funds -there is a lack of focus or structure

Although we will get into more detail about interviews, questionnaires, and focus groups, it is important to understand them early on and when to use them and not to use them. In a nutshell, I like to use personal interviews if it is a personal contact, a sensitive issue, and a complex issue that requires discussion. I like to use telephone interviews when I need to do it fast and with little cost and the issues are fairly simple to convey. I like to use questionnaires when the data is more quantitative or requires structured thought based on structured questions. Finally, I like to use focus groups when I need to gain consensus or brainstorm. Those are good to communicate issues at key milestones in your project as well.

Keys to Success

The keys to researching alternative solutions are as follows:

- Think out of the box. Don't narrow your research to just look at your specific issues in your specific industry. Some of the most breakthrough improvements have come from a project teams ability to think outside of the box. See Exhibit 1-5 for a list of out of the box improvement examples.
- Ensure research is accurate, reliable and relevant. If someone gives you data that is garbage the phrase 'garbage in is garbage out' comes into play. Make sure your sources are credible.
- Be willing to give what you get. If you are asking for information from a primary source be prepared to share with them in an equal manner. Many companies will write up a summary of their project when it is finished and send it to these benchmark partners.
- Be prepared. Don't start research until you have some good questions and issues you are researching. That is why it is important to understand your As Is environment before researching the Should Be environment.

Exhibit 1-5 Out-of-the-Box Benchmarking Examples
Source: Arthur Andersen Global Best Practices Knowledge Base; "Out of the Box Benchmarking Examples," 1995

Company: Construction Aggregate Co Process: Order Fulfillment Description: At this supplier of construction materials, gravel and crushed rock were typically measured by the loader-bucketful as they were poured into trucks--a messy and imprecise system. Taking a cue from the automatic teller machine, the company devised a new process. Drivers now roll into a building where their trucks sit on an electronic scale. They slip a data card into the slot, and punch in the amount and type of material needed. The truck then proceeds to the loading facility, where it is automatically filled to the desired weight. The system works around the clock and has cut truck turnaround time to 9 minutes from 24 minutes.

Company: Telecommunications Company Process: Customer Satisfaction Description: Finding that customers were expecting to have their requests resolved in one phone call, the company sought out a specialist in single-point-of-contact customer service: the a major catalog clothing company. Error rates in the company's customer information and billing systems were unacceptably high. To remedy the problem, the company sought inspiration from an organization that processes hundreds of millions of transactions a day with extraordinary levels of accuracy. That organization processes all the daily transactions for the New York Stock Exchange, the American Stock Exchange, and other exchanges. The telecom company learned from the exchange processor various methods for ensuring the integrity of data before it enters the system.

Company: Gas Utility
Process: Outsourcing
Description:
The company's sales and marketing director heard a presentation by a fast food chain restaurant executive on how the restaurant chain outsourced food preparation activities--slicing tomatoes, for one example--in order to focus on its core competency: selling food. The utility applied the same idea by outsourcing the sales function to its installation contractors. The change allowed the company to eliminate its 16-person sales force, and focus its own efforts on the business of providing gas. Customer surveys show that customers are pleased with the change.

Company: Insurance Provider
Process: Collections
Description:
The insurance provider, a property and casualty underwriter, gained significant insights from a chain of retail stores in how to speed up the collection of premiums. The insurer observed that its agents were much like the individual stores in a chain in their need to transfer funds and remittance information efficiently to a central location. Where the insurance provider used a lockbox approach, the retailer employed a sophisticated system in which the stores entered remittance data on line and then concentrated the funds using an automated clearinghouse. In the reengineered insurance provider collection system, agents electronically send information the premiums collected and the accounts to which payments should be credited. The agents authorize the insurance provider to then debit their bank accounts accordingly. Savings in the first year totaled $200,000.

Company: Gasoline Retailer
Process: Premium pricing for premium service
Description:
Gasoline retailers have competed viciously in price wars to woo customers away from their competitors. When this retailer's research showed that only 20% of its customers buy gas solely on the basis of price, it decided that a different approach might boost sales as well as profitability. Rather than offering trading stamps or free glassware, as the industry did in the 1950s, this retailer decided that the answer was to "blow the customer away with quality product and service." For ideas, executives visited companies who have succeeded in commanding premium prices for a premium level of service: premium department stores and premium hotels.

Company: Electronics manufacturer
Process: Procurement
Description:
This company continually benchmarks its customers to gather ideas that can be adapted to its own work processes. For example, the company was very interested in one of their customers purchasing card program in which certain employees are issued credit cards to make small purchases. The system eliminated processing requisitions and lowered processing costs. But the electronics manufacturer didn't simply copy their customer's program because they didn't want to take on the liabilities involved in credit card purchases. Rather they switched to a blanket purchase order system in which suppliers provide collective billing weekly or monthly. This cut processing costs for small orders by 90%.

Company: Firearms manufacturer
Process: Product Development
Description:
When the company's customers demanded smoother, shinier ammunition shells, it went to a cosmetics company to find out how they manufactured their smooth lipstick containers. Obviously this is the kind of information that would be very difficult to get from the competition.

Company: Chemical manufacturer
Process: Logistics
Description:
This company has looked outside its industry on numerous occasions. In the case of logistics, the company was looking for ways to reduce its shipment costs, which were discovered to be six times previous company estimates. They looked at a major shipping provider's distribution system; all shipments regardless of origin or destination are handled through a central distribution center. The chemical company, on the other hand, typically shipped its products to regional sites. For example, the company would ship chemicals from one plant in Texas to another plant also in Texas. The product would be transferred from rail car to barge and shipped on to the company's Chicago terminal. Inspired by the shipping company example, the company analyzed its process and discovered that despite the low cost of shipping by barge, it would be cheaper to ship directly to Chicago by rail.

Company: Computer Manufacturer
Process: Inventory Management
Description:
An employee learned from a magazine article that a cosmetics manufacturer had not made any inventory errors in several consecutive years and had a cycle time of 24 hours. Since the division's own cycle time was 8 days, this provided them with the impetus to examine how other companies operated. They conducted benchmarking visits with 6 companies with similar picking procedures, compiling a "best of the best" flow chart for this process. They were able to cut their cycle time in half.

Company: Electronics manufacturer
Process: On-time deliveries
Description:
The company was hoping to improve delivery speed. They looked at how a major pizza delivery company delivers their pizzas so fast.

Company: Paper products manufacturer
Process: Productivity measurement
Description:
This paper manufacturer sought to raise profits in an industry where overcapacity and foreign competition soak up any increase in demand, making it impossible to raise prices. Instead of embarking on a traditional cost-cutting effort, the company's CEO looked for a company that earned brisk profits in another mature industry in which prices were flat. In an appliance and lighting business, he found a formula for measuring productivity that focused on things that managers could control. The new formula also revealed shortcomings in their own performance. The company sent its managers out to visit the appliance and light bulb company to observe their productivity improvement efforts.

Step 4. Document the Gaps

<u>Organize and Prioritize</u>

So know you have understood your own process and researched the best practices. The difference between the two is the performance gap. The larger the gap, the more opportunity for improvement.

When determining the gaps try and classify them in multiple ways. I suggest classifying the gap along the following dimensions so you can see them from different perspectives:

1. Benefit versus cost
2. Opportunity to eliminate rather than shift problems
3. Low hanging fruit versus significant process overhauls
4. Strategic versus tactical changes

A cost benefit analysis is something that a lot of managers like to see. Here you try and monetize potential benefits of changes compared to the costs of implementing them. It is always important to point out the cost or business risk of not making the change, as that can often overshadow everything else. For example, if you don't change the way you process invoices you might not get paid in a timely manner or your invoices will go out the door with incorrect pricing. That can result in lost revenue and unhappy customers.

Second, although as a new manager you may see your area of ownership somewhat limited, you must make decisions that impact more than just your domain. If your correction of a problem shifts the problem elsewhere in your organization than you are part of the problem and not the solution. Think through the effects of your changes and try and focus on complete elimination of problems not shifting of them.

Third, analyze the different gaps from the simple versus the complex. I've seen suggestions such as implementing a new ERP system that is a very costly, time consuming and complex process but could generate great long-term returns. I've also seen simple suggestions such as photocopy the documents before you ship them to the main office or set materiality thresholds for manager review. These are not costly and time consuming to implement and they could be the changes that make a big difference in your process. Keep in mind, if your suggestions are all time consuming and costly to implement, you're not showing quick wins and that may cause a project to stall or run out of steam. It is good to always suggest some quick wins to keep momentum strong.

Finally lets look at the strategic versus the tactical. Organize your gaps in a way that shows a link to strategy. This is taking a long-term perspective. Also organize the gaps in terms of the tactical ones this takes an operational perspective.

Communicate the Gaps

As a new manager it will be important to communicate the gaps in an appropriate manner. There are multiple ways to communicate the gaps. Exhibit 1-6 summarizes these communication types.

Exhibit 1-6 Communication Types

Type of strategy	When to use this strategy	What should be accomplished
Workshop	-intent to immediately implement the change -participants are motivated and bought into the concept of change	-present proposed changes and resulting benefits -decide on next steps (goals, timelines, and accountable roles)
Focus Group	-implementation not immediate -motivation and buy-in are needed	-present proposed changes and resulting benefits -discuss and consider the results and ramifications of change -determine next steps (move forward with implementation or not)
Formal Presentation	-implementation not immediate -motivation and buy-in needed -a later date for focus group or workshop	-debrief project accomplishments -present proposed changes and resulting benefits - determine next steps (move forward with implementation or not)
Internal Communication	-finding documentation of findings and conclusions	-to create awareness that this phase of the project has concluded

Keys to Success

When you determine the gaps in your process, remember these keys to success:

- Involve team members in the process. Get your team involved in identifying gaps. The more perspective on the issues the better. Also, remember the team composition, they are stakeholders with skin in the game and their roles might be impacted by any changes. To this end, get them involved in these decisions. This way if any changes take place down the road they feel less intimidated by them.
- Don't over rationalize. Attitudes like "we can't control this", "it's not our problem", and my personal favorite "we're not like anything else so what others do can't be applied here" stifle creativity. Be objective document your gaps for what they are: the difference between your As Is and the Should Be.
- Try and quantify gaps, where possible. Numbers are like pictures they speak a thousand words. If you can say that your cycle time is 48 hours and the best practice is 2 hours that is powerful. If you can communicate that it costs you $15.00 to process an invoice versus the best practice of $5.00 that is articulating a wide gap. You get my point, try and communicate through less wordy diatribes and more focused statements.

- Consider change management implications. A solid gap analysis will be forward thinking. If you know that the culture of your organization may stifle a change mention this as an element of risk. Gaps cannot be narrowed or eliminated by force and fear. Don't assume implementation will be happily accepted.

Step 4. Adapt Action Plans

<u>Create Action Plans</u>

We'll discuss action planning later in the book but for know let's just say that this is important to clearly articulate a road map for implementation. A clear action plan communicates the agreed upon recommendations that will be resolved through changes in people, process, technology or strategy. In short, an action plan does not have to be a thousand pages but you should make sure it has the following components:

- Statement of the problem
- Statement of the recommendation (and how it will resolve the problem)
- Key parties responsible for implementation
- Key steps needed to implement the change
- Timing for each step to begin and end
- Rewards if successfully implemented on time
- Performance measures to monitor progress over time

<u>Develop a Change Management Program</u>

Like action plans, we'll discuss change management in more detail but for now let's just set the stage for it by saying it is often overlooked and mismanaged and causes many projects to fail during implementation. To prevent this from happening, follow these change management steps:

- Create the case for change.
- Define a vision for the future.
- Conduct a change readiness assessment.
- Conduct a change leadership workshop.
- Design the change management plan.

<u>Keys to Success</u>

To adapt appropriate action plans that have a probable chance of successful implementation, remember the following:

- Consider training needs. Most implementations require behavior changes. To put people at ease and ensure change is implemented correctly develop appropriate training programs.
- Consider ripple effects to other areas. We've already stated that you don't want to solve a problem that really shifts it elsewhere.

But also consider how your changes will impact not just the activities within the group you manage but also any inputs to your process and outputs to your process.

- Avoid false starts. A false start is beginning to make change when you're not ready for it. That can destroy credibility and damage moral.
- Don't over simplify. Recognize that some changes such as the implementation of a new system may involve multiple action plans and steps. Don't sugar coat the change with simplicity if it won't be.

Step 5. Measure and Monitor

Performance Measures

This step is an umbrella over the entire methodology. It really is the true sense of continuous improvement. You can't be expected to do a costly and time-consuming project for every little issue that transpires. In addition, if you do spend significant resources to make a change you'll want to know if the change was beneficial. To this end, you'll want to devise a small, yet well-balanced family of performance measures to monitor the process. We'll discuss performance measures later in the book. But, we'll give you a brief overview below.

Types of Measures

The key to performance measurement is good balance. I recall a project a few years ago where I was helping a company improve their payroll processing function. The payroll manager was very interested in the results because he felt he was a best practice performer. I ran a high level diagnostic and benchmarked the company's payroll process to around 100 other organizations. The process was great for a variety of benchmarks that were linked to cost initiatives. However, he was under performing where the benchmarks were tied to quality, productivity, customer satisfaction and timeliness issues.

Upon seeing this the payroll manager quickly realized that he had executed on a strategy to cut costs based on a corporate initiative the CFO had launched the prior year. The payroll manager gave early retirement to a few senior payroll clerks that were commanding high salaries and hired more junior staff to fill the roles. The outcome was evident. The payroll manager achieved his goal of cost cutting and the performance measures proved that. However, he did not focus on other issues that were equally important and thus was suffering in those areas. We envisioned that the other areas he was lagging in would eventually wipe away any cost efficiencies he had achieved.

The moral of the above story is balance your measures. We suggest a balance across cost, quality, time, productivity, and customer satisfaction. If you are having trouble thinking through them try to think broader at what the major corporate objectives typically are. In my experience those corporate objectives are:

- Increase revenue
- Decrease cost
- Increase productivity
- Increase quality
- Increase customer satisfaction
- Increase employee retention

Almost any initiative you do is probably geared toward accomplishing one of the above objectives. So try and shadow these with performance measures that link to them.

Keys to Success

The keys to successful measuring and monitoring can be summed up as follows:

- Use a small set of measures. You don't need a thousand measures. Remember you can't spend all day calculating statistics and analyzing them, you do have a regular job to do! Keep it small, I would say if you have more than ten it is too many. I like a number between 5 to 7 myself.
- Ensure measures are well balanced. We discussed the need to be multi-dimensional in your measurement. Review each measure and ensure you are addressing the right objectives.
- Use baselines from historic data to set goals and compare against. Once you create measures measure past performance. This is a good way to see if you can efficiently and effectively compute your measures but it also tells you where you're at so you can set goals for improvement.
- Visually measure. Use graphs and pictures rather than tables of numbers. Motivate by example by placing the key graphs around the office so employees can be reminded of them and see results changing over time.

Summing It Up

Now that you have been introduced to this methodology let's get more tactical and explore how you can attack these steps with some tools and tips that make it actionable and meaningful.

Remember, methodologies can be adjusted to fit your needs. Don't let methodologies collect dust on a shelf; use them to help you improve your performance. As a new manager you need to get out there and make changes and prove you can do things better than they're being done now.

Chapter Two: Continuous Improvement Movements

Defining Quality

Before drilling deeper into continuous improvement tools I wanted to take a moment to familiarize you with some continuous improvement movements. A continuous improvement movement is a popular quality initiative that has been endorsed by reputable organizations and applied by world-class companies from a variety of business disciplines.

The three continuous improvement movements I will discuss are Six Sigma, ISO, and Baldrige. At a minimum, the goal here is to orient you on what these movements are trying to achieve and to compare and contrast the movements. Ultimately, in building your own continuous improvement program, you can find one of these or bits and pieces of them all to help you create your own quality process.

I just mentioned the word quality. These movements are really about quality. So before I go any further I'd like to define quality with a little more detail.

The best place you'll find information about quality is from the American Society for Quality (ASQ). The ASQ has been shaping America's thought leadership on quality for over fifty years. It offers many tools to assist a new manager in thinking about quality and I encourage visiting their website to learn more about them. They are found at www.asq.org.

The ASQ among others will tell you that quality is really a state of mind as much as anything else. Quality can be described as follows:

- An approach to business rather than a program or "flavor of the month."
- A collection of tools and concepts that have been proven to work.
- Quality is ultimately defined by the customer's satisfaction.
- Continuous improvement is a subset of quality.
- Quality can be applied to all business processes.
- The goal of quality is excellence. All else is opportunity to improve.
- Quality applies to all industries including government and non-profit organizations.
- Performance results such as increased productivity and improved profitability are derivatives of excellent quality management.

When we think of quality and continuous improvement we tend to also think of business process re-engineering (BPR) and total quality management (TQM). TQM is broadly defined as a set of continuous improvement principles to facilitate change on a constant and progressive basis. BPR promotes larger changes using formalized and structured techniques to change a process. Some researchers argue that TQM is a good starter for BPR.

If you think about it, the methodology presented in chapter two is a hybrid of TQM and BPR. TQM, being continuous and progressive improvement steps is synergistic to the 'manage and monitor' process. While the formalized and structured approach of identifying issues, mapping the process, researching best practices, documenting gaps, and creating action plans to narrow the gaps links nicely to BPR.

Both TQM and BPR are well-accepted approaches to problem solving. Six Sigma, ISO and Baldrige are movements that support these concepts in their own unique ways. In fact, the argument can be made that TQM and BPR are dead management fads while concepts like Six Sigma, ISO and Baldrige are going strong.

However, the point of this rant is to tell you that no matter what you call it, your continuous improvement movement must be sound and embraced by your organization. Not to be discouraging, but reality is that Baldrige award winners go bankrupt, ISO-9000 registered companies have been known to produce poor quality goods and services, and those practicing Six Sigma programs might not be at Three Sigma. So, read on but do so knowing that quality can be nothing more than a fad or a flavor of the month in your organization if it is not embraced, championed, formalized and resource committed.

ISO Facts

First, a great source to learn more about ISO is by visiting a website located at http://www.iso.ch/. Many of the following ISO facts are summarized from this website.

ISO stands for the International Standards Organization. ISO is a set of rules and guidelines to ensure quality processes are in place. The rules were developed by industry consensus and voluntary submissions.

There are a few ISO quality certifications. These are as follows:

- ISO 9000 provides a framework for quality management and assurance
- QS 9000 a common supplier quality standard used by the Ford, General Motors and Chrysler
- ISO 14000 provides a framework for environmental management

To learn how to implement the standards managers from various organizations will go to seminars or use consultants. However, implementation is voluntary in most industries with the exception of certain industries that require it. However, in certain industries, certification sends a signal to competitors, suppliers and customers that your quality standards are in place. It can be a real advantage.

Once certified by an ISO auditor, the ISO auditors monitor certification through surveillance. The auditors can revoke certification if quality standards are not maintained.

ISO Principles

There are eight main principles to ISO certification.

1. *Customer focus* this looks at how the organization is meeting customer needs and strives to exceed customer expectations
2. *Leadership* this looks at the strength of management and their ability to establish unity and purpose of direction within the organization
3. *Involvement of people* this looks at the skill levels, experiences, and training of people and how people are fully involved in the organization
4. *Process approach* this looks at how inputs, activities and outputs are managed collectively and harmoniously, efficiently and effectively
5. *System approach to management* this looks at the way the organization manages interrelated processes to contribute to the organizations objectives
6. *Continual improvement* this looks at the program(s) in place to ensure that organizational performance continuously progresses and is a permanent organizational objective
7. *Factual approach to decision-making* this looks at how the organization makes decisions recognizing that effective decisions are based on data analysis and factual information
8. *Mutually beneficial supplier relationships* this looks at the strength of supplier relationships recognizing that a mutually beneficial relationship can enhance the value of both organizations

Understanding the guiding principles of ISO, let's look at the advantages and disadvantages of adapting this type of quality program.

Advantages of ISO

- Promotes unity through generic management principles
- Provides a framework for continual improvement
- Ability to attract new business and bid on new contracts
- Documented system that is a useful training tool
- The potential and hope for fewer errors and rejects
- The need to maintain standards in lieu of lost certification
- A marketing and PR tool that promotes the organization's commitment to quality

Disadvantages of ISO

- It is often costly and time consuming to obtain certification
- It is often costly and time consuming to maintain certification
- It is often a challenge to implement based on strict ISO guidelines
- Documentation can be overwhelming at times
- Strict procedures can stifle out-of-the-box improvement ideas
- Uses a pass/fail mentality for certification

Several organizations have adopted ISO as a part of their quality process. For example, Ford Motor Company, Chrysler Corporation and General Motors Corporation adapted a version of ISO known as QS-9000. These guidelines represent the automotive interpretation of the standards. Many suppliers to these automotive manufacturers must be QS-9000 certified before they can do business with these companies.

Remember, quality programs are not fail-proof. One need only look at the Ford/Firestone situation to understand this clearly. Firestone passed the surveillance audit but the end results still did not guarantee the customer total protection against defects.

Nonetheless, ISO programs have proven to be an effective means of establishing baseline quality programs that have formality and rigor. For example, Frymaster Corporation, a Louisiana-based manufacturer of deep-fat friers, ISO is used as one component to their overall Quality Assurance (QA) strategy. They use internal testing, inspection and auditing to meet both internal and external requirements.

Frymaster began their goal of being ISO certified in 1990 and reached it by late 1992. The ISO registration signals to Frymaster customers that they are a supplier of quality products. The rigor of the ISO application process forced Frymaster to make significant adaptations to their quality documentation standards. Additionally, because the standards need to be maintained, the company was forced to scrutinize and streamline many underlying processes throughout the organization saving them time and money.

ISO Company In Action: Industrial Product Company A

Industrial Product Company A. has maintained a long history of creating and marketing unique products to serve the needs of industrial consumers. A key ingredient contributing to their success is its adherence to long-term principles such as innovation, customer service and extraordinary quality. In the 1980's Industrial Product Company A, a privately held company, was acquired by Chemical Company B.

Along with this acquisition came Chemical Company B's unique business philosophy, which encourages its operating companies to operate independently and establish synergies where feasible. During the mid 1990's Chemical Company B's operating companies, including Industrial Product Company A, geared up for expansion into global markets and were confronted by many barriers. An important asset that helped alleviate some of these barriers was the synergies between Chemical Company B's operating companies. Many new entrants were able to gain global access through previously established Chemical Company B's operating companies. To further reduce entry barriers Chemical Company B mandated that all of its operating companies actively pursue ISO 9001 certification. Certification would assure both domestic and international customers that products designed and managed by these operating companies would maintain a consistent level of quality. In addition, those companies that utilized the synergies among Chemical Company B's operating companies would be assured of these standards.

Prior to ISO 9001, Industrial Product Company A's operations could have been described as reactive and chaotic. Things were done a certain way because they were always done that way. Its operations lacked the procedures to consistently produce and monitor products and services. Many internal business units failed to effectively communicate critical information to one another. Resulting in costly delays, poor customer service and countless production errors. Somehow, Industrial Product Company A beat all the odds. Sales and profits continued to grow at a record pace. Industrial Product Company A was a model company for all other Chemical Company B companies to follow. However, many of the details previously mentioned went undetected by Chemical Company B due to its lack of controls and the autonomy it granted to its operating companies. As global sales continued to expand Industrial Product Company A was at risk of loosing current and future business if it did not establish a standardized process to monitor and record its operations.

The initial launch of ISO 9001 at Industrial Product Company A was met with much resistance. It was extremely difficult to implement this process due to top management's lack of support for certification. Again, ISO 9001 certification was mandated to all operating companies by Chemical Company B's headquarters. Many of the operating company leaders shared this resistance to comply because they felt that this was the first in many steps to rid the operating companies of their autonomy. Thereby, threatening the success of many divisions. Companies with a track record of success greatly feared this new process. It was a drastic change from the way things were historically done. In an effort to reduce these internal barriers and gain compliance Chemical Company B devised a compensation plan that would greatly benefit those managers who met the established deadlines for ISO 9001 certification.

Industrial Product Company A began its ISO 9001 certification program in the late 1990's by developing a committee that would implement and oversee ISO training, procedures and documentation. This committee was comprised of individuals from various departments including, sales, quality control, customer service, operations and research and development. This committee was responsible for establishing and standardizing processes within the organization. In addition, they would continuously review and make adjustments to these procedures if needed. Processes were prioritized based on the principles of the organization and a timeline was established. This would lay the basis for Industrial Product Company A's short- and long-term strategic planning.

The ISO certification program began in manufacturing. The current manufacturing process was a just-in-time system. The main focus of the ISO implementation was to establish a standardized just-in-time process for producing products. Prior to the new ISO procedures vendors, line operators and technical support were not held accountable. ISO established a streamline process, which included a paper trail that detailed batch production processes, thereby, assigning accountability. As a result, batch errors, rework and inferior raw materials were significantly reduced. In addition, many of the current vendors were urged to become ISO certified otherwise, Industrial Product Company A would be unable to continue their business relationship.

Next, the focus was on customer service, which included order taking and complaint resolution. In the order-taking department employees were trained on new procedures and documentation to track orders, credits and resolve complaints. Shipping and logistics were also trained on these new processes. In addition, common carriers with similar processes and values were sought out by the Director of Logistics. Quality control established procedures to review and monitor databases of customer complaints and batch retains. Previously, less than ten percent of all customer complaints were logged into a database. Both internal (consumer affairs) and external (sales) customer support have been trained on these new procedures and documentation. Since the ISO certification complaint recording is accurate and customer complaints have declined.

Finally, procedures were established for communicating and developing new products. Traditionally, the technical department and upper management generated new product ideas resulting in numerous successes and several costly disappointments. When a decision to produce a new product was made it generally did not include input from Industrial Product Company A 's customers base. With the establishment of ISO 9001 procedures Industrial Product Company A now had a formal process for developing new products and restructuring existing products to meet market demands. This helped to streamline costs and reduce the communication gaps between critical internal departments. Through the use of new documentation, procedures and regularly schedule cross-functional meetings, new product introductions are more successful than ever.

In conclusion, since the implementation of ISO 9001 several years ago the management I spoke with has noticed dramatic positive changes in product quality and customer service. In their industry, Industrial Product Company A is considered the benchmark for providing exceptional customer service and unmatched product quality. However, top management at Industrial Product Company A continues to show resentment toward Chemical Company B for mandating this costly and time-consuming procedure. It seems that egos were bruised, and the benefits of ISO 9001 have not fully been embraced. This continues to be evident particularly in the new product development process. For example, product managers were instructed to utilize the procedures put into place by the ISO committee. On a daily basis they were challenged by Industrial Product Company A's President and sales management to bypass these guidelines in order to bring products to market quicker, which potentially could result in costly errors. Until Industrial Product Company A's top management fully accepts and appreciates the benefits of ISO 9001, policies will be ignored and things will be done as they have always been done in the past.

ISO Company In Action: Safety Product Company A

Competition in product safety industry is fierce. The constant introduction of new products manufactured by foreign entities shrinks the market share of many US companies and reduces their already eroding profit margins. Safety Product Company A is one of the leading US safety products companies. Safety Product Company B is a determined competitor to A. Both have adopted ISO 9001 standards to stay competitive.

Safety Product Company A manufactures and markets safety equipment and apparel. The apparel produced by the company must meet standards set forth by national safety organizations. Powerful industry associations mandate that certain apparel must be manufactured in a facility with ISO 9001 registration. According to Safety Product Company A's Technical Manager, the adoption of this standard is what led to the company's beginning the process of seeking ISO 9001 certification. While they initially brought in a consultant to work with them on this process, they quickly dismissed this plan. According to the company's ISO Coordinator, the consultants just didn't have the same knowledge of their business that the company's own internal resources had.

Even before the company began to migrate to ISO9001 had very strict quality control procedures. It was only the documentation of these procedures that was the bulk of their required work for ISO. Having these strict internal procedures prior to even consideration of seeking ISO registration greatly aided in the process and was a main contributor to their earning registration only 18 months after beginning the process. Yet it was the documentation of these processes that was still key, because it wasn't until they achieved consistency that they could then work towards true continuous improvement. Safety Product Company A's ISO registrar is experienced in their industry, which also helped speed the process along.

Safety Product Company A has found that their ISO 9001 registration has impacted their business in a variety of ways. For starters it was a requirement for them to be able to sell certain safety gear, so the simple ability to continue to do this was critical. Secondly, it has had a positive impact on their relationship with suppliers. They have pushed their quality controls back the supply chain on to their own suppliers, and now inquire about ISO certification on their Supplier Application Forms. From a quality of product perspective, Safety Product Company A has quality production meetings every morning where they review the master database of product yields by SKU. By regularly analyzing these results they can look for irregularities and then research the root causes.

Safety Product Company B's journey towards ISO 9001 certification began from a similar motivation. Safety Product Company B is a domestic manufacturer of safety equipment. While a great deal of sales are in the US, they have grown their sales by exporting products all over the world. Several of the products they manufacture are required to be done in an ISO 9001 registered facility.

According Safety Product Company B's QA and Regulatory Affairs Manager, while meeting the requirements was the primary initial goal of seeking ISO 9001 registration they found that its benefits were much more wide reaching. The company attributes the fact it has been able to continue manufacturing in the US while many of their competitors has been pressured to move production elsewhere directly to its continuous improvement processes.

One of the biggest obstacles that Best needed to overcome while working towards registration were from within their own organization. The QA and Regulatory Affairs Manager estimates that a very high level of functional illiteracy made the necessary documentation even more cumbersome. This is a main reason that it took almost 3 years, for them to receive its ISO registration. Their registrar was chosen due to its global presence and its ability to keep Safety Product Company B informed of the regulatory issues in a large number of different countries.

The biggest improvement that Safety Product Company B notes between the earlier ISO standards and the latest 2000 standards is the scope of information. Earlier standards were much more focused on a narrow manufacturing perspective. ISO 2000 is more focused on an overall management/business focus; meeting the goals of the company (making money) by producing products that your customers will purchase. It is this greater scope of accountability by management that the company estimates is the primary cause behind a 10-15% drop in ISO registered companies. Yet Safety Product Company B's Manufacturing continues to thrive as a world leader.

Baldrige Award Facts

First, a great source to learn more about the Baldrige Award is by visiting a website located at http://www.quality.nist.gov/. Many of the following Baldrige facts are summarized from this website.

The Baldrige Award was named in honor of Malcolm Baldrige. Baldrige was the Secretary of Commerce under President Ronald Reagan. He was notorious for his managerial excellence.

In recognition of Baldrige, who passed away several years ago, the government recognizes organizations that achieve performance excellence by focusing on their overall performance management system.

The President of the United States gives the award. The awards process is managed by the National Institute of Standards and Technology.

Baldrige Principles

Baldrige has criteria available for business, healthcare and education sectors. Below are the criteria for the business sector.

Leadership this looks at senior management and how they guide the organization and practice good corporate citizenship

Strategic planning this examines how the organization sets strategic direction and creates action plans to accomplish the strategy

Customer and market focus this examines how the organization determines the requirements and expectations for markets and customers

Information and analysis this examines how the organization uses data and information to support key organizational processes and maintain their performance management system

Human resource focus this examines how the organization enables its workforce to develop its full potential and how the workforce is aligned with organizational objectives

Process management this examines how key production, delivery and support processes are designed, managed and improved

Business results this examines organizational performance and improvement in key business areas such as customer satisfaction, financial and marketplace performance, human resources, supplier and partner performance, and operational performance. The category also examines how the organization performs relative to competitors

With the Baldrige award, a company does not have to win the award to use the principles inherent in the program. In fact, you don't even have to apply for the award. Many organizations use the structure and rigor of the award criteria to help guide them in their own customized continuous improvement process.

Like ISO standards, Baldrige has its advantages and disadvantages.

Advantages of Baldrige

- A widely accepted standard of performance excellence
- An excellent credential to have for marketing and PR purposes (if you are one of the rare few who win this coveted award)
- A great way to promote continuous improvement amongst the ranks within the organization
- Provides a solid framework for organizations to establish their own continuous improvement process

Disadvantages of Baldrige

- Only US headquartered companies can receive the award
- Sometimes the mystique of getting the award overshadows the purpose of quality improvement
- The award can be very costly and time consuming to apply for

Baldrige Company In Action: The Ritz Carlton Hotel

The Ritz Carlton Hotel Company is the only two-time recipient of the Malcolm Baldrige National Quality Award in the service area. The company competes against ten other hotel groups in the luxury and up-scale hotel market with its largest business segment being meeting and events planners followed by leisure travelers.

Prior to 1983, the hotel industry had dramatically increased in size creating a structure operated by functional departments with each hotel. The leader of the functional department had the responsibility of maintaining the quality and operations of the department. All functional areas reported to the general manager of the specific hotel location. This coupled with increasing product complexity caused and almost complete separation between the planning and execution functions. The end result was that problems were unrealized until they reached the customer, segregation between divisions and departments and lack of involvement by upper-management in quality initiates.

In 1983 Horst Schultz became President and Chief Operating Officer, he decided that managing for quality could not be delegated. Schultz developed a team to take charge of all quality initiates. In 1989 he selected the Malcolm Baldrige criteria to provide a more comprehensive structure to optimize performance.   Through the assessment tool they created a "Roadmap" that resulted in the becoming the first ever two-time recipient of the award.

Summary of Procedures
1. Upper Management Participation (Initiated between 1983-1988): Upper management defined the traits of all company products in The Credo. They then translated The Credo into a basic standard of quality and responsibility for the employees. The most important standards included the anticipation of the guest's needs, resolution of guest problems and the presentation of a caring attitude toward guests and others.
2. Business Excellence Roadmap (Initiated between 1989-1999): This "Roadmap" incorporated a continuous improvement methodology by establishing with a team of Senior Leaders and employees that would be affected by the results of the planning. The team applied the continuous improvement mythology which consisted of four parts: (1) The Approach "Plan" (2) Deployment "Do" (3) Results "Check" (4) Improvement "Act," to each of the seven Malcolm Baldrige criteria.
   Leadership:
   - Plan: Senior Leaders collectively set the direction for business excellence by establishing seven decisions including: 10 Year Vision, 5 Year Mission, 3 Year Objectives, 1 Year Tactics, Strategy, Methods and Foundation.
   - Do: Senior leaders work with hotel workers before each new opening using a combination of hands-on behavior models and reinforcement.   They also distribute the results of the strategic

planning session to employees in the form of a "Pyramid Concept." Finally, senior management reinforces the Gold Standards daily.

- Check: Semi-annual employees satisfaction surveys and audits on public responsibility.
- Act: Development and training programs, a leadership center located at the company headquarters, and developmental job assignments address gaps in leadership.

Strategic Planning:
- Plan: Senior Leaders conduct a Macro-Environmental Analysis that details the current stage of the environment and results in a future projection of the state of The Ritz-Carlton.
- Do: Senior leaders deploy Vital-Few objectives. These objectives are then divided and sub-divided by process owner at the corporate level. Processes are developed and resources are allocated.
- Checks/Act: Monthly performance reviews of the strategic plan are conducted by upper management and translated into opportunities for improvement and innovation.

Customer and Market Focus:
- Plan: Market research is conducted to determine market segments, potential customers, and the relative priorities of customers, individual dissatisfaction, widespread dissatisfaction, competitive quality status and opportunities for improving revenues through quality.
- Do: The Sales and Marketing deploy the results of research through four major processes: (1) The 6P's concept (2) Operations of the CLASS database (3) Complaint Resolution Process and (4) Standard Performance Measurements.
- Check: The effectiveness of the Customer and Market Focus are measured by daily, monthly and annual standard performance reviews.
- Act: Review and identify gaps to be corrected.

Information and Analysis:
- Plan: The Ritz-Carlton selects organization measurements for upper managers and operation measurements to evaluate planning. The company also performs three forms of comparative benchmarks to evaluate performance including industry competitors, companies outside the industry and internal.
- Do: Senior leaders deploy information based on the concept of individual process owners.
- Check: Employees are charged with the collection of data and a consultant is brought in to analyze the information.
- Act: Changes are made based on third party findings.

Human Resource Focus:
- Plan: Senior Leaders develop a plan to improve employee satisfaction. It is based on the notion that employees know the procedures of their jobs, have learned and use the Gold Standards, and generate ideas for improvement.

- Do: The company selects employees based on The Quality Selection Process and provides education and training designed to keep individuals up to date with business needs.
- Check: Continuous training for each employee is provided in a number of ways. Employee appraisals and surveys identify weaknesses in training procedures.
- Act: Improvements are made based on internal audits, surveys and appraisals.

Process Management:
- Plan: Market research identifies key production processes. Additional information is obtained via formal discussions between support/operations employees and internal/external customers that identify and support processes that impact the company's mission.
- Do: Action including incorporating change, assigning process owners, emphasizing the employee handbook, and hotel development processes are taken to deploy the company's annual process management approach.
- Check: The Ritz-Carlton Corporation puts its results in numbers.
- Act: Improvements are implemented through the traditional hierarchy and through executive process owners.

Business Results:
- Plan: Senior Leaders use strategic objectives to define long-term targets and use tactical processes to set annual targets.
- Do: The Ritz-Carlton deploys the plan by leading people, managing processes and determining standard performance measures.
- Check: Actual versus Planned Performance is evaluated quarterly by Senior Leader and daily operations are reviewed by the workforce.
- Act: Continuous Improvement

The Continuous Improvement procedures have delivered positive results. The percentage of meeting planners that were "extremely satisfied" with their experience was up from just under 70 percent in 1998 to over 80 percent in 1999, while 99 percent said they were satisfied. Overnight guest satisfaction also increased. Financial performance has increased as well, 1999 revenues were up to $1.5 billion, a 40 percent increase over the previous five years.

Baldrige Company In Action: Clarke American

Clarke American, one of the largest printers of financial institution checks in the United States, was selected as a recipient of the Malcolm Baldrige National Quality Award for 2001 in the category of manufacturing. Clarke American began its quality improvement initiatives in 1986 when it developed its "First in Service" quality program.

In 1993 and 1994 Clarke American applied for the Malcolm Baldrige National Quality Award. This was the point when they understand that in order to achieve world-class levels of performance excellence that it would be a long journey. Through time, their internal assessment process evolved from the Quest Quality Fitness Review, a performance measure developed by Quest Quality, a London-based consulting firm that assisted Clarke American in their implementation of the "First in Service" disciplines, to the Business Excellence Assessment that is modeled as a mirror image of the Baldrige Model, which includes: Leadership, Strategic Planning, Customer and Market Focus, Information and Analysis, Human Resources Focus, Process Management, and Business Results.

Some of the highlights within the Business Excellence Assessment model that Clarke American implemented include:

LEADERSHIP
The base of Clarke American's success is solid values. Clarke American's Key Leadership Team (KLT), which includes the President and Chief Executive Officer, the Chief Operating Officer, the General Managers of each business division, and the Vice Presidents, is the group that establishes and deploys values, direction, and performance expectations.

The Key Leadership Team encourages an environment of empowerment, which includes the S.T.A.R. program in which employees propose and quantify improvements of any size.

STRATEGIC PLANNING
Clarke American establishes long-term strategic objectives during development of the strategic vision. Shorter-term objectives are linked to the vision during goal deployment. In order to implement their strategic objectives, action plans are established al every level of the organization.

CUSTOMER AND MARKET FOCUS
Clarke American is continually creating value for current and prospective partners and customers. This is accomplished through strategic studies and market research and uses both quantitative and qualitative tools to gather information regarding satisfaction relative to competitors.

INFORMATION ANALYSIS
Clarke American gathers information through performance metrics in order to continually set goals and to analyze performance. Clarke American uses benchmarking to compare themselves to competitors. The CEO and other executives have been personally involved in the adoption of numerous best practices that have been gleaned from "study tours".

HUMAN RESOURCES FOCUS
Clarke American's Human Resource focus is to empower and to motivate its employees. One philosophy used to motivate employees to excel is "Start Anywhere, Go Anywhere". Another practice that Clarke American has implemented in a pay for performance compensation practice that is designed to reward teams and individuals for customer focused high performance.

PROCESS MANAGEMENT

All of Clarke American's processes are aimed at satisfying partners and customers. Clarke American uses a proactive approach to build in quality to its design, production, and delivery processes.

BUSINESS RESULTS

Clarke American uses various tools to measure results, such as:

Customer Focused Results

On-time service

Financial and Market Results

Revenue trend and growth rate

Inventory turns

Human Resource Results

Associate satisfaction

401K plan participation

Organizational Effectiveness Results

Manufacturing cycle time

Check manufacturing units per hour

Revenue per associate

Linking ISO and Baldrige

As you probably recognized, there are some similarities between ISO and Baldrige programs. In case you didn't let's summarize the similarities and then discuss the differences.

Similarities between ISO and Baldrige

Similarities:

- Both are quality movements
- Use many of the same tools and methodologies (reengineering, root cause analysis)
- Dependent upon the thinking of quality giant W. Edwards Demming
- Both focus on customer, process and continuous improvement

Differences:

- ISO is international whereas Baldrige is limited to the US
- ISO recognition covers less than 10% of the Baldrige criteria
- ISO is more concerned with conformance standards
- Baldrige winners can do poorly afterwards and not lose the award
- Baldrige criteria is points based (on 1000 points) vs. ISO is conform/nonconformist

Because of the above, some quality leaders have proposed a merger amongst the two programs. Nicknamed MB9000, the program would have both Baldrige and ISO criteria. Please note that such a program has yet to be formally recognized. For more information about what the merged criteria might look like, refer to the article "Integrating ISO 9001: 2000 And the Baldrige Criteria" by Hampton

Scott Tonk, in the August 2000 issue of *Quality Progress*. There you'll find a schematic showing the merger of the two programs.

Six Sigma Facts

First, a great source to learn more about the Six Sigma is by visiting a website located at http://www.isixsigma.com/.

Six Sigma has its origins as a Greek letter that is a statistical unit of measurement used to define the standard deviation of a population. Six Sigma is the equivalent of 3.4 defects per million opportunities. It is equivalent to a 99.99966% success rate.

To illustrate the magnitude of achieving six sigma consider the following:

- At 3 Sigma there are 54,000 wrong drug prescriptions per year, at Six Sigma there is 1 wrong prescription in 25 years.
- At 3 Sigma there are 40,500 dropped newborn babies per year, at Six Sigma there is 3 newborns dropped in 100 years
- At 3 Sigma there is unsafe drinking water released 2 hours per month, at Six Sigma there is 1 second of unsafe drinking water every 16 years
- At 3 Sigma there are 5 crash landings per day at the busiest airports, at Six Sigma there is 1 crash landing in 10 years
- At 3 Sigma there are 54,000 pieces of lost mail per hour, at Six Sigma there is 35 lost pieces of mail per year.

The Six Sigma program was started by Bill Smith, a reliability engineer at Motorola, that sold the idea to CEO Robert Galvin. Smith concluded that higher quality was necessary to prevent field failure. Motorola subsequently won a Baldrige Award for its Six Sigma efforts.

Six Sigma has now been used by many large and small organizations. Some of the more highly publicized users of Six Sigma include the following organizations:

Financial services sector: GE Capital, JP Morgan, AIG Insurance, American Express, Citibank, American General, and LG Insurance

Manufacturing sector: Motorola, Allied Signal, General Electric, Eaton, LG Group (Korea), Sony (Japan), Philips Lighting – Europe, and Johnson & Johnson

High tech sector: Seagate Technologies, Gateway, Compaq, Toshiba, and Microsoft

Government sector: US Postal Service, and US Mint

Chemical sector: Dow Chemical, DuPont, and Air Products

Aerospace/Automotive sector: Lockheed Martin, Penske, Navistar, Ford, and Dana Corp.

Six Sigma Principles

Below is a high-level framework for the Six Sigma Process. It is often referred to as the DMAIC process (Define, Measure, Analyze, Improve, Control).

Define
- Define project goals and deliverables
- Define in terms of internal and external customers
- Determine and define the critical requirements

Measure
- Select CTQ (critical to quality) characteristic
- Define performance standards
- Validate measurement system

Analyze
- Establish product capability
- Define performance objectives
- Identify variation sources

Improve
- Screen potential causes
- Discover variable relationships
- Establish operating tolerances

Control
- Validate measurement system
- Determine process capability
- Implement process controls

In addition to the steps in the process, Six Sigma followers certify their practitioners to ensure they have the appropriate training and experience to lead Six Sigma projects. The certification components are as follows:

Green Belts - - Employees participating on a Six Sigma team.

Black Belts - - Manager assigned responsibility to implement Six Sigma. Black Belts have an in-depth understanding of Six Sigma philosophy, theory, strategy, tactics, and quality management tools

Master Black Belts - - Company-wide Six Sigma quality experts. The Master Black Belt is qualified to teach other Six Sigma Black Belts, Green Belts or champions the methodologies, tools, and applications in all functions and levels of the company.

Like ISO and Baldrige, Six Sigma has its advantages and disadvantages.

Advantages of Six Sigma

- integrates a deep sense of quality (centered around defects) into the organization
- addresses the importance of failure and quality
- addresses leadership tools and infrastructure issues
- promotes company wide excellence
- it is disciplined and statistical (data driven approach)

Disadvantages of Six Sigma

- little to offer that can't be found elsewhere (a marketing ploy)
- it is more of an appraisal system or corrective system, rather than preventative
- it may be unreasonable to attain such low defect rates for all processes
- it is difficult to implement as it requires the support and training of many
- it may take years to reach 6 sigma

Six Sigma in practice

Organizations that have applied Six Sigma believe its benefits definitely exceed the costs. GE is probably the best-known case for this. For example, In GE's 1998 Annual Report they attributed $1.2B profit to one strategic initiative - Six Sigma. This initiative was driving growth and cost reduction. Exhibit 2-1 showcases the costs vs. benefits from GE's Six Sigma initiative:

Exhibit 2-1 GE's Six Sigma Costs vs. Benefits

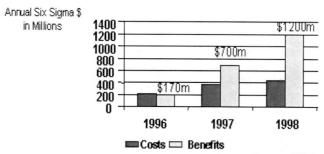

Source: 1998 GE Annual Report

Other organizations such as Citibank claim they have increased their customer loyalty by applying Six Sigma processes. Citibank began its quality initiative in 1997 and in six months trained over 600 managers. Within two years, over 90,000 employees received training. They have reduced cycle time elements of their funds availability process by up to 75 percent. They attribute their success to the Six Sigma program coupled with training and process mapping.

Six Sigma Company In Action: Motorola

Motorola has been at the forefront of the quality movement for decades. However, the company learned about quality by facing hard times such as when a Japanese firm took over a US factory due to quality problems. The management takeover actually proved to be a very positive sign for Motorola. Under Japanese management, the factory was producing products with $1/20^{th}$ the number of defects it had produced under Motorola management. From these tough experiences, Motorola began the process of improving quality.

Since undertaking Six Sigma initiatives to root out defects the company has been rewarded. For example, in 1988, Motorola won the Malcolm Baldrige National Quality Award. In addition, Motorola has been universally recognized for its quality practices and is often sought out as a benchmark partner and trainer on Six Sigma initiatives and processes.

Currently the company continues its emphasis on Six Sigma but has broadened it to include a new program of Performance Excellence, based on the Baldrige Model. This model demands a commitment to quality through visionary leadership, organizational learning, company agility, employee engagement, shrewd management, and a focus on results. While Six Sigma remains at the heart of the internal processes, the vision at Motorola has widened to ensure that excellence is permeated through every aspect of the business.

Motorola is the thought leader behind Six Sigma, having invented it to measure defects on a parts per million (or in some cases per billion) basis. The company strives to obtain a 99.99966% quality perfection rate in order to improve customer satisfaction, maximize process efficiencies, increase competitive advantage and market share, and save millions of dollars in operating expenses. In order to achieve such a high perfection rate, Motorola must continually and consistently communicate quality initiatives in order ensure that the entire company understands the processes.

Six Sigma has been successful at Motorola because of management involvement and commitment. Management takes quality seriously. They hold management meetings to review quality programs. In addition, employees are involved in the Participative Management Program (PMP) to assess progress toward meeting quality goals, identify new quality initiatives and work out problems.

Motorola developed a framework to continuous improvement based on six process steps:

- Identify the type of product or service provide
- Identify customers and their requirements
- Determine needs and suppliers
- Define the process for approaching and doing work
- Eliminate defect sources and optimize processes
- Continuously improve the Sigma level

This framework allows Motorola to continuously work toward capturing, measuring, and eliminating defects in every process. It also allows the company to maintain focus on the processes, not the people. The company believes that if the processes are designed to be flawless, then the people will perform flawlessly while using the process. If flawless results are produced, then Motorola should have the ability to produce high-quality products, which will allow the company to stay ahead of its competition. Nevertheless, the company still conducts benchmarking programs that analyze all aspects of a competitor's products to assess their manufacturability, reliability, manufacturing cost, and performance.

In addition to internal quality efforts, Motorola is known for benchmarking externally. They have participated in benchmarking programs to analyze manufacturability, reliability, manufacturing cost, and performance.

Motorola's intense focus on producing high-quality products is only one of the main initiatives of the company. Total customer satisfaction is another very important initiative that the company focuses on. By delivering high-quality products that are competitively priced as well as shaping customer perceptions by creating an environment of trust through customer communication and engagement, Motorola believes that total customer satisfaction can be achieved. Company research proves that customer satisfaction rates are very high and most customers plan to continue to purchase Motorola products. Motorola is continuously striving to build relationships with customers that are built on a solid foundation of trust through the anticipation of customer needs, demonstration of innovation, and customer loyalty.

Motorola plans to continue their intense focus on perfecting their processes while increasing their focus on the concept of total customer satisfaction. The company believes the best way to accomplish this is through the successful implementation of the Performance Excellence Business System. This program changes the way the company manages its organization by becoming even more focused on the customer. This program is based on seven key ideas:

- Leadership
- Strategic Planning
- Customer and Market Focus
- Fact-Based Decisions
- Human Resources
- Process Management
- Business Results

Motorola's success with Six Sigma and quality management did not come easy. During their rise to the top, the company learned many lessons that allowed them to determine the best ways to succeed in the competitive market. Some of the tools that they learned and currently use to maintain success include: top down commitment and involvement, measurement systems to track progress, tough goal setting, provide required education, spread the success stories, never lose sight of the customer's priorities, and never be satisfied. Motorola's commitment to quality and continuous improvement in its business and relationships with its customers will allow it to remain a top companies for many more years to come.

Six Sigma Company In Action: Ford

Ford Motor Company has made significantly strides in its quality movement by adapting the principles of Six Sigma. Ford made "Quality Is Job 1" their slogan in the 1980's, while trying to drive down costs and capture market share. The TQM movement was a success and by 1986 had helped Ford become the most profitable American Automotive Company. The TQM project saved Ford millions of dollars and improved customer satisfaction. Unfortunately, the principles implemented with TQM were not routinely practiced in the years that followed and Ford has once again run into some quality issues.

Over these past few years Ford has had struggled with quality in both perception and reality. The Firestone/Explorer controversy, costly model recalls and delays on new product introductions, Ford has taken knocks in the public for quality. In order to get back on track Ford decided to adopt the Six Sigma methodology.

Ford has implemented Six Sigma throughout their enterprise and is firmly committed in continuously looking for new ways to improve quality and take advantage of substantial cost savings. Ford has gained the buy in of top management, and has been successful in improving and implementing standards uncovered through this Six Sigma initiative. From Six Sigma, Ford has placed a greater emphasis on working closely with suppliers on the design and manufacturing of automobiles. They have also realized the importance of avoiding slight variations in the design and production processes. Most importantly, and unlike TQM, Ford has learned to take a cost benefit approach to their new quality projects.

Six Sigma is an enterprise wide quality initiative where discoveries can be shared across the organization to improve processes. Ford has three main criteria that must be met before they assume a Six Sigma project. First, each project has to improve processes 70 percent. Second, each project must produce at least $250,000 in cost savings. Third, the process must relate to customer satisfaction. Some recent projects have included fixing the hoods on their Focus, investigating a misalignment of motor mounts, and reducing the number of exterior surface defects on vehicles being delivered overseas. Ford has also worked on fixing the pressure needed to close the hood of their Mustang, and also improving the consistency of their Explorer and Expedition manufacturing processes.

Ford uses the Define, Measure, Analyze, Improve, Control or DMAIC methodology and will not consider a project until Ford can audit the results to see the effect on customers and the bottom line. Six Sigma program is being implemented in all the company's divisions, including engineering, manufacturing, sales and service. According to a Ford executive, "Consumer

Driven 6-Sigma allowed us to look at the interactions between all the components to find the true root cause" of the problems.

Ford separates their employees involved in this quality movement into four different categories. These categories include green belts, black belts, master black belts and project champions. Ultimately, green belts are responsible for maintaining the improvement once the projects are completed and assist black belts in their day-to-day activities. Black belts are generally full-time employees who typically use "tools such as process mapping, cause-and-effect diagrams, failure mode and effects analysis, design of experiments, and mistake proofing in their daily work." Black belts are employees who are involved in the daily analytical, measurement, defining and control cycles of the project. Master black belts tend to be handpicked by upper management and their main duties are to teach, coach and mentor black and green belt classes. Finally, the project champions are managers who work with master black belts to identify projects and provide the necessary resources to the key persons involved.

In the first year and a half of the initiative, Ford trained nearly 10,000 employees in Six Sigma. They already have more than 6,000 Green Belts and 2,300 Black Belts and have a goal to train all of their salaried professional employees to be Green Belts within next four years.

Once projects have been identified and assigned, the Black Belts begin to work through the DMAIC cycle, asking key questions, using a variety of tools and focusing on delivering specific results. Specifically the process of making the hoods easy to close will be reviewed in this paper.

Define- Many Ford Mustang owners expressed dissatisfaction with the amount of effort it took to close the hoods on their vehicles. "They like to get under the hood," says Mike Stock, a Ford Master Black Belt. "But in some cases, they had to drop the hood from as high as 20 inches in order to get it to latch." The project team worked to identify the customers involved and what matters to them. They defined the scope of the project and form a team charter. The tools they used at this stage included a process scope contract, process mapping and a CT matrix.

Measure- The team used design of experiments to simulate how parts could be changed and what their effects would be. For example, the team altered the height of the hood latch bumper, or changed the angle and position of the latch relative to the hood-mounted striker, and dropped the hood to study the effect. Such "line trials" identified other areas where variations in product occur. Process mapping enabled the team to walk the entire manufacturing process to see where any variance occurred and where components were not matching specifications. The tools they used at this stage included process mapping, cause-and-affect diagrams, failure mode and effects analysis, gage R&R, and graphical techniques.

Analyze- Much of the testing was done on a "coordination fixture," a representation of the vehicle that was used to measure the suspected gaps, margins and fits. The coordination fixture showed where each component is located in relationship to another. The team measured hood-drop heights with a gage that showed the effects of closing from various distances.

The team prioritized the input variables that caused variation in process performance, analyzed data to determine the root causes of problems and opportunities for improvement, and validated process input variables with data. They also looked at possible combinations of process variables to see their effect on the process. At this stage, the team began to look at the effect of changing process inputs on the process performance and how similar processes function at different locations. The tools they used at this stage included process mapping, graphical techniques, multivariate studies, hypothesis testing, and correlation and regression analysis.

Improve- One of the major trouble spots in the Mustang hood-closing system involved the angle at which the latch and striker met. The team found the solution by changing the geometry of a support bracket to allow for expected variations. Process mapping and assembly evaluation also showed variation in the way hood latches were installed. The hood latch was changed so that it will only fit one way, making it impossible to install the latch improperly. The tools they used at this stage included design of experiments, simulation and optimization.

Control -Although Ford is still calculating final customer satisfaction figures on the adjusted hood-closing system, the team expects a 97-percent drop in related reported vehicle concerns. Ford stands to save $283,000 a year in reduced scrap, rework and non-value-added activity caused by the hood issue and vehicle-warranty work. Additionally, customer satisfaction with the Mustang gets a boost. The team completed a control plan, documented the project, translated the opportunities identified to other parts of the organization, built systems and structures to institutionalize the improvement, and completed an audit plan. The tools they used at this stage included control plans, statistical process control, gage control plans, preventive maintenance and poka yoke ("mistake proofing").

Unfortunately, with any large corporation, a project of this nature generally doesn't come without its problems. According to Ford, three of the biggest problems with Six Sigma were employee skepticism, resource allocation and data availability. Ford said they had to work hard and get employees to buy into Six Sigma. They had to show value to Ford employees and build enthusiasm about improving day-to-day activities. Next, the commitment of resources, in particular people, was also difficult. Ford stated they had to take time to train employees, ask them to take on added responsibilities while balancing their daily duties. Last, Ford had to commit to improving current infrastructure capabilities to make this project work. Prior to Six Sigma, Ford didn't have to technology or networks in place to handle the data necessary to run and analyze Six Sigma process initiatives. With all this said, Ford did work with their employees, gave them training, worked to build enthusiasm and devoted the means necessary to get their infrastructure up to par.

Since introducing Six Sigma, Ford has been able to see a great improvement in their standard of quality. Ford's CEO Jacques Nasser said, "Our data shows that customers who are highly satisfied remain loyal." These days, customers appear to be satisfied for Ford has stated that their warranty costs dropped by 32 percent last year and initial data for 2002 showed an additional 17 percent improvement. In 2000, Ford believes Six Sigma contributed to a $52 million bottom line increase and nearly a two-point increase in customer satisfaction in 2001. It appears that Ford is headed in the right direction with their Six Sigma initiative. They have devoted the resources necessary to make this work and are strongly committed in growing and implementing to this new method of quality across their organization.

Chapter Three: Improvement Tools

Quick recap: we've discussed our methodology and we've discussed some continuous improvement movements. Now let's take some time and talk about a few tools you can use to take action on the methodology or in your quality movement.

What are tools?

In it is probably helpful if I explain the concept of tools before actually diving into specifics. A tool is a device with a specific purpose. Tools are used to understand, analyze and improve processes. For example, if I am a sales person I may use a contact management tool to manage my network of contacts. That's a tool. The contact management device has a clear purpose.

Contrast a tool with a technique and a system. A technique is a collection of tools. For example, benchmarking is a technique because you may be using multiple tools such as focus groups and process mapping to form a comprehensive benchmark exercise.

Moving up the food chain is the system. A system provides effective integration of many techniques or tools. For example, 6 Sigma is a system. It relies on a technique, statistical process control. Statistical process control uses a variety of tools such as control charts and histograms.

Although the above information is more anecdotal than practical, it is helpful to understand the relationship between tools, techniques and systems. By doing so, you can better understand the set of resources available to you to bring to bear on your performance improvement initiative.

Why use tools?

Another obvious question is why use tools? Just as a carpenter uses a saw to make a table, or a chef uses a mixer to stir up the ingredients, performance improvement professionals use their tools to perform the steps in the methodology they are applying on their business process problem.

The major benefits to understanding and then utilizing accepted performance improvement tools are many, but below are some of the major points:

- **See the invisible**. Tools provide creative insight by allowing you to see what may not always be apparent. For example, a correlation tool can show how one variable is related to another. Until you take the time to do the analysis using the tool it might not be so obvious.
- **Job aids**. Tools help train less than experienced staff on key problem solving, data analysis, and project management concepts that may be extraordinarily difficult to grasp without the tool. For example, a Gantt

chart that visually depicts the timing and steps of a project is a great job aid for someone who has little expertise in planning a large project.

- **Common lexicon**. Because many tools used by performance improvement practitioners are fairly standardized in their application they serve as a common tool that many people can understand without getting lost in the definition and jargon.
- **Communication device**. Almost all tools result in a set of reportable outcomes. In doing so these are great vehicles for communication. Being able to take the results of a control chart and show it to a stakeholder in the project is a way to be more articulate in your communications process.
- **Credibility**. Tools turn opinion and subjectivity into more credible, hard data. For example, it is far more credible to tell the CFO that that sales returns doubled last year because you correlated the cause of the returns to product recalls versus a mere assumption that the recall caused the returns.
- **Efficiency and Effectiveness**. Tools by their nature allow the project teams to be more efficient and effective. Imagine a physician trying to operate without a scalpel or a firefighter trying to fight a fire without a hose, you get my point.
- **Completeness**. Tools help you from an audit perspective because they assist you in ensuring you are being complete and thorough in your research.

Getting Started:

When using performance improvement tools take the crawl, walk, run approach. What that means is start small and build up over time.

The most basic starting point when deploying any tool on a project is ensuring it is the right fit for the job. This is important because the right tool increases the likelihood of achieving the desired result but will also decrease the risk of wasted time on the wrong solution. When a carpenter eyes his toolbox he must think carefully about the type of tool to use otherwise it could have serious ramifications on what he is building. The same principle holds true when using performance improvement tools. Take the time to really understand what the purpose of the tool is and how it might be applied in a positive manner on your project.

Let's consider an example. If you are at the very beginning of a project and nothing has been done yet, you might want to use project management tools like a Gantt chart to prepare for the project. Or, say you are assessing the "as is" environment trying to document what the current process does. You might be using a process flow chart or process map to accomplish this task.

So how do you know the right tool for the right situation? Well, hopefully there was some training involved up front that describes some general principles on performance improvement. In addition, there should be training specific to each tool. Finally, the project team should be led by a person with experience in performance improvement that can coach and mentor the staff on appropriately using these tools. Think of it this way, you would not have someone use a forklift if they did not know how to operate it. They probably went through training and certification then were closely watched prior to using it on a regular basis.

The Basic Seven:

Now that we have touched upon the background of tools, I want to talk about the basic 7 tools as you may run into them either as a group or individually.

The basic seven tool tools have their origins in Japanese quality management. The basic seven were created so that practitioners in the quality control arena could be more efficient. Dr. Kaoru Ishikawa put these tools together and Japanese workers have used them since the 1960's. The seven tools are primarily used for analyzing discrete processes that usually produce numeric data. They are the foundation of effective, efficient, improvement activities.

Below is a brief overview of each of the seven basic tools:

Check sheet: A simple data collection and analysis form to record observed and collected data. Check sheets help to get timely, accurate information and house it centrally.

Process flow chart: A graph of the steps of a process and their relationship to one another. Flowcharts show inputs, activities and outputs with an emphasis on the activities. They are a very useful tool in understanding the "as is " process because you are forced to think through every step in the process.

Cause and effect diagram: also known as a fish-bone diagram or Ishikawa chart, this tool is a qualitative tool summarizing the results of cause-effect analysis. The tool's purpose is to bring the root cause of a problem to the surface. A facilitator using this tool must constantly ask "why" to ultimately get at the root cause.

Pareto chart: This tool is based on the "Pareto Principle" promoting the 80/20 rule attempts to find the problem that has the greatest effect with the premise being that the principle cause is a high priority candidate for improvement. The Pareto chart will categorize problems and then order them by frequency of occurrence. A risk you want to avoid in using Pareto charts is lumping distinct problems together blinding you from seeing the real problem.

Control chart/run chart: This tool distinguishes between normal and abnormal variation. Charts such as these help you see if your process is stable and predictable or where there is variation and if the variation is due to an unusual cause.

The run chart is sometimes lumped with the control chart but is actually plotting data over periods of time to provide trends and patterns. Run charts are very simple yet powerful. Any time you plot data over time you are creating a run chart. Time is on the horizontal axis and frequency on the vertical axis.

Histogram: The histogram chart represents the distribution from the mean (or average). The histogram is typically plotted as a bar chart and shows the distribution of variance. This will help understand how data is distributed. In doing so you can see the frequency of distribution of a set of measurements.

Scatter diagram: A method of plotting one variable against another variable to see trends and relationships. Keep in mind that although you can see relationships it may not necessarily be a cause-and-effect relationship.

The check sheet, process flow chart, cause and effect diagram and pareto charts are used more in the "as is" stage of an improvement project to identify problems and collect data. The control chart/run chart, histogram and scatter diagram are more data analysis tools than collection tools.

The 'New' Seven

Because the basic seven are highly numbers oriented, a new set of tools was formulated in the 1980's. These tools focus on the softer side of things. Items like strategy, planning, qualitative data are at the heart of the new seven tools. These tools, as a group, are often referred to as management and planning tools. They are based on the principles of added value over basic needs and problem prevention versus problem correction.

Below is a brief overview of each of the seven 'new' tools.

Affinity diagram: A graphical, brainstorming tool developed by cultural anthropologist Jiro Kawakita. The tool attempts to produce a natural hierarchy of requirements by grouping facts, opinions and ideas under related themes.

Relations diagram: Also known as an interrelationship digraph or wheel diagram. It is a descriptive tool to document a central problem at the hub (hence the term wheel which is sometimes used). Related issues are arranged in a circle and arrows map connection points. These are predominantly used to understand complex relationships. They too are themselves are often complex to master.

Matrix diagram: A tabular tool to facilitate the identification of relationships between two or more sets of factors. For example, in a 2x2 matrix you might plot performance and importance. If a customer is asked how important a product feature is to their needs and also asked how well your product performs in terms of meeting those needs, plotting the two variables of performance and importance in a matrix can help you see the relationship between them in a clearer light.

Tree diagrams: These are sometimes referred to as vine and leaves diagrams or hierarchy diagrams or systematic diagrams. Breaks down a topic from the top down into successive levels of detail until implementation. The trunk of the tree is the primary objective and branches are the tasks. These are useful to show the hierarchy and subsets of a process.

Process decision program charts: A planning tool that comes from reliability engineering and is used along with failure mode defect analysis to analyze reliability issues. This tool maps out every step of a plan at every conceivable point that might cause problems along with countermeasures. The key question when using this tool is to ask "What can happen here?"

Activities diagram: A planning and project management tool to schedule the completion of complex tasks. It displays each task and the time to complete the task along with the jobs that precede, proceed and simultaneously occur. Compared to the Gantt chart you get more sequencing detail as well as activity duration.

Matrix data analysis charts: The only one of the new seven tools that analyzes numeric data. It presents the results of multivariate statistical analysis data. Results are in a rectangular or triangular matrix. The degree of relationships is determined by subjective weights or statistical analysis.

Summary

The importance of tools cannot be overstated. They are an essential element of any performance improvement project. The key is finding the right tools that work for you. According to research and experience of TQM International, remember the following best practices when using performance improvement tools:

1. Maintain consistency. It takes time for people to get up to speed and reach their comfort zone in using a particular tool. Don't constantly switch tools before you get a chance to truly learn those you have just begun to use.

2. Rely on the results of the tools. The tools are meant to uncover items you cannot uncover without the aide of the tool. Don't explain away the results of the tools just because it might not agree with your original hypothesis.

3. Implement your action plans. If a tool helped you objectively conclude on a course of action then take the next step and implement the action. Otherwise you have a binder of tool results and great ideas that collect dust.

4. Encourage the use of tools. Provide your people with the skills, resources, and training necessary to use tools efficiently and effectively to aid them in their performance improvement efforts.

Detailed Examples:

In order to further extrapolate on some of the tools discussed above and present a few new tools, this next section takes a deeper look at 9 tools by providing descriptions and illustrative examples.

Keep in mind, that it is not the intent of this book to provide an overload of information on the intimacies of each tool but rather to help the reader understand the existence and purpose of tools. In achieving this, the reader may have a better sense of what tools are available for their business need and then seek the appropriate training to educate his or her team on those tools prior to their rollout and usage.

1) Affinity diagrams
2) Cause and effect diagrams
3) Control charts
4) Gantt charts
5) Process flow charts
6) 2x2 Matrix diagram
7) Pareto chart
8) Scatter diagram
9) Staff analysis/activity profile

We will frame each tool using the following outline so that you can understand them better and determine their applicability with more clarity.

Description: a definition of the tool
Benefits: describes why you would want to use the tool
Limitations: documents the disadvantages to applying the tool
Resources: describes the data sources you will need to use this tool appropriately
How to Use It: bullet points the key action steps you should take to use the tool
Example: a mini case illustrating application of the tool

Finally, before we explain the tools let me make a few suggestions. For more information on continuous improvement tools you might take a look at The Memory Jogger. Michael Brassard and Diane Ritter wrote The Memory Jogger™ II- A Pocket Guide of Tools for Continuous Improvement and Effective Planning. Goal/QPC publishes it. You can go to their web site at http://www.goalqpc.com/. The Memory Jogger offers a lot of benefit for very little cost. It's less than $10 US dollars.

In addition, more tools and their explanations are available online through The Quality Tools Cookbook by Professor Syd Sytsma and Dr. Katherine Manley of Ferris State University. In their words the Quality Tools Cookbook is "a free, comprehensive, reference to the quality tools for students, faculty, or anyone on the Internet who may find it useful." You can find the Quality Tools Cookbook at http://www.sytsma.com/tqmtools/tqmtoolmenu.html.

Affinity Diagrams

Description
A tool that gathers large amounts of ideas and organizes them into categories based on natural or meaningful relationships between each item.

This tool allows the continuous improvement team to generate a large number of ideas/issues and organize them into logical groupings. It allows the project team to understand the root cause of a problem from many diverse viewpoints in a natural, meaningful way.

Benefits
- Quickly and collectively organize ideas, opinions, issues, quickly.
- Achieve creative ideas to expand the team's thinking when the only solutions are old solutions.
- Get group consensus around ideas and issues
- Gather input from a cross-functional and diverse group of people working on a problem
- A forum to give all ideas an equal opportunity to be voiced
- To creatively brainstorm on issues, needs, and opportunities
- Not a costly or technical tool to deploy

Limitations
- Some team members may monopolize the session with their ideas
- Some team members may be uncomfortable speaking candidly in front of others so you might not get honest inputs
- A group that is too diverse may tend to get off subject with comments and opinions

Resources
- A meeting place. A comfortable room with a white board or place to tack up ideas.
- Time. Busy people need to block out some quality time to have this session. It should not be an ad-hoc meeting but a scheduled meeting with a definite purpose.
- Preparation. Attendees should come prepared with some thought to the issues so they don't enter the session completely unaware of its purpose.

How to Use It
1. Assemble a cross-functional team that has a diverse set of opinions on the issues.
2. Construct a problem or issue statement that the team can begin to brainstorm about.
3. Silently list the root causes, risks and outcomes surrounding the problem or issues
4. List responses on 3x5 cards or Post-It notes, one response per card.
5. Spread the cards out on a table so that all can read them and have group members read for clarification. Team members can add cards/responses at

this point since they may have additional ideas based on reading other group members ideas.

6. Have team members clarify, group and categorize the cards .
7. When the groupings are complete, create header cards that captures the central idea and theme that ties groups together. Designate this card as the title card for each group.
8. Once this is completed, tape these cards or rewrite the ideas on a flipchart for the entire group to see.

Example

You are asked to improve how people in your group work in teams. Some workflows will be changing requiring a more cohesive team and you need to understand how they can work in a team environment better.

1. Set up a meeting with the key stakeholders including staff and management that are a part of the future team. Inform them in advance that this exercise is about team building.
2. Once in a room together, create the problem or issues statement "What are the key steps to effective teamwork?"
3. Brainstorm about how the group can create more effective teams.
4. Document the ideas on 3x5 cards.
5. Group the ideas into logical elements
6. Label the groupings
7. Post the groupings.

See Exhibit 3-1 for an example of the posted groupings:

Exhibit 3-1 Affinity Diagram Example

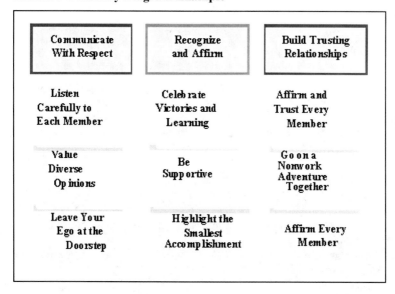

Cause and Effect Diagrams

Description
An approach to illustrate interdependent relationships systematically, looking at the effects and the causes that create or contribute to those effects. Dr. W. Edwards Deming as a helpful tool in improving quality adopted this tool.

Benefits
- Facilitate a session in a problem-solving effort
- Visually identifies root causes of known problems
- Clearly communicates cause and effect relationships

Limitations
- Requires that additional tools be used to determine how to eliminate root causes.
- Generally does not focus on the relative degree of impact among various causes.
- Extensive interviews and analysis may be required to adequately identify the real causes of a specific effect.

Resources
- An experience-based understanding of various cause and effect relationships will be helpful in using this analytical tool. The facilitator should have a general knowledge of the cause areas (four Ms) in the organization to allow a thorough evaluation of all the possible causes.

How to Use It
1. Identify a single problem or process to be examined.
2. Develop a high-level understanding of the process related to the problem identified.
3. Draw a horizontal arrow pointing to the right. This arrow represents the problem to be examined. Write the problem statement at the right end of the arrow.
4. Draw four lines branching off the main arrow; these lines represent the major causes of the problem. The major causes are usually defined as the four Ms: Materials, Methods, Machinery, and Manpower. However, the causes should be customized to fit the issue being examined. One alternative is the four Ps: Policy, Procedure, People, and Plant. This approach may be more appropriate for administrative groups.
5. Lead the group in brainstorming the underlying issues for each major cause contributing to the problem. These issues are entered on the chart as minor causes, branching off the line that represents the major causes they influence.
6. Look for causes that appear repeatedly. Gather data to determine the relative frequencies of the different causes.
7. Help the team reach a consensus on the critical root causes, then work to develop ways to eliminate them.

Example
You are the new manager in a department experiencing high employee turnover. You are asked to determine the cause of this turnover and develop ways to reduce it. You use a cause and effect diagram to begin your analysis.

1. Once the appropriate people are assembled, you begin by drawing a horizontal arrow across the page and label it "Why do we have employee turnover?"
2. You then draw branches off this arrow. Typically you could use the four Ms: Materials, Methods, Machinery, and Manpower or the four Ps: Policy, Procedure, People, and Plant for administrative issues. However, you brainstorm with your team and take a broader perspective grouping your branches into People, Process, Technology, Culture, and Externalities as these relate well to the four Ps and to the major causes of change identified in chapter two that help you understand when something is in need of improvement.
3. You then brainstorm further and group the derivative causes of these main causes to form your diagram.

See the diagram in exhibit 3-2 below.

Exhibit 3-2 Cause and Effect Diagram Example

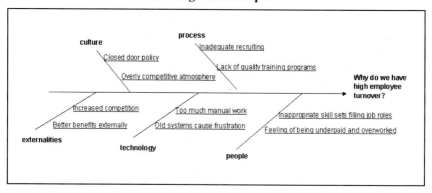

Control Charts

Description
Control Charts help assess how much variability in a process is random and how much is due to unique events or individual actions by plotting data collected over time.

Benefits
- To evaluate if a process is in or out of control
- Understand cause and magnitude of variation
- A quantifiable way of articulating quality control of a process

Limitations
- Inappropriate for "soft" issues that cannot be easily quantified

- Not very effective for manages who don't like statistics and quantitative methods
- A suitable set of historic data is required to draw control charts, requiring data collection rigor

Resources
- Data related to the process being analyzed needs to be collected over time.
- A rigorous process in place to collect the data consistently over time
- A knowledgeable person to translate the data into the control chart

How to Use It (Basic Control Chart - - please note more detailed control charts can be done)
1. Collect data by running the process as usual.
2. Calculate the Center Line (average), Upper Control Limit (UCL) and the Lower Control Limit (LCL).
   a. These limits represent the highest and lowest measure (size, weight, purity, etc.,) that are deemed as acceptable quality for the product.
3. Set up the Control Chart graph.
   a. Y-Axis is usually a measurement of data. X-Axis usually represents time or a sequence.
4. Draw lines across the graph to represent the centerline, upper and lower control limits.
5. Plot points on the graph to represent the sample data and connect with a running line.
6. Analyze the graph.
   a. Fluctuation within the control limits results from variation built into the process.
   b. If any points fall outside the control limits, the process is said to be "out of control."
   c. What may have affected the process (temperature, environment)?
   d. Has there been any significant alterations to the process inputs, activities or outputs?
   e. Have normal conditions in the process caused this?
   f. Did the personnel change at any time?
   g. Was there a change in the policies, procedures, or workflows?
   h. Was there a change in the technology or automation elements of the process?
   i. Has the way the process is monitored and measured changed at all?
   j. Has there been a change in management objectives that may have changed behavior patterns within the process?
   k. Were there any maintenance issues within the process?
   l. Are any externalities impacting the process?
   m. When using this tool, the term "control" does not imply that the product or service meets customer or management needs. It only means that the process is consistent; however, it may be consistently bad.

<u>Example</u>
30 newly hired professionals in your organization must begin with a 2-week (10 day) training program. At the end of each day, the new hires rate the day using the following helpfulness scale:
1= not at all   2= Not very 3=Moderately 4=Very 5=Extremely   N= 10 evaluations randomly sampled each day (10 from the population of 30)

Step One: Collect Data
Step Two: Compute center-line (mean) and UCL and LCL
Step Three: plot
• plot days on x-axis and average score for sample on y-axis
• draw lines for CL, UCL, LCL
• plot averages for each day and connect lines
• look at the items near control limits and outside the limits
Step Four: analyze (differentiate between the common and special causes - work on changing the process so that common causes are mitigated. Special causes are outside the system and not a normal part of the process anyway.)

Exhibit 3-3 illustrates the Control Chart table and Exhibit 3-4 illustrates the Control Chart graph.

Exhibit 3-3 Control Chart Table

sample/day	1	2	3	4	5	6	7	8	9	10	Overall
Student 1	3	2	1	4	5	3	4	2	3	4	
Student 2	4	2	2	4	4	3	4	3	1	4	
Student 3	3	3	1	4	4	3	4	3	3	4	
Student 4	4	3	2	3	4	3	3	3	3	4	
Student 5	4	3	2	4	5	3	3	3	3	4	
Student 6	5	3	2	3	4	3	4	3	2	3	
Student 7	2	4	3	3	3	3	3	2	2	4	
Student 8	3	4	3	3	2	4	4	4	3	4	
Student 9	3	3	3	3	5	3	3	3	2	3	
Student 10	3	2	3	4	4	3	4	3	3	3	
Average (mean)	3.4	2.9	2.2	3.5	4	3.1	3.6	2.9	2.5	3.7	3.18 center line (X bar)
Standard Deviation	0.84	0.7	0.8	0.5	0.9	0.3	0.5	0.6	0.7	0.5	0.643 average std. dev.
constant		1									
(from lookup table of constants)											
UCL mean+(contstant x std dev)				3.8							
LCL mean - (contstant x std dev)				2.6							

Mean - statistical average
Standard deviation - how widely values are dispersed from the average
Constant - based on whether it is attribute or variable data and how large n (the population is)

Exhibit 3-4 Control Chart Graph

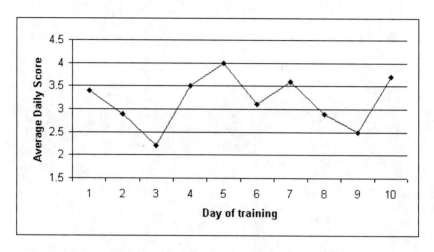

Gantt Charts

Description
An activity chart laying out the tasks of a project in sequential order and shows when each must take place. The activities are related to the steps defined in a more detailed project plan.

Benefits
- clearer objectives to accomplish goals
- visual aid in management key milestones and timelines
- great communication tool to articulate progress and project duration
- great tool to understand compliance with more detailed project plan

Limitations
- a simplistic view and does not analyze the project thoroughly
- does not reveal potential bottlenecks in project
- does not reveal tasks that are dependent on other tasks

Resources
- A detailed project plan is really the backbone of the Gantt chart. The Gantt chart is merely a high-level summary of the work plan over time.

How to Use It
1. Identify the tasks that need to be done to complete the project. This may be done by using a project plan (if applicable) or by brainstorming a list,

Champions of Change

drawing a flowchart, storyboard, or arrow diagram for the project. Identify the time required for each task. Finally, identify the sequence. Which tasks must be finished before a following task can begin, and which can happen simultaneously?

2. Draw a horizontal time axis along the top of a page. Mark it off in an appropriate scale for the length of the project (for example, days, weeks).

3. Down the left side of the page, write each task of the project in order. For events that happen at a point in time (such as a presentation), draw a diamond under the time the event must happen. For activities that occur over a period of time (such as developing a plan or holding a series of interviews), draw a bar under the appropriate time on the timeline. Align the left end of the bar with the time the activity begins, and align the right end with the time that activity concludes. Draw just the outlines of the bars and diamonds; don't fill them in.

4. Check that every task of the project is on the activity chart as a bar.

5. As events and activities take place, fill in the diamonds and bars to show completion. For activities in progress, estimate how far along you are and fill in that much of the bar.

6. Place a vertical marker to show where you are on the timeline. If the chart is posted on the wall, an easy way to show the current time is with a heavy dark string and two thumbtacks.

Example

You are a new manager in charge of a continuous improvement project. You have prepared a project plan, assigned roles and responsibilities and are ready to begin your project. You wish to create a Gantt chart that can serve as a visual aide of the projects progress to project team members and management.

1. You estimated the project would take approximately 8 weeks to do. You list the time period (in weeks) along the top of your chart.

2. You then believe there are 9 key steps to accomplishing the project plan. You list those 9 steps along with the person(s) accountable for accomplishing those steps along the left hand side of the chart.

3. The events that are occurring at a point in time are our key milestones. They are a status report presentation to management and the presentation of the final results. We could mark these with a diamond but we color code them differently from other events to make them more noteworthy to the project team.

4. Uncompleted tasks are denoted by a different color (or no color) and completed tasks are colored in.

5. A marker indicates where we are at in the process.

See Exhibit 3-5 for the Gantt Chart Example of our process.

Exhibit 3-5 Gantt chart Example

Steps	Person	(weeks)							
		1-Jul	7-Jul	14-Jul	21-Jul	28-Jul	7-Aug	14-Aug	21-Aug
Determine what to benchmark	All Team								
Complete surveys	Jeff								
Process mapping	Bob								
Present status report	All Team		July 14th						
Select site visit partners	Jane								
Site visits	All Team								
Determine gaps	Jeff								
Create action plan	Bob/Jane								
Present final results	All Team								Aug 25th

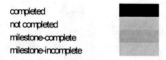

completed
not completed
milestone-complete
milestone-incomplete

current position in the process |

Process Flow Charts

Description
A graphic representation of all the steps within a process. It depicts the relationships between multiple functions, individuals, and systems.

Benefits
- To better show the relationships between departments and groups
- To provide a better understanding of the activities involved within a process.
- To help identify any critical points or bottlenecks within the process

Limitations
- Difficult to draw when many functions are involved.
- Difficult to read when many functions are involved and there are redundancies in the process or multiple handoffs and exchanges.

Resources
- Individual(s) with comprehensive knowledge of all steps within the process
- Individuals(s) with flowcharting skills

How to Use It

1. Decide what function or process will be flowcharted and state a clear beginning and ending point for the process.
2. Decide how many groups and individuals (or operations and systems) fall within this function.
3. Discuss the major activities of the process without concern for sequence.
4. On paper, arrange the activities in order from left to right or top to bottom, within their respective sequential order of operations. Connect them with arrows. This forms the basis of the flowchart.
5. Go through the steps again adding any other relevant details left out.
6. Go through the steps and add the appropriate flow chart symbols to finalize the chart. (see Exhibit 3-6 below.)
7. If the flowchart requires more than one page, use flow connectors as in flowchart preparation.
8. For group sessions, ensure that participants are in agreement with the process that has been drawn.
9. Analyze information by asking:
   a. "Is one operation responsible for many more activities in the process than other operations?"
   b. "Are certain types of activities frequently repeated?"
   c. "Is the sequence of activities efficient?"
10. Compare the activities of systems and operations.
    a. "Are there too few or too many interfaces between systems?"
    b. "Are systems used to document the same information for which other operations are responsible?"
11. If so, it may make sense to let the systems provide documentation of information instead of obtaining it from individuals responsible for other operations.

Exhibit 3-6 Sample Flow Chart Symbols

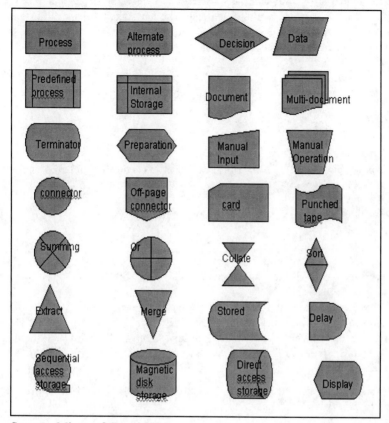

Source: Microsoft Excel 2000

Example

You are the manager of your company's accounts receivable department. You are new to the job. As a way to understand what takes place within the department you now manage, you decide to draw a flowchart. Assume your company is a consumer products distributor.

Please note that this is for illustration purposes only. A more complex receivables process would most likely exist in most organizations.

Below are the key steps to the process:

1. A customer order is processed.
2. Credit application might be filled out if the order exceeds a certain amount
3. The product is delivered.
4. The customer is sent a bill.
5. A receivable is established in the customer's name.
5. Cash is received.
6. Cash is applied to account.
7. If cash is not received reminder notices are sent.
8. If not received within 360 days the account is written off.

Below is the flowchart resulting from the above steps. You'll note it is not the prettiest flowchart in the history of flowcharts. But, that is precisely why I am illustrating it. Certainly this could have been done much nicer. However, this is a real flowchart someone gave me that worked amazingly well for their organization.

Exhibit 3-7 Process Flowchart Example

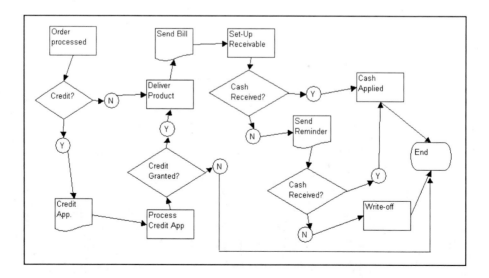

2x2 Matrix Diagram

Description
This tool organizes information based on 2 perspectives. It places one perspective on the X-axis (horizontal) and another on the Y-axis (vertical). It then examines the relationship between the two perspectives to aide in decision-making. The tool is inspired by the Boston Consulting Group (BCG) Matrix that analyzes SBU's on a market growth relative to market share 2x2 matrix and then categories each quadrant.

Benefits
- Shows the strength of a relationship and direction of influence
- Help prioritize future action items based on strength of relationship

Limitations
- Relationships addressed in the matrix tend to be high-level requiring more discussion to understand root cause of problems

Resources
- An individual(s) with viewpoints on a particular topic

How to Use It
1. Prepare for the "Matrix Diagram" session.
    a. Document the key elements that you would like to compare along dual dimensions (these could be a series of questions or statements that you would like respondents to provide responses to along two dimensions)
2. Agree on the two dimensions to be mapped on the Matrix.
    a. The categories could be the following or whatever you create as comparison variables:
        i. performance vs. importance
        ii. business risk vs. strength of control
        iii. market share vs. growth (this is the Boston Consulting Group (BCG) Matrix)
3. Determine the appropriate scale to rate the dimensions.
4. Collect information from respondents along the two dimensions for each question or statement.
5. Graph the responses in the 2x2 matrix.
6. Analyze the responses based upon their placement within the quadrants of the matrix.

Example
You are a new manager in your organization's procurement department. You are trying to understand some of the viewpoints on major elements of the purchasing process. Many people you have had initial discussions with have several ideas on what is important and needs to change. You want to understand this in a more logical fashion. You use a 2x2 Matrix.

1. First you establish the questions or statements you want to formalize in your analysis. Based on your research you have chosen the following 3 issues you'll put into statements:

Statement 1 (S1): The purchasing department has an optimized supplier base.
Statement 2 (S2): The purchasing department has adequate ethical guidelines for suppliers.
Statement 3 (S3): The purchasing department leverages technology to optimize the process.

2. The dimensions you will use for the matrix are performance and importance. Each respondent will respond to the statements from both of these perspectives. For example "How good do you think our performance is?" and "How important is it to the process that it is done right?"

3. The scale we decide to use is a basic likert scale using a 1 to 5-response set. We provide guidance to the respondents for the scale as follows:

Performance: Importance:
1=Do not perform   1=Not at all important
2=Poor performance   2=Minor importance
3=Average performance   3=Somewhat important
4=Above average performance   4=Very important
5=Exceptional performance   5=Essential

4. We collect information from managers and staff personnel. We then average the responses for these two groups. The results are as follows:

Statement 1:

	Importance Score	Performance Score
Managers	4	2
Staff	4	3

Statement 2:

Managers	5	2
Staff	3	3

Statement 3:

Managers	3	4
Staff	5	1

5. See exhibit 3-8 – 2x2 Matrix Example

Exhibit 3-8 2x2 Matrix Example

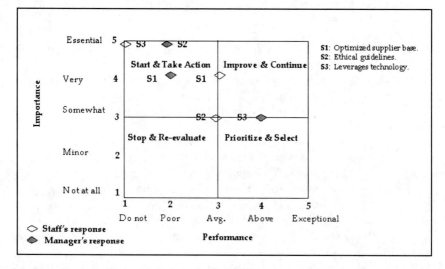

6. The diagram is then labeled to show what each quadrant represents. The diagram from our example shows some lack of consensus between management and staff, especially in the statement about technology leverage.

Pareto Chart

Description
A bar chart that focuses on an organization's most significant activities, problems, costs, or other issues. Problems are analyzed in descending order of occurrence.

Benefits
- Displays the importance of all problems or conditions
- A starting point for problem solving
- An effective tool for presentations because it is a good visual

Limitations
- Only deals with characteristics of a product or services
- The most frequent problems are not always the most costly
- If clear differences don't emerge, you will need to group the data

Resources
- Historic data and a mechanism to collect it

How to Use It
1. Using existing data or brainstorming, select the problems (or activities, costs, etc.) that are to be compared and ranked.

2. Select the unit of measurement to be used as a standard for comparison (e.g. annual cost, frequency).
3. Select the time period to be studied.
4. Gather the necessary data for each category (e.g., "Defect A occurred X times in last 6 months").
5. Compare the frequency or cost of each category relative to the other categories (e.g., "Defect A happened 74 times, Defect B happened 107 times, Defect C happened 35 times").
6. List the categories from left to right on the horizontal axis in their order of decreasing frequency or cost. The categories containing the fewest items can be combined into an "other" category, which is placed on the extreme right as the last bar.
   a. There are many variations of Pareto Charts and many kinds of problems that can be analyzed using them, including:
      - Analyzing which costs are most significant.
      - Focusing efforts on problems that occur most frequently.
      - Demonstrating which activities take the most time in a department.
      - Analyzing different groupings of data, e.g., defects by product, by machine, and by shift.
      - Measuring the impact of changes made to a process, e.g., before and after comparisons.
      - Breaking down causes into more and more specific parts.

Example
You are a new manager asked to investigate why there is so much rework in the purchasing process. You decide to use a Pareto diagram to help in your analysis.

1. You brainstorm about the possible causes of rework and list them out.
   -no manager approval
   -wrong quantity
   -wrong quality
   -unauthorized items
   -unauthorized supplier
   -system downtime

2. The unit of measurement you select is both frequency and cost. You want to know the frequency of occurrence and the cost of the occurrences.

3. You decide to record sample data over a 3-month period.

The data is then graphed and analyzed. See Exhibit 3-9

Exhibit 3-9 Pareto Diagram

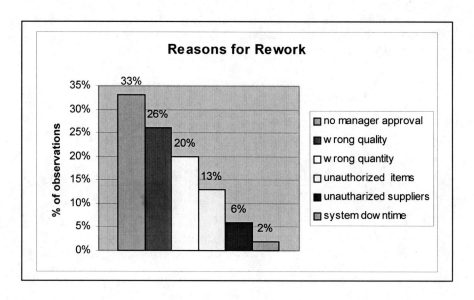

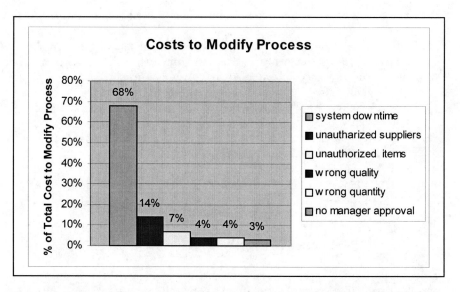

As seen from the Pareto example, although system downtime is the least frequent occurrence it is the most costly. Although lack of management approval is the least costly it is the most frequent. This indicates that for a "quick win" that is not so costly to rectify and will help curb a lot of the current problems more rigorous authorization may need to be enforced. In the long run, enhancing systems to prevent downtime can avoid very costly problems that occur less frequently.

Scatter Diagram

Description

A Scatter Diagram studies the possible relationship between two variables, determining if they have a cause-and-effect relationship, and analyzing the strength of the relationship.

Benefits

- Visually depicts the relationship between two variables
- Display what happens to one variable when another variable changes

Limitations

- Requires a significant amount of data
- Graph only shows relationship between variables not root cause of problems

Resources

- Data containing a list of potentially related pairs of data. Fifty to one hundred paired samples are suggested, but a smaller sample may be accurate.

How to Use It

1. Collect a sample of potentially related pairs of data and construct a data sheet.
2. Draw the horizontal and vertical axes of the diagram. Each axis will represent the measurement value of one of the two variables. The variable that is being investigated as the possible "cause" is usually on the horizontal axis, and the "effect" is usually on the vertical.
3. Plot the data on the diagram. If the values repeat, circle that point as many times as appropriate.
4. To analyze the data, notice how the plotted points form a clustered pattern. The direction and "tightness" of the cluster are an indication of the strength of the relationship between variable one and variable two. The more that this resembles a straight line, the stronger the correlation between the variables.

Example

The examples illustrate positive, negative and no correlation.

Positive correlation is when an increase in one variable depends on an increase in another variable. For example, if you're trying to see how training relates to job performance you would hope to see positive correlation, that better job performance results from more training. See Exhibit 3-10 for positive correlation.

Negative correlation is when an increase in one variable causes a decreased in another variable. For example, if you increase your internal controls you will decrease fraudulent activity. See Exhibit 3-11 for negative correlation.

No correlation is when the two variables are unrelated. For example, if you eat apples there is hopefully no correlation to being a world-class violinist. See Exhibit 3-12 for no correlation.

Exhibit 3-10 Positive Correlation

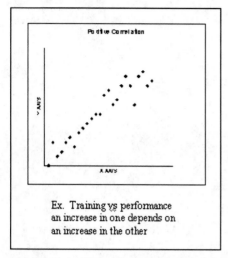

Ex. Training vs performance
an increase in one depends on
an increase in the other

Exhibit 3-11 Negative Correlation

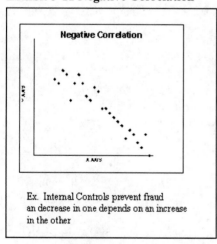

Ex. Internal Controls prevent fraud
an decrease in one depends on an increase
in the other

Exhibit 3-12 No Correlation

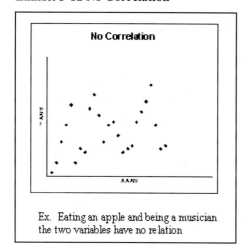

Ex. Eating an apple and being a musician
the two variables have no relation

Staff Analysis/Activity Profile

Description
A staffing profile illustrates the job functions performing activities within a process. They help to identify the span of control within a process. Span of control is the staff to management ratio.

Benefits
- To determine reporting relationships within a process
- To determine where accountability and responsibility lie
- Visually depicts the relationship between people in a process
- A way to determine where job overlaps may be occurring

Limitations
- Can be time consuming to do

Resources
- The cooperation of all of the management and staff in the process. An honest and truthful evaluation of their time and activities.

How to Use It
1. Clearly define the process and its activities
2. Identify all the parties involved in the process.
3. Separate people into managerial (with supervisory responsibilities) and staff.
4. Draw an organizational chart of the staff and management.
5. Label the people on the chart in terms of Full Time Equivalents (FTEs) where one FTE is equivalent to a 40-hour workweek.

6. List the activities for which each staff and management person is responsible.
7. Label the activities as being value-added, control/oversight, or transaction processing (use other labels suitable for the specific process, these labels are typical for administrative functions but not necessarily operational functions)
8. Try to identify the timing and handoffs of the activities in the process, this will help identify bottlenecks.

Example
You are the accounts payable manager. You want to understand who does what in this process and understand the organizational hierarchy within the process. You use a staff analysis/activity profile tool.

Below is a listing of the key inputs, activities and outputs in the process. In bold parentheses we list the title of the person responsible for that job. In addition we add additional information to help clearly define what the person does and then label the task as value added, transaction processing or control/oversight.

Key Activities of the Accounts Payable Process:
• gather and compile A/P documentation, including company purchase orders, vendor invoices, receiving information, etc. (other, internal and vendor invoices) (AP staff) (batches arrive from warehousemen and matched to invoices (can take hours to track and match)TRANS.PROCESS
•establish new vendor accounts
(AP manager) (1 week review time from purchasing mgr) VALUE ADDED
•obtain verification of receipt of goods/services
(AP staff) (from warehouse who don't always notify us and we don't have linked systems) CONTROL/OVERSIGHT
•approve invoices and payments
(AP manager) (1 day, approve by next day, approve all) CONTROL/OVERSIGHT
•post payments to General Ledger accounts
(AP staff)(system does this) TRANS. PROCESS
•evaluate and review A/P balances, including account analysis
(Acct. and AP mgr)(Acct mgr does monthly, AP mgr weekly- takes a few hours) (CONTROL/OVERSIGHT)
•resolve vendor billing discrepancies and related inquiries
(Financial mgr and AP mgr) (each dispute can take minutes or months to resolve) (Trans Proc)
•process A/P adjustments for errors or omissions
(AP staff) (takes minutes to do but errors are hard to find) (TRAN PROCESSING)
•create and produce A/P-related reports for management or other review
(Acct mgr) (takes a few hours to prepare and a few more to review before giving it to management)(CONTROL AND OVERSIGHT)
•Working to determine how to improve cash flow, decrease errors, and have better AP turns
(AP manager) (not doing) Value Added

We then create a traditional organizational chart and tie FTEs (full time equivalents) to the process. See Exhibit 3-13 for the organizational chart for this department. In our example we find that there are 5.35 total FTEs in the process. Some fall outside the direct department, like the Internal Audit person.

The total managerial time allotted to this process is 1.2 FTEs compared to 4.6 staff personnel for a span of control that is 3.833. As a new manager, comparing this to other span of controls within the organization and externally can help you understand if managers are doing staff tasks and thus having less time to supervise and strategize or if it is the exact opposite.

Exhibit 3-13 Organizational Chart Example

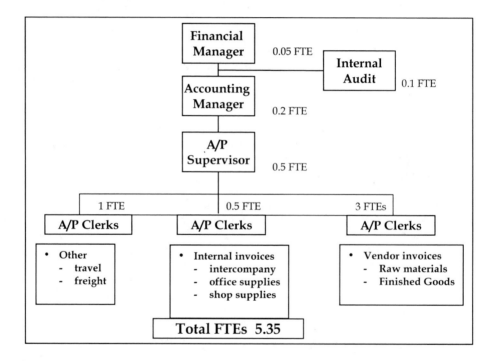

Tool Wrap Up
Continuous improvement tools are great to help you apply methodologies and sink your teeth into a process. The key is to not get overwhelmed with the technicalities. Take what works for you with each tool and apply it in a way that works for you and your organization.

Chapter Four: Diagnostic Tools

This brief chapter discusses a tool known as a diagnostic. We will explain what it is and why you use it. We will also discuss how it matches up against the concept of needs assessment.

What it is:

You go to a doctor not knowing what ailment you have but you know you don't feel healthy. The doctor needs to do a little probing, ask some questions, run some initial tests to diagnose your symptoms and offer the right medicines to help you get better. Remember how the doctor tool the stethoscope out of her lab coat and listened to your chest? Or how about that long list of questions on that clipboard you had to answer yes or no to? Remember that? The doctor was using simple diagnostic tools prior to running more time consuming, expensive and perhaps painful tests that might not be necessary. Further, the initial scan was certainly a step to be taken before any medicine was to be prescribed.

Now let's cast the light of the "diagnostic tool" on performance improvement projects. Before making shotgun recommendations about improvement you need to understand your process. We understand from prior chapters in this book about the importance of assessing the "as is" state. However, even prior to that, before the project is fully "baked" so to speak, you need to run a diagnostic tool to help you determine if you are even looking at the right process and if so is your early notions about the problem really correct or are you barking up the wrong tree?

A diagnostic tool can help you with this initial scooping and confirmation. It is a high-level, process scan that attempts to do the following:

Determine alignment to best practices. A high level review of a process against some previously researched and industry accepted best practices may help you understand how close or far removed you really are from world-class performance prior to any substantial improvement efforts taking place.

For example, if you are trying to improve your training function, you can easily find great research from most of the major training periodicals on the attributes of award winning training organizations and quickly review the one's your current training process shares in common with the award winners.

Define the problem. Sometimes you might not know what the problem is at all. You know the outcomes or results of it. The diagnostic tool can help you unearth some of the root causes.

For example, Say you know that the number of days to close the books has been creeping upward each and every month which is not a good thing because management is needing that information for decision making, regulatory and shareholder stakeholders. A high level group meeting to discuss the situation by asking some broad questions reveals that a system malfunction from 6 months ago that was eventually fixed resulted in the systems now being less reliable than prior to the malfunction and they seem to have more system downtime than before. Although this is perhaps not the only problem, it is a very good direction to point your flashlight if you are otherwise in the dark.

Identify the needs. A diagnostic tool will help you identify what the requirements and desires of the process stakeholders are. This is the moment of strategic relevance where you ask "What business problem are we really trying to solve here?" Another question to get at needs would be to ask "Has the process met or exceeded your expectations?" Taking time to diagnose needs is just as important as time to diagnose problems. In fact, a serious problem could very well be that the existing process does not meet the needs of your stakeholders. Identifying those needs will help you solve those problems.

Determine the scope of the problem. Diagnostic tools are broad. They try and ask a variety of questions around a process or an issue to help in the refining, scooping and narrowing tasks. It is far better to spend time early in the process ruling out specific details than ruling them out after analyzing them for countless hours. Sometimes that is hard to do, but the diagnostic done up front before the beginning of your improvement process can help weed out the out of scope and give you a more manageable scope.

For example, you are the supply chain manager responsible for items such as procurement, inventory management and logistics. You know that your supply chain needs improvement due to the lack of responsiveness you have in being able to get product on shelves quickly and replenish stock outs. You could either begin a full improvement initiative turning over every activity in your procurement, inventory management and logistics processes or you could perform a higher level diagnostic tool on each of these and determine where the biggest problems are at to focus on those first.

Confirm or reject an initial hypothesis. It is not uncommon for management or staff to think they know the reason why they have a problem and should therefore move right to fixing the problem. If you know this with certainty there probably is not a need to dispense with other probing and questions. But, would a doctor move straight to the prescription of drugs without a few more questions? Probably not. I cannot recall a time when I went to a doctor where I was not asked countless questions and completed at least one form. A high level interview or survey that at least checks off or rules out the other issues is good for peace of mind. It might reveal other issues that were not thought of before.

Look before you leap. Performance improvement can be a black hole. It can be a dark and expansive place where many resources can get lost only never to be recovered again. The diagnostic tool can help you explore the process holistically before jumping into an unmanageable task. It is truly a process of simply looking before leaping because once you convince management of a performance improvement project you are accountable for seeing it through. Take some time and do some upfront homework first.

Diagnostic Tool vs. Needs Assessments

Sometimes people get diagnostic tools confused with needs assessments. When you read about needs assessments in the TQM literature or training literature you may see that the scope of such projects is dramatically different than what is defined in this text. It typically conjures up rigorous, elaborate, and time-consuming academic research that dives into the root causes of a performance problem.

For example, General Motors did a needs analysis in its metal fabrication plant back in the late 1990's. They created a team and conducted the following five-step process to identify needs:

1. Identify symptoms and causes
2. Plan data-gathering techniques
3. Collect the data
4. Analyze and interpret the data
5. Report results and suggest solutions

At the end of the day, GM came up with several significant ways to improve the plant. As a result of such improvements GM saw a 30 percent reduction in scrap and an annualized cost savings of over $500,000. However, this "needs assessment" was a significantly larger scope than what we will discuss. In fact, I would argue that this was the performance improvement project whereby a formal methodology was deployed to not only assess needs, but also determine the features of the existing and desired processes, identify gaps and make suggestions to narrow the gaps.

The "needs assessment" may very well be the full-blown performance improvement project cloaked in a catchy phrase people like to hear. Management likes to know you'll be looking at the needs of customers. You cannot solve a problem without understanding the needs of the stakeholders. All of this is very true. A needs analysis is very important to do. But, to label the entire performance improvement process a needs assessment is incorrect.

Hence, we use the term diagnostic tool to describe the act of conducting that high level scan of needs and problems to scope and clarify a potential project. The key attributes of the diagnostic tool are the following:

- High level.
- Broad.
- Efficient to administer.
- Efficient to report.
- Best practice oriented.

The tool itself can be in the form of a qualitative, quantitative or hybrid type data collection instrument.

- Qualitative. This type of tool asks questions that are more subjective and self-reported but can be scored for quantification. For example, asking a series of likert questions that the respondent completes can be averaged into a score. If I am conducting a diagnostic tool around procurement, for example, a qualitative diagnostic question might ask "Our procurement vendor base is currently optimized with the right mix of vendors to satisfy our future needs." The respondent can answer 1 to 5 with 1 indicating they strongly disagree and 5 indicating they strongly agree.

- Quantitative. A question that is really a performance metric that can be compared internally, historically, or externally. For example, "how many vendors are currently in your procurement database?" Typically one respondent not many answers this. If the answer is 100 and you compare it historically, internally or externally it can help you diagnose if your vendor base is optimized.

- Hybrid. A diagnostic tool that gathers both qualitative and quantitative questions. It is best to gather the majority of the questions as qualitative, scoring where appropriate and a few key performance indicators as the quantitative (3 to 5). Again, you want it to be high level and efficient so typically qualitative questions that the user can provide their opinion on in the form of a 1 to 5 (or whatever rating you chose) rating is both efficient and effective during this initial data gathering stage.

Why do a diagnostic?

A diagnostic is often one of the first steps in a continuous improvement project. It is hard to come up with solutions when you don't have a firm grasp on the problem, thus the diagnostic really helps clarify the problem and think about what potential future outcomes are desired.

The key reasons why you should consider a diagnostic as a precursor to your next performance improvement project is as follows:

- **Prioritize next steps**: Sometimes you think you know the cause of a problem and are willing to invest substantial resources in solving it. However, a diagnostic done before doing more extensive process reengineering can help you determine if your instincts were correct.

- **Plan future projects:** A diagnostic can reveal that your problem is really several problems. To try and fix them all at once could result in organizational chaos. Hence the diagnostic might result in a prioritized set of next steps that really become future projects.

- **Allocate resources more effectively:** We all live and work in a world of resource constraints. Because there is limited financial, physical and human resources to tackle any particular process you need to be sure that the process you select is the right one for the right time. The diagnostic tool can help you determine this with more assurance.

- **Strengthen your business case if you can demonstrate unfilled needs or defined problems:** When you are attempting to convince management to provide resources for your performance improvement initiative, it is much more credible to have documented the unmet needs or defined problems formally and articulately. Just saying "I think my order entry process is broken, can I have 2 weeks and $10,000 to look into it?" is not the best way to position your project proposal. But the results of a high level diagnostic can paint a more objective and realistic picture.

- **Pinpoint the weaker areas in more dire need of improvement:** Because the diagnostic has elements of best practices embedded within it, it is a tool to help you prioritize areas to be within the scope of your performance improvement project when not everything can be in scope.

- **Guide the mission, goals and strategy within the processes:** Diagnostic tools as organizational scans or health checks can certainly guide the strategic intent of a process. If your diagnostic reveals that you are less competitive than others in the marketplace, that may help reshape the mission of your process.

- **Facilitate a healthy discussion about critical issues:** Anytime you ask people to discuss a process and to tell you what they think, you will get a healthy debate about the way things are and the way things should be. The high level diagnostic gives people the opportunity to lay out some of the larger, broader items that may not have been discussed or documented previously.

- **A precursor to a performance improvement project**: Last but not least, a properly conducted diagnostic tool will either lead to a performance improvement project or it wont. If does the diagnostic helped shape the scope of the project. If it did not it avoided allocating resources to a potential project that did not need to happen.

Constructing a diagnostic tool

There are two ways I would suggest getting your hands on a diagnostic tool: buy it or create it.

Buying a diagnostic tool is my way of saying get one externally. In fact, "buying it" does not necessarily mean you need to spend thousands of dollars, in fact it may even be free.

<u>Sources of Diagnostic Tools</u>
Consulting firms. Consultants are known for using diagnostic tools in everything they do. In fact, it is a necessary part of their job. If they do not set the proper scope for their project they could incur cost overruns and mismanage

client expectations. A great first step might be to ask a consultant if they happen to have a high level questionnaire or tool you can complete for a particular process. Most firms with expertise in that area should be able to quickly provide you with at least a 10 to 25-question document on that process that walks you through some of the major considerations for creating a world-class process. In fact, several firms may be willing to administer it for a nominal charge or for free in hopes of helping you with the more detailed performance improvement project and ultimately in the implementation of any action steps from that project.

A great example is PriceWaterhouseCoopers who has a site known as Global Best Practices (www.globalbestpractices.com) that has hundreds of qualitative process tools on the site so you can compare a particular process to best practices.

Trade and Industry Associations. It is within the mission and intent of most of these organizations to conduct research on behalf of its membership. Often times these organizations collaborate with consulting firms or major periodicals to conduct exhaustive research on a variety of relevant and future-oriented topics specific to the trade or industry. Members typically receive questionnaires that are chock full of excellent 'diagnostic' style questions and a few months later, they will receive a report outlining the results. It helps participating organizations do a quick sanity check on how their process aligns with the rest of the pack. It saves the participating organizations time and money because they can leverage research already created without having to reinvent the wheel. Often times, the associations will archive and offer to its members and even nonmembers past research results or data collection instruments.

A great example here is the National Association of Manufacturing (NAM). They conduct studies all the time on items such as workforce trends and technology in manufacturing.

Periodicals. Most major periodicals will do research projects for the benefits of its readership. It could be an annual survey or a host of mini research projects on hot topics throughout the year. Subscribers are asked to participate in the studies and typically get a summary version of the results in the periodical but can also purchase more detailed reports from the publisher directly.

A great examples is Industry Week Magazine who has conducted a Best Plants survey that takes an exhaustive look at multiple processes within a plant and honors the best one's each year with an award. They also offer for sale the database of those plants along with multiple other studies they have conducted over the past several years.

Acadamia. It is not uncommon for universities to conduct research on specific business processes. In doing so they develop excellent data collection instruments and publish detailed findings. For example, Michigan State University has been intimately involved in the Customer Satisfaction Index (CSI) that surveys consumers and then tabulates ratings of major businesses from multiple industries relative to their customer service. Information such as this is available to those interested in obtaining it.

<u>Building a Diagnostic Tool</u>
 A diagnostic tool can be created in a variety of ways and can have multiple project management and needs analysis input sources such as those listed below.

Project Management Tools:
1. Proposals
2. Project Management Process
3. Letter of Understanding
4. Project Plan
5. Reporting Plans
6. Communication Plans
7. Escalation Plans
8. Team Communication Form
9. Responsibility Matrix
10. Quality Control Data
11. Project Progress Report
12. Project Checklist
13. Project Change Notice
14. Project Audit Plan
15. Meeting Agenda Templates
16. Conference Call Agenda Template
17. PERT Time Estimates
18. Team Directory
19. Instructor Profile
20. Developer Profile
21. Technical Profile
22. Tracking Summary Report
23. Work Review Process
24. Work Confirmation Form
25. Feasibility Analysis Template

Needs Analysis Tools:
1. Project Management Process
2. Needs Analysis Process
3. Vendor Assessment
4. Task Inventory Lists
5. Scoping questions
6. Needs Assessment Matrix
7. Decision Aid
8. Focus Group Protocol
9. Needs Interview Protocol
10. Needs Questionnaire
11. Surveys –respondents'
12. Surveys – Sites
13. Job Content Analysis
14. Analysis Report Templates
15. Project Estimation Rules

Champions of Change

16. Project Estimation Worksheet
17. Assumption checklist
18. Assessment checklist
19. User Characteristics
20. Assessment Matrices
21. Objectives Specifications Tool
22. Object Review Checklist
23. Multimedia Feasibility Survey
24. Evaluation Plan Template
25. Plan of Bidders Session
26. Text Design Guidelines
27. RFP Template
28. Vendor Contracts

The delivery of the tool can be any of the following:

- **Interview**. A face-to-face meeting with the respondent to gather the information using structured questions.
- **Focus group**. A group meeting with several stakeholders to gather the information using structured facilitation techniques.
- **Questionnaire**. A formal set of questions that respondents complete and return to you for analysis.

We will focus our attention on the questionnaire as the delivery mechanism for our diagnostic tool because it has the following benefits:

- Reusable. The format of the tool and even content could be made into a template and re-used on future diagnostic endeavors.
- Quantifiable. The tool questions should be scored for output and reporting purposes. A questionnaire lends itself better to scoring than interviews and focus groups.
- Easier to document. Results of surveys are easier to report specific findings because they are highly structured and easy to automate in terms of analysis.

To construct the diagnostic tool questionnaire, it is organized around sets of grouped questions called constructs. There are usually 5 to 10 constructs but you could have more or less.

Once you have identified these groupings you prepare discussion questions or data items that you would like to receive that relate to the each grouping.

In order to make your diagnostic tool more powerful, each question should be assigned a score. In this manner, you can tabulate the responses up to the construct level and for the entire assessment. It then allows you to showcase for your constituents where the greatest needs exist. In that manner it helps prioritize your next steps in the process of improvement.

How should you know when to use the diagnostic tool?

Now that this tool has been explained, you are probably curious as to how you know when to use it. You'll recall from earlier in this book, we discussed the first step of our methodology, *Identify the Need*. You'll also recall that we identified five forces that could impact you as a new manager and send up a red flag that the process may need to be examined. Those five factors are as follows:

1. Strategic Change
2. Process Change
3. Personnel Change
4. Technology Change
5. External Shifts

If there are changes in any of these you may want to assess needs and determine if problem areas exist.

First, let's take strategic change. Some key elements here are to look at the following:
- "Flavor the month" changes these are those key management initiatives that tend to be in vogue one day and pitched aside the next. You must be on top of these changes because your span of control could be impacted by it. For example, if Six Sigma is the hot program management is really interested in, how will that impact your domain?
- Long-term shifts. Examples include:
  o dropping product lines
  o moving from being the low cost provider to the high value player
  o Business drivers emphasized and de-emphasized, these include:
    ▪ Customer satisfaction
    ▪ Quality initiatives
    ▪ Cost reductions and cuts
    ▪ Revenue growth
    ▪ Employee retention
    ▪ Productivity gains

Next let's discuss process change. Some key elements here are to look at the following:
- Changes in policies and procedures
- Changes in organizational structure (centralized to decentralized for example)
- Merger, acquisition, divestiture
- Change in the way performance is measured and managed
- Change in organizational culture

Then there are personnel changes. Some key elements here are as follows:
- Management and staff turnover
- Loss of a key employee(s)
- Addition of people with different ideas and ways of doing things
- Addition or loss of skill, knowledge and experience

Champions of Change

93

Technology change is another indicator of a potential needs assessment. Some key elements here are as follows:

- Implementation of a new system
- Major system upgrade or downgrade
- Automation of manual tasks
- Phase out of legacy systems

Finally, we must not forget external shifts. Key elements here are as follows:

- Marketplace shifts
- Economic swings
- Sporadic customer growth or turnover
- Loss of key suppliers
- Competitive maneuvers

All of the aforementioned changes can signal the need for you to assess needs. You just need to be careful not to go overboard every time a minor change occurs. You should always have your pulse on the day-to-day operations of your managerial domain through a well-balanced performance measurement system (which we'll discuss in the next chapter). Nonetheless, you can probably think back in your career at some of the above changes and most of the time, those types of changes impacted what you did or how your department was run. Understanding the needs based on these changes is a first step in the right direction to reacting quickly in the face of change.

Example

Let's say you are the manager of the training and development group. A new senior management team is reviewing your group for the first time. Your budget is approximately 4% of company-wide revenue, a significant number to the senior management team. They would like to understand how the investment in training is paying off.

They want to make sure that the employees in return for the investment that is being made are receiving the best training. To date, very little has been done to support this effort so management asks that you understand the needs of the employees better and devise a way to help them understand if their needs are being met appropriately.

So, because of this management change, you must change. You can use a diagnostic tool to determine employee needs and report back to management the current state of affairs as it relates to training and development.

To begin, you do some research and discuss with business unit managers what they are looking for from training and development. You also review literature on the web, take a look at various publications on training evaluation and talk to the vendors and in-house folks who design and deliver your training. You come up with the following key constructs to build your needs assessment around:

- Instructor
- Course Design
- Training Facilities
- Customer Service
- On the Job Support
- Applicability to the job
- Impact on the Job

You feel that if you can assess your needs along these dimensions, management would have enough information to help you with your budget.

You begin your assessment by putting together some key questions beneath each construct. Let's look at a few we created for the Instructor construct:

1. Do instructors have adequate subject matter knowledge?
2. Do instructors have good presentation skills?
3. Do instructors make good use of exercises and labs?

Now you hope to quantify these responses. You use a traditional Likert scale to do so. Likert, in case you are not familiar, developed a method to measure attitudes that would be easy for respondents to fill out and easy for administrators to score. Our Likert scale is the original 1 to 5 and we place our own descriptions next to each scale option to guide our respondents:

1=no
2=poor
3=fair
4=good
5=excellent

You instruct a random sample of management and staff employees to answer each question by rating their belief about it from 1 to 5.

Once you have created questions and the scoring model for all of your constructs you administer the assessment to business unit managers to get their feedback on where the needs are met and falling short. You would probably have some open ended questions in there as well to ensure you capture all of their feedback. You might follow-up with a debrief to capture their commentary as well.

The data is then tabulated and quantified by question and by construct and rolled up to an overall summary layer of detail. You can even get fancy and show the data in a graphical way. I like to use a "stop light" effect. The "stop light" effect is where any scores falling below a certain threshold are red, indicating a problem area. Those areas that score very well are indicated by a green color. Finally, those scores that are within a range of indifference are scored yellow.

For our needs assessment, see Exhibit 4-1 for an example of each constructs score and the Instructor construct broken out by the questions. In color, items between less than 2 are red, items greater than 4 are green and in between items are yellow.

Exhibit 4-1 Needs Assessment Report Example

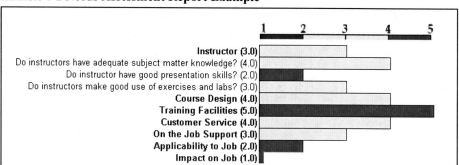

From the example above, we can quickly see that learners think the training and development group needs to improve in presentation skills for instructors as well as applicability to Job and Impact on Job. The lower scores evidence this.

Conversely, the training facility scored high. Other notable high scores included course design and customer service.

Armed with this analysis, as the training and development manager, you know where to invest some resources in improving this process, or at a minimum where to look deeper for root causes of problems. You can go back to senior management with this analysis and provide them some next steps to help improve the process where it needs it.

Senior management has a clearer picture of its training investment. They agree with your assertion that a larger portion of this year's budget should be focused on the weak points identified in the analysis. They would like to see a similar analysis at the end of the first quarter to determine if improvements were made.

Companies like Ford Motor Company use this type of analysis when they develop courses within their Education, Training and Development (ET&D) department. This needs analysis is helpful to Ford to ensure they are aligning training with desired skill sets.

Other organizations like Trident Precision Manufacturing Inc., a precision parts manufacturer in Webster New York used diagnostic tools to help reduce turnover from 50% to less than 5% and increase customer quality from around 70% to over 99%. Trident, a 1996 Malcolm Baldrige National Quality Award Winner assesses needs in a Total Quality Roundtable that meets twice a year to find solutions to troublesome processes. From 1991 to 1995 over 97% of the 5000 process improvements identified by employees were implemented.

In a similar story, the smallest company ever to win a Malcolm Baldrige National Quality Award, Texas Nameplate has regular meetings to discuss key business drivers, customer complaints, and on-time delivery. Staying on top of the needs in these areas is something that CEO Dale Crownover sees a competitive advantage.

Conclusion

Diagnostic tools are like flashlights in the dark, they help you find your way around much easier. My example, although fictitious is not far from fact. Organizations like General Motors collaborated with the United Auto Workers Union to conduct a training needs assessment. That team deployed a five-step methodology to understand training as it related to production scheduling, efficiency, and cost goals. Their methodology focused on:
1. identification of the performance problems
2. planning the data gathering techniques
3. data gathering through interviews and surveys of workers and supervisors
4. analysis of and interpretation of data
5. presented findings to management with nine suggestions to solve problems not meeting needs

Use needs assessments if for nothing else, to at least keep a pulse on what your stakeholders value most. Just asking them can yield a wealth of information to help you improve your process and be a better manager.

Chapter Five: Historic Data Analysis

This is a brief chapter to familiarize you with the use of historical data to analyze processes and improve future performance.

Lots of organizations use historical data analysis to help in their continuous improvement projects. For example, in an effort to improve ergonomics in the workplace, Boeing used historical data coupled with employee feedback to identify opportunities for improvement.

In another example, John Hancock Funds (JHF) used historical data to flag brokers whose purchases were dropping off. The data analysis was the catalyst in a broker retention campaign that helped JHF regain $33 million in sales from brokers who had been taking business elsewhere.

Recreational Equipment Inc., (REI) used historical data analysis based upon transaction histories, lifestyle data, accounting data, and demographic data to come up with a model of the perfect customer. The model helped REI move from a 1% to a 4% response rate to its 2000 holiday season mailing.

Still yet, Rockwell Collins, a manufacturer of cockpit instruments and ground – communication tools used historical data to help it realize the need for computer-based training. The result was an 82 page strategic plan that transitioned its training to "alternative" learning formats like self-paced Web based-training.

Let's begin our discussion of historical data by reviewing some of the common data collection techniques that are available.

- Surveys. Surveys allow the collection of qualitative and quantitative data of current and past results to build a data bank and assess needs
- Observation. Observation is a verification technique that validates results.
- Interviews. Interviews are on-on-one, personal collections of qualitative information.
- Focus groups. Focus groups are a way to measure consensus and gather data collectively.
- Historical data. Historical data is a quantitative review of past results and trends.

Exhibit 5-1 illustrates the advantages and disadvantages of using each of the above-mentioned data collection techniques.

Exhibit 5-1 Data Collection Techniques

Technique	Advantage	Disadvantage
Surveys	-easy to quantify -easy to summarize -low cost to administer -obtain large amounts of data	-self reported bias -often a time consuming -low response rates
Observation	-collect data on behavior -real time analysis -paints a true picture	-high cost -observation bias -difficult to summarize
Interviews	-powerful if credible sources -collection on range of subjects	-high cost -interviewer/interviewee bias
Focus groups	-reach multiple people at once -see consensus or lack there of	-difficult to set-up -not always honest, candid -a few monopolize time
Historic data	-quick and easy to gather -easy to segment -low cost -spot trends	-can at times be difficult to gather -often hard to quantify and collect "soft" data -time consuming to continuously collect data over time

In Chapter six we will take a look at surveys, interviews and focus groups in more detail as they are commonly applied tools. For now, lets take a closer look at historical data.

Why use historical data?

Now that you know a little about historical data it makes sense to let you know why you should use it as part of your continuous improvement efforts. First, historical data can be used to determine baselines of performance. A baseline is good to set goals for future performance and as a comparison to benchmark against other organizations performances.

Second, historic data can help you establish trend lines. Trend lines help understand the fluctuation in a process over time.

Historical data is good in identifying key sources of variation in the data. Processes that are out of control need to be adjusted, historical data helps you pinpoint those processes.

Organizations will use data warehouses to facilitate access to their historical data. For example, Garden Ride, a retailer of home decorating products, uses data warehouses to help them see historical data coming from their enterprise resource planning system to look at product, location, and time data, which in turn helps them, understand consumer trends and habits.

In another example, Florida's Broward County School District uses data mining and analysis tools to help improve student academic performance. A new data warehouse helps the district analyze historic data on its 237,000 students in terms of academic achievement and other relevant information. This helps the district implement best practices and improve student achievement.

What is data mining?

The old adage "garbage in is garbage out" is of particular relevance when talking about data. That is why organizations have begun to use data mining techniques to manage the massive amounts of data they collect. It is estimated that the average Fortune 500 company generates up to 500 million documents annually. Thus, it is important to manage and leverage that data appropriately.

Data mining is the process of finding patterns and correlations in large amounts of data. There are several software programs available that combine pattern recognition with statistical and mathematical techniques to root through data and make sense of it.

Companies like LTV Steel used data mining to save $10 million by reducing defects in their steel manufacturing process. They used data mining to determine which furnaces were creating the defects and then predicted when deterioration would occur.

Another example of a company leveraging data analysis is Dana Corp., an automotive parts supplier. Dana reduced its supplier parts per million defects by 50%. They use a real-time system to monitor supplier metrics and data mining is built into this process.

Additional data management tools you can use to manage historic data include the following:

data warehouse: A collection of data that has been extracted from operational databases and then cleansed to remove redundant data and bring in additional information as needed. These can be set up as a centralized database of information from disparate systems.

neural networks: Models designed to simulate the human brain. From an analytical tool standpoint they have been shown to outperform statistical techniques where relationships among data are nonstandard.

decision tree analysis: A data analysis tool that searches through data to identify which predictor is most important to correctly predict the dependent variable. It can be used to rank the importance of various attributes and identify performance targets for customer satisfaction attributes.

OLAP tools: OLAP is an Online Analytic Processing tool. It is a technology that allows users of multidimensional database to generate data summaries and query data.

statistical and mathematical techniques: multiple statistics can be used to sort, analyze, and mine data. Please see the section *employing statistics* later in this chapter for more information on statistics.

When do you use historical data?

Although historical data can be gathered at any point in a continuous improvement process, it is most valuable to gather that data at early stages when attempting to understand your current process. This early data can help point you in the right direction to source root causes. It can also help you compare your process to others along the way.

Another point where historical data collection is helpful is part of your measurement and monitoring process. Once you implement changes, having the right performance measurement system in place to compute key performance indicators and trend them over time is powerful and essential to keep your improvements on track. We'll discuss performance measurement principles later in this book.

Finally, ever heard of the balanced scorecard? Maybe it was a flavor of the month at your company a little while ago? Maybe it's still in use. It is a good tool for the most part. It's a set of key performance indicators to measure and manage a process. Historical data is a core element of a balanced scorecard system.

Organizations like Sallie Mae, which funds approximately 40 percent of all insured student loans used historical data when it created specific Key Performance Indicators (KPI's) to increase employee performance and customer satisfaction. A detailed study, which used historical data collection along with operational reviews and employee interviews, helped them refine their call center process. They collect data for any hour of the day and use this data to make operational changes in a timely manner.

Develop Performance Measures

Establish your data collection goals by devising the right performance measures. You need to define the types of data you want to collect. This means defining your performance measures. Try and breakdown your performance measures into categories. This way you make sure you have a well-balanced family of measures.

The types of measures that help ensure this balance are cost, quality, time, productivity and customer satisfaction-based measures. For example, let's say you are a finance department manager trying to collect data in preparation for a balanced scorecard. What measures would you suggest that ensure this balance? Exhibit 5-2 illustrates these measures.

Exhibit 5-2 Performance Measures for a finance department's balanced scorecard

Measure	Measurement Type
Finance department cost as a percent of revenue	Cost measure
Percent of fixed asset transactions misclassified	Quality measure
Number of days to close the accounting books	Time measure
Number of accounts payable invoices processed per full time equivalents	Productivity measure
Management satisfaction with month-end financial reports	Customer satisfaction measure

Once you have these measures be sure you collect the data in a manner that is consistent and comparable. Consistency ensures your historical data can be appropriately trended with reliability in the numbers. Comparability ensures that the manner in which you collect your data is common enough to be benchmarked against other organizations or internally.

Employing Statistics

What would a book on continuous improvement be without a mention of statistics in your quantitative data analysis? When you collect data keep in mind you can use statistics as tools to enhance your analysis of the data. If understood, statistics can help you better interpret data.

We'll discuss some basic statistics: mean, standard deviation and confidence intervals. However, see Table 5-1 for a summary of the major statistics that might be used in data analysis. It is suggested you consult a statistics guide for use of more advanced statistics to deploy on data such as Pareto Charts, ANOVA diagrams (analysis of variance) and Chi-Square analysis.

Mean

Definition: The average of a set of data

Formula:

$$\frac{\sum x}{n}$$

Example. 10, 7, 9, 27, 2
The mean is 11 (10+7+9+27+2)/5

Standard deviation

Definition: A measure of how widely values are dispersed from the average value (the mean).

This statistic tells you how tightly all the various examples are clustered around the mean in a set of data. When the examples are pretty tightly bunched together, the standard deviation is small. When the examples are spread apart that indicates you have a relatively large standard deviation.

High standard deviation values occur when the data item being analyzed (e.g., prices or an indicator) is changing dramatically. Similarly, low standard deviation values occur when data are stable.

The standard deviation can help point you in the right direction when asking why data is the way it is. A bigger standard deviation for a class tells you that there are relatively more evaluations for that class scoring toward one extreme or the other.

Formula:

$$\sqrt{\frac{n\sum x^2 - \left(\sum x\right)^2}{n(n-1)}}$$

Example:
Suppose 10 tools stamped from the same machine during a production run are collected as a random sample and measured for breaking strength. The sample values (1345, 1301, 1368, 1322, 1310, 1370, 1318, 1350, 1303, 1299). The standard deviation is 27.46

Confidence interval

Definition: A range on either side of a sample mean. For example, if you order a product through the mail, you can determine, with a particular level of confidence, the earliest and latest the product will arrive.

The confidence level is the probability value (1-std dev) associated with a confidence interval. Ex. If std dev is .05 (5%) than 1-.05 is a 95% confidence interval.

The width of the confidence interval gives us some idea about how uncertain we are about the unknown population parameter, in this case the mean. A very wide interval may indicate that more data should be collected before anything very definite can be said about the parameter.

Formula:

$$\bar{x} \pm 1.96 \left(\frac{\sigma}{\sqrt{n}} \right)$$

Example:
Suppose we observe that, in our sample of 50 commuters, the average length of travel to work is 30 minutes with a population standard deviation of 2.5. We can be 95 percent confident that the population mean is in the interval:

$$30 \pm 1.96 \left(\frac{2.5}{\sqrt{50}} \right)$$

or: CONFIDENCE(0.05,2.5,50) equals 0.692951. In other words, the average length of travel to work equals 30 ± 0.692951 minutes, or 29.3 to 30.7 minutes.

Table 5-1 Key Statistics Used in Data Analysis

source: *The Internet Glossary of Statistical Terms* written by Howard S. Hoffman, Professor Emeritus of Psychology, Bryn Mawr College and Programmed by Russell D. Hoffman, Owner and Chief Programmer, The Animated Software Company

Statistic	Definition
Alpha	The probability of rejecting the statistical hypothesis tested when the hypothesis is true.
Alternative Hypothesis	The test of a statistical hypothesis that assesses if the sample yielded a statistic that is among the cases that would occur alpha proportion of the time if the hypothesis were true.
ANOVA	Analysis of Variance. Uses the F statistic to test statistical significance of the differences among the obtained means of two or more random samples from a given population.
Average Deviation	An index of variability to characterize the dispersion among the measures in a given population
Beta	The probability of failing to reject the statistical hypothesis tested when the hypothesis is false and an alternative hypothesis is true.
Central Limit Theorem	Describes the characteristics of the distribution of values one would obtain if one were to draw an infinite number of random samples of a given size from a given population and the mean was calculated for each sample.
Chi Square	Compares the frequencies of various kinds of items in a random sample to the frequencies that are expected if the population frequencies are as hypothesized by the investigator.
Confounding factor.	Term used to describe the unsuspecting systematic differences in the way groups were treated in addition to the intended treatment conditions.
Correlation	The degree to which paired measures (X and Y) co-vary in a linear fashion.
Critical Region	The area or areas, of the sampling distribution of as statistic that will lead to the rejection of the hypothesis tested when the hypothesis is true.
Critical Value	The value(s) that cut off the proportion of the sampling distribution designated as the alpha region.
Degrees of Freedom	The number of values in the final calculation of a statistic that are free to vary.

Statistic	Definition
F Statistic	The ratio of two s squares (estimates of a population variance, based on the information in two or more random samples.)
F Test	Uses the F Statistic to test various statistical hypothesis about the mean of the distribution from which a sample has been drawn.
Histogram	Shows the characteristics of the distribution of items in a given population.
Mean	The average scores of the population.
Mean Square	An estimate of the population variance based on the variability among a given set of measures.
Median	The point that divides the distribution scores in half.
Mode	The score of the population that occurs most frequently.
Null Hypothesis	The statistical hypothesis tested.
One-tailed test	Test of a statistical hypothesis in which only a value of the statistic will lead to rejection of the hypothesis tested.
Parameter	A measurement on a population that characterizes one of its features.
Population	The entire collection of items that is the focus of concern.
Power	The probability that the test will reject the hypothesis tested when a specific alternative hypothesis is true.
Prediction	In regression, the regression line indicates the predicted value of Y for each value of X
Random Sample	Set of items drawn from a population in such a way that each time an item is selected, every item in the population had an equal opportunity to appear in the sample.
Range	The distance between the highest and lowest scores.
Regression	Given related measures (X and Y), the manner in which one of the measures change as the other measure changes.
Regression Towards the Mean	The property of a scatter plot where the linear relationship is less than perfect such that the regression of Y on X will have a slope less than 45 degrees.
Related Measures	The population of paired numbers so one can measure more than one feature.
Sample Mean	The average mean of the sample population. Repeated random samples of the same size from the same population would cluster around the exact value of the population mean.
Sampling Distribution	The set of values that one would obtain if one drew an infinite number of random samples from a given population and calculated the statistic on each sample.
Sample Variance	Measures the variance of the population from which the sample is drawn. It is the sum of the squared deviations around the mean of a random sample divided by the sample size minus one.
Standard Deviation	Calculates the dispersion among the measures in a given population. It is the square root of the variance.
Standard Error	An estimate of the standard deviation of the sampling distribution of the means. It is the square root of the quantity obtained when s **squared** is divided by the size of the sample.
Statistic	A measure on the items in a random sample done to estimate a corresponding parameter of the population from which the sample was drawn.
Statistical Hypothesis	The hypothesis that is tested. The null hypothesis.
Statistical Significance	A finding where it is demonstrated that the probability of obtaining such a difference by chance only, is relatively low.
Statistical Test	A procedure for deciding whether an assertion about a quantitative feature of a population is true or false.

Statistic	Definition
T statistic	A measure of a random sample in which the mean appears in the numerator and an estimate of the numerator's standard deviation appears in the denominator.
T Test	Employs the statistic **t** to test a given statistical hypothesis about the mean of a population
Transformation Rules	Term used to describe the changes in the mean, variance and standard deviation of a distribution when every item in a distribution is either increased or decreased by a constant amount.
Two-Tailed Test	Test of a given statistical hypothesis in which a value of the statistic that is either sufficiently small or sufficiently large will lead to the rejection of the hypothesis tested.
Type One Error	Rejecting the hypothesis tested when it was true.
Type Two Error	Failing to reject the hypothesis tested when a given alternative hypothesis was true.
Unbiased Estimate	Occurs when the mean of the sampling distribution of that statistic can be shown to be equal to the parameter being estimated.
Variance	Characterizes the dispersion among the measures in a given population.
Z Statistic	A measure on a random sample in which a mean appears in the numerator and the numerator's standard deviation appears in the denominator.
Z Score	Indicates how far and in what direction the item deviates from its distribution's mean, expressed in units of its distribution's standard deviation.

Chapter Six: Questionnaires, Interviews and Focus Groups

As you've probably observed, many of the examples and tools discussed gathered information through questionnaires, interviews or focus groups. It is only appropriate to teach you some techniques to optimizing these tools.

Lots of organizations use these techniques in their day-to-day operations. For example, Asea Brown Boveri (ABB) uses internal questionnaires as a part of its internal audit process. The surveys help ABB collect the necessary data to create quality metrics to measure and manage their internal audit department.

Another organization, Respironics Inc., a medical equipment manufacturer, began an employee survey process in its commitment to be viewed as a great place to work. A team was assembled and they brainstormed around questions related to ten topical areas. The questions were gauged to reflect both employee satisfaction and importance to the customer. In addition senior management provided input to the survey process to help provide important strategic business issues. Employees completed the surveys during one-hour meetings. Confidentiality was a key to getting honest and high response rates. Managers analyzed the results using a SWOT analysis (strengths-weaknesses-opportunities-threats). The survey resulted in many opportunities for improvement. It helped management realize the need to focus on improving their 401(k) plan, add a gain sharing plan, improve facilities, IT systems and internal communications.

At Aetna Insurance Company, the retirement services division uses the power of surveying to help identify customer issues. Customers complete surveys right after a service transaction. Aetna calls the customer back in a timely manner in reaction to the data received in this survey.

Interviewing has been used at Cigna Corporation as a part of the hiring process. Cigna uses behavioral interviewing techniques when hiring employees. The behavioral interviewing approach is used to detect proficiency, deficiency, and aptitude for behaviors such as customer service, working in a team environment, and problem solving. The interviews help Cigna match skills with positions more appropriately.

This chapter's objective is to articulate the ways in which you can use questionnaires, interviews and focus groups to best gather data to improve your process.

Questionnaires
Below is a ten-step process to effectively designing and using questionnaires.
1. Conduct background research
2. Determine the scope
3. Categorize the issues
4. Create performance measures

5. Design the survey instrument
6. Select the sample population
7. Administer the questionnaire
8. Review respondent data
9. Compile and analyze data
10. Report data

Step 1: Conduct background research

1. Conduct article searches on the general subject (ex. Databases like Lexus/Nexus, internet, reference books)
2. Contact an industry or trade association to find additional articles, books, studies, and seminars on the subject
3. Use process mapping within your process to understand it better and identify its inputs, activities, outputs, efficiencies, bottlenecks, redundancies
4. Talk with management and others outside the process to understand what their perception of the process is and what they think it should be like
5. Use your network such as with academics, consultants, and your internal auditors to gather more background on the topic

Step 2: Determine the scope

1. Based on the research and understanding your own environment determine the process or processes under consideration.
2. Prioritize the issues based upon what is determined to be the most important, what has the greatest business risk, short term vs. long term 'wins', fit with strategy, size of gap between importance and performance, by urgency, or by cost
3. Understand what type of resources are available to work on this project. How many people? How much money in the budget? How much time?
4. Determine if the resources are aligned with the priorities. If not re-examine.
5. Once scope is set, create a timeline (it might be helpful to use a Gantt chart) that has the following date: performance measures complete, draft survey complete, survey review and finalization, survey dissemination, survey deadline, data review and follow-up, data analysis, data reporting.

Step 3: Categorize the issues

1. Group the issues into smaller sub-categories that share common themes. For example, cost, quality, time, productivity, technology
2. Prioritize the issues *again* based upon what is determined to be the most important, what has the greatest business risk, short term vs. long term 'wins', fit with strategy, size of gap between importance and performance, by urgency, or by cost

Step 4: Create performance measures

1. Involve core stakeholders (shareholders, customers, and employees) in the development of measures
2. Create a small, balanced family of measures that address cost, quality, timeliness and productivity across the process
3. If possible, align performance measures with other measures used by management, internally and externally and with strategy and other business processes.

4. Set goals which support continuous improvement and stimulate breakthrough performance (may need to do after data is collected)
5. Begin to create a monitoring mechanism for performance measures, which allows management and the process owners to identify a need for action on a timely basis.
6. Communicate to the key stakeholders the finalized list of measures and why they were chosen

Step 5: Design the questionnaire instrument
1. In general, the approach to survey design should be to 1) convey a single thought in a single message, 2) avoid using ambiguous terminology, and 3) start with easy questions and progress to more difficult or sensitive questions (this is sometimes true - -with online surveys easy questions are said to work better at the end)
2. Include relevant company and contact information for demographic and reference purposes (unless anonymity is required). Information such as revenue, size, industry, products and services, and organizational structure are desirable. It can be placed at the beginning or end of the survey. For long surveys it is good to place it at the beginning. For online surveys placing it at the end allows the respondent to "warm-up" to the survey.
3. Include an introduction and statement of purpose. Include the amount of time it will take to complete the survey in this text. (ex. The survey is 25 questions and will take approximately 1 hour to complete.)
4. Create questions that lead to the compilation of the performance measures determined in the prior step. (For example: cost per purchase order is a performance measure so you need to ask questions that yield the cost and the number of purchase orders so this measure can be computed
5. Structure questions into categories (hopefully aligned with overall performance measure categories) to ensure they flow smoothly
6. Challenge each question you want to ask. Is it too trivial? Too sensitive? Too complex? Does it ask questions already answered through publicly available information? Are there too many questions? Are there too few?
7. Try and limit the questionnaire to 40 or fewer questions, depending on the complexity of individual questions. Include parenthetically any brief interpretive guidance and create a separate instruction set for more detailed guidance. Consider page length, not just questions, a survey 4 to 8 pages is normal.
8. Place the format of the data required above each data entry box. For example, if you require a percentage state percentage, if the respondent is to check all that apply state 'check all that apply.'
9. For certain questions that are required, state that clearly. For example, if you need to have their contact name for future follow-up make that clear. Sometimes indicating the required versus optional questions is helpful. If the survey is online, you can build in validation routines that prevent the user from moving on or submitting the survey without the required information entered.
10. Ensure questions are designed to unearth best practices or optimal ways to perform the process. For example if the purchasing department has an objective to use the internet to process purchase orders ask respondents for their percentage of purchase orders processed via the internet.

Champions of Change

11. When asking questions regarding a ranking of performance, also ask their rank regarding importance.
12. Try and avoid 'and' questions. For example "Does your company's customer support center have friendly and knowledgeable representatives?"
13. Instruct respondents to leave blank questions they are not sure of in order to prevent the respondent from merely guessing with a shot in the dark.
14. Ensure there are some open-ended questions. For example, "other" as the last option in a multiple-choice question is desirable. Leave space for the respondent to explain what "other" is.
15. Ensure the survey is edited, proofread, reviewed by stakeholders, pre-tested with a small group and finalized prior to sending out.

Step 6: Select the sample population
1. Try and research best companies to compare against based on criteria important to your project. Use trade associations and benchmarking associations as potential resources for finding the right companies to benchmark against.
2. To collect large amounts of data mass mailings use list brokers may be an option, but it can be expensive considering response rates to surveys are typically 1 to 5 %.
3. If you are interested in speaking with 2 or 3 companies qualitatively, try and have a list of 30 to 50 potential candidates.
4. It makes sense to not only pick companies within your industry, size, or geographic region, but also organizations outside these areas for additional insight and perspective.
5. For quantitative results, it is good to have a minimum of 20 respondents in your sample to help diminish any data discrepancies inherent in a few organizations that are surveyed and provided unreasonable data.
6. It may make sense to send a higher level, screener survey to potential benchmark candidates first and then use the screener to pick, which you want to 1) talk with qualitatively or 2) complete a more detailed quantitative survey.
7. Always use a cover letter to explain the survey. Position the benefits of the survey to the respondent from their perspective. Be clear on what they will receive in return and address the confidentiality of their data.

Step 7: Administer the Questionnaire
1. Personal interview
    - For sensitive issues
    - To build a relationship
    - For more qualitative, longer, more complex, discussion-type questions (open-ended, essay)
2. Telephone interview
    - To interview large numbers of people for short, precise and easy questions
    - To interview people with whom you have had little or no contact
3. Written survey document
    - For more quantitative questions that require research to obtain responses
    - To obtain structured responses

- When information is needed from many sources
4. Focus group
   - For brainstorming
   - To gain consensus
   - To speak to many people in a short time
   - For more qualitative, discussion-type questions
5. Online surveys
   - For high level, short, precise and easy questions
   - To reach a large number of people in a cost efficient manner

Provide plenty of time and advance preparation regardless of the data collection method used.

Step 8: Review Respondent Data
1. Try and review information shortly after the responses have been gathered so it is still fresh in the minds of all the parties. It is a good idea to at least read over the responses and make notes to you within hours after an interview or after receiving a returned survey.
2. Review data individually (survey by survey) and as a whole (as a benchmark population) and try and identify any outliers in the population.
3. Review the data for completeness. Were all the questions answered? If not why? Was something not applicable?
4. Make sure a response of zero is truly zero and not "NA" a response of zero may be averaged into calculations when computing benchmark results.
5. Develop a high level list of validation controls (if possible input into the database systems that process and report the data) to detect any unusual or unreasonable data. (Ex. If you ask in one question for the number of employees and in another you ask how many employees are paid by direct deposit vs. check vs. other and the two questions have very different numbers for total employees there is a potential problem.)
6. Follow-up with the respondent with all of your questions at once so as to avoid continuing to question them on their information, but leave the door open for additional follow-up.

Step 9: Compile and analyze the data
1. Organize data for analysis in a meaningful manner. (Ex. Cost, quality, time, productivity issues - - create an affinity diagram as a model for data organization)
2. Identify and classify the areas where there is obvious differences between your process and others either good or bad.
3. Highlight any judgments, opinions or benchmarks gathered from experts as "best practice" (for example - - a person with 20 years of experience is more credible than a person with 2 months of experience)
4. Note the instances where the same practices are regularly occurring among benchmark partners. These will help identify the standards.
5. Note the instances where a few companies are more innovative and creative or have exceptional performance. These will help identify the best practice organizations.
6. Note instances where automation and technology are leveraged.
7. Note instances where policies and procedures may be different.

Champions of Change   111

8. Compare process maps. Compare the inputs, activities and outputs.
9. Identify differences in activities performed by management vs. staff.
10. Identify differences in organizational structure. Is the activity decentralized or centralized?

*Gather data (Steps 3,4 and 5) with the end results in mind. Make sure that the questions you are asking are going to yield what you want to analyze in this step.

Step 10: Report Data
1. Explain the survey methodology and background and how you arrived at the results.
2. Include chart explanation text if needed (example - How to read a quartile)
3. Present numeric data graphically and in table format. Separate your company's responses from the benchmark group so it is clear to see where your company is positioned.
4. Provide high-level summary analysis for each measure you report. Point out the process, operational , or structural differences. Provide high-level suggestions for next steps and action items.
5. Try and prioritize the report based upon what the team feels needs to be addressed now vs. later. Prioritization can be based upon ease of implementation, cost of implementation, urgency, degree of fit with strategy, gap between performance and benchmark, gap between performance and importance, or greatest opportunity for overall improvement.
6. Present the results in an executive summary format as well as a detailed format.
7. Note constraints or barriers to implementation for each high level suggestion.
8. Distribute the report to all parties who championed the project and had bought into it.
9. Communicate the results first through a written report followed up by a group meeting to provide expanded interpretation.
10. Ensure the respondent organizations receive some condensed report back in exchange for their data and time.

Interviews

When gathering information, interview skills are important. A good interviewer will always know the right questions to ask, and more importantly the right follow-up questions in response to answers provided. Below are some interviewing tips to help you master this craft:

1. Be courteous and respectful. Make an appointment.
2. Do your homework. In order to establish good chemistry with the person you are interviewing you need to have some knowledge about who they are and what they do. Ignorance is a quick way to lose credibility as an interviewer. Knowledge allows the interviewee to be more candid and may give you more of their time.

3. Provide the context. Provide a background on the purpose of your discussion, but not too specific.
4. Be prepared. Have specific questions and open-ended questions. The questions should not be quantitative but something you can expect a reasonable answer to during the course of the interview.
5. Be a good listener. Let your interviewee elaborate on the issues.
6. Be ready with follow-up questions. Those come in response to listening to good listening and are not the questions you prepared-for.
7. Be involved. The more you give the more you get. Help them forget they're being interviewed and make it feel like they're having a conversation with a real person.
8. Be careful on wording of questions. Don't ask, "What are the inefficiencies of failures of your department?" Do ask "What are the major obstacles or challenges being faced by your department and what improvement opportunities do you see?"
9. Try and ask for examples. Examples illustrate a point far better than any methodological or procedural explanation. Trying to articulate to others a complex issue is difficult, but an example of what went wrong can make it very clear.
10. Be grateful. Thank the interviewee for their time and insights.
11. Leave the door open. Ensure you can follow-up with any further questions
12. Send the interviewee a copy of how you used their material in your work. Do so in advance for their review purposes to ensure you did not misstate any events.

Focus Groups

Focus groups are a great way to get stakeholders together to help map the process. It is also a great way to see where people converge and diverge on the issues at stake. Below are some keys to facilitating a successful focus group.

1. Get commitment from managers. This could be a 1/2 day session in which a number of employees will need to attend. Ensure they are willing to commit the resources.
2. Set expectations. This may be the first time employees feel listened to. If you cannot take their comments and produce actions from them that might be a problem. Ensure that if the focus group is held, next steps regarding development of opportunities for improvement can and will occur.
3. Know your deliverables. Be prepared to present a summary of where the process could be improved as a result of this focus group activity.
4. Gather the right attendees. Obtain broad coverage across all relevant functions, if needed obtain coverage from suppliers and customers too. A focus group of 6 to 12 people is manageable. If your group has more you may question the project scope or break it up into sub-components.
5. Set up the room. Arrange participants in a semi-circle facing the facilitator. Have large sheets of blank paper tacked on the wall so you can physically 'map' the process in a real time manner.

6. Do a warm up. Get participants comfortable and relaxed. Introduce yourself, provide a summary of the project and day's events, have everyone introduce him or herself to break the ice.
7. Explain the rules. Everyone should participate. All ideas and suggestions are welcome and feedback to them should be positive not negative. For the duration of the meeting all participants are equal so everyone during the meeting is free to speak their minds. Ensure people are mindful of others and do not monopolize the meeting with their own agendas or ideas- - caution to everyone they may be asked to 'give up the microphone' when they begin to monopolize the meeting.
8. Set the boundaries. Label the input processes on one blank paper, the core process for discussion on a second and the output processes on a third.
9. Ensure agreement from the group before you finalize additions on the paper.
10. Focus most of the time on the activities of the core process.
11. Use a separate paper for "obstacles"
12. Towards the end of the session, try and prioritize the obstacles and briefly discuss solutions you can write in beside each obstacle.

Good Starter Questions

It's always good to break the ice with some starter questions that help you engage your respondents in a healthy debate about the issues and about continuous improvement. Below is an excerpt from Dorine C. Andrews and Susan K. Stalick book, Business Reengineering, The Survival Guide.

The following questions help identify process improvement opportunities and assess if change is necessary. They can be used in interviews or focus groups to stimulate the discussion.

1. What in the business process you perform, prevents you from satisfying your customers and creating quality products and services?

○ Time delays	○ handoffs
○ Transaction errors	○ lack of controls
○ rigid procedures	○ exception processing
○ facility problems	○ paperwork problems
○ approval layers	○ review cycles
○ duplication of work	○ lack of standards
○ documentation errors	○ transaction volatility
○ fragmentation of work	○ inconsistent inputs to work
○ inaccurate outputs to work	○ unclear work outputs
○ incomplete work outputs	○ policy problems
○ procedure problems	○ content complexities

2. What does technology (automation, computers, communications, and so on) or lack of it do to enhance or inhibit effective process performance?

    ○ communication   ○ information access
    ○ decision support   ○ data creation, updating
    ○ transaction processing   ○ outcome production
    ○ information timeliness   ○ information availability
    ○ performance monitoring   ○ work flow handling

3. What does the organization structure do to enhance or inhibit effective process performance?

    ○ job position structure   ○ job reporting relationships
    ○ job content   ○ job requirements
    ○ job accountabilities   ○ job complexity
    ○ organization structure   ○ job groupings
    ○ work group relationships ○ organization type

4. What do reward structures (financial, non-financial, formal and informal) do to enhance or inhibit effective process performance?

    ○ alignment/nonalignment with process performance objectives
    ○ consistency of application
    ○ clarity of definition/understandability
    ○ relationship with actual process performance
    ○ discrepancies

5. What do measurement systems or lack of them do to enhance or inhibit process performance?

    ○ customer satisfaction
    ○ quality of process outcomes
    ○ process performance

6. What do the management methods or lack of them do to enhance or inhibit process performance?

    ○ leadership capabilities   ○ leadership style
    ○ control of decision making   ○ management style
    ○ performance development support ○ experience
    ○ decision style   ○ rule predictability
    ○ praise from managers   ○ staff involvement
    ○ punishment from managers

7. What does the culture do to enhance or inhibit process performance?

    ○ rituals, symbols, myths   ○ language
    ○ attention/focus   ○ what is important
    ○ position in industry   ○ position to customers

8. What does the political power within the organization do to enhance or inhibit process performance?
   - ○ coercive/abusive of power
   - ○ legitimate power sources
   - ○ power styles (confrontational)
   - ○ focus on power
   - ○ influence
   - ○ personal power
   - ○ empowerment

9. What do belief systems of individuals do to enhance or inhibit process performance?
   - ○ customers
   - ○ how things work
   - ○ competency of others
   - ○ products and services
   - ○ organizational culture
   - ○ work environment
   - ○ change
   - ○ accountability
   - ○ trust in leaders
   - ○ org. mission
   - ○ themselves
   - ○ influence others

Additional Warm Up Questions

In addition to the <u>Business Reengineering, The Survival Guide</u> questions, the following questions help you engage the interviewee better and elicit information to help you better understand the root of problems.

These questions are problem specific: You already know a problem exists and are hoping to learn more about it.

1. Can you please explain briefly the history of the process, your role and the process' role within the organization?

2. Can you please tell us a little bit about the types of issues or challenges you are currently facing?

3. What is it that your customers want and need from you?

4. What problem are you trying to resolve? What prompted this in the first place? Who is the driving force behind this initiative?

5. What would it take for your managers and constituents to feel that you had contributed high value in this process and resolved this issue? What would they want to see demonstrated?

6. What are the major obstacles you feel have or might hinder improvement? Are there any barriers that might inhibit this problem from being resolved?

7. What are the major strengths you feel you can leverage to foster improvement?

8. If there are a few things that keep you up at night regarding this issue, what are they? Do you have any ideas on how to approach solving them?

9. Is this a new problem or has it been addressed in the past?

10. Has anyone else had a similar issue? If so how have they dealt with it?

The following questions are more general and not specific to a particular problem. Perhaps there is a sense of an issue within the process and these questions help you understand the process better.

1. What is the process like? Can you briefly explain its inputs, activities and outputs at a high level so I understand it better?

2. Are there any areas in the process you feel might be in need of some fresh thinking?

3. If you could manage this process with just 3 measures what would those be?

4. If you could teach someone about your process, what are the most critical elements you would try and educate him or her on?

5. What issues have been the most challenging to solve in the past few months?

6. What activities have you undertaken to help improve the process?

7. What are the areas of this process that have the greatest impact on the overall business and its customers?

8. Can you give me some examples of what you would describe as a value-added activity versus a routine activity in the process? What percent of total activities are these composed of?

9. What does your management want to see from you to indicate this process is adding value? What are the key attributes they look for? How do you think you are doing in regard to meeting those expectations?

10. What are your expectations for this process? At the end of the day, what would have had to have happened in this process for you to step back and say "I am totally satisfied with this process and how it is running."

11. What are the top three areas that you would want to improve or change, if you could?

12. What are the top three activities you feel you do really, really well?

13. If you could change one element of your process and nothing else, what would that be and how would that make your job and the process better?

Chapter Seven: Checklist for Excellence in Business Processes

In my class I invite guest speakers to lecture to my class. I don't know everything and I learn from the guest speakers as much as my students do. One guest speaker that was a profound influence on my class and me was Manny Rosenfeld. Manny is a Director of Internal Audit for a large corporation. Manny has worked on many continuous improvement projects in his colorful career.

Manny's presentation to my class was one that he has presented before to internal auditors as a way to articulate to them how to improve business processes. This chapter focuses on Manny's principles of excellence in business processes. In summary, Manny's tips are as follows:

1. know the customer orientation
2. understand the business requirements
3. focus on simplicity
4. keep adequate process documentation
5. leverage cross-functional management
6. keep process-based performance measures
7. keep an eye on time management
8. use adequate internal controls
9. minimize rework loops
10. build quality into the process
11. cultivate cohesive supplier relationships
12. keep an eye on cost management
13. learn from the best
14. leverage automation and technology
15. create a learning organization
16. focus on employee morale
17. build effective teams

Know the customer orientation

As a new manager, it is vital to your success to understand the customer needs and wants. A customer can be an internal customer as easily as it is an external customer. As a process owner you need to not only understand your customer requirements but to deliver upon them on time and with high quality and integrity. This is essential to your credibility as a manager.

As a part of the continuous improvement process, your ability to constantly gather data from customer through a variety of formal and informal means is very important. Formally, tools like surveys, interviews and focus groups are helpful. Informally, looking at trends in the marketplace, observing customer behavior, and talking to your sales and marketing folks are steps in the right direction.

At the top of your game, you'll be creating products and services that anticipate rather than react to customer desires. You'll get to the point where you will know what your customer needs before they need it. This is how you stay ahead of the competition and how you stay on the offensive rather than the defensive with your customers.

Remember, your objective, the reason you are working is to delight someone with a product or service. Keep this in mind with everything you do.

Understand business requirements

Business requirements are the objectives that a process has to meet in order to satisfy other stakeholders besides customers. For example, let's suppose you are the new manager in charge of a new product launch. You know the customer requirements but other stakeholders also have requirements. Senior management has a requirement such as a profitability hurdle rate of 15%.

Business requirements are just as important as customer requirements. In my example above, if you solely looked at customer requirements, a customer would desire your product be free of charge. However, the business requirements don't permit it as senior management demands your profitability hurdle rate.

So, the key to excellence in business processes is in understanding all of your stakeholders requirements. You may not be able to exceed expectations in all areas because the diversity in the requirements may overlap or contradict each other. You need to balance these needs and manage expectations to be a successful manager.

Who are key stakeholders you should pay attention to in improving your process? What are the key considerations you need to think about when making continuous improvement decisions? Below is a short list of stakeholders and considerations.

- Internal or external customers
- Suppliers
- Logistics contractors
- Senior management
- Board of directors
- Finance managers
- Sales/Marketing managers
- Legal/regulatory issues
- Ethical issues

Focus on Simplicity

Whenever you map your process and you compare it to others or against a desired state, you hopefully look at a revised state that is less complex than your current one. I am always amazed at how complex and cumbersome existing processes appear to be. There is most always a simpler way of doing things. Keeping the process simple makes it more controllable and manageable. Your goal as a new manager should be to assess the existing process and look for redundancies, overlaps, duplication of efforts, and manual tasks that can be performed through technology or automation.

As a first action item, reduce the number of steps in the process. If you map the process and there are 81 steps to do a process and you can reduce it to 75 that is a step in the right direction. The key to saving money, reducing cycle time and increasing productivity is in streamlining the number of steps it takes to do a process.

As an additional action item, look at your process steps. Look at the complexity of the steps. Those that are more complex should rely on business judgment versus those that are less complex should rely on technology and automation.

Keep adequate process documentation

Process documentation is vital whenever there is turnover. If you're a new manager you'd want to review a decent transaction trail on how your process works from the beginning to the end. Thus, adequate documentation is essential to success.

If you have inadequate or an absence of process documentation, start out by mapping the process. Utilize interviews, focus groups, and surveys to understand your process. Combine it with a flowchart of the process and a staffing profile. This will help you wrap your arms around the process.

For all critical areas it is good to have adequate policies and procedures. As a helpful guide I like to create policy and procedure manuals with the following organizational structure. You can use this as a starting point and customize it as you go along.

- Policy Statement
- Reason for Policy
- Who Should Know this Policy
- Related Information
- Contacts for questions
- Exclusions
- History of Policy
- Policy Definitions
- Responsibilities
- Procedures
- Forms/Instructions
- Frequently Asked Questions
- Appendices

Leverage Cross Functional Management

Think of your company as a puzzle. Your group makes up a piece of this puzzle. All the pieces need to fit together to form the finished product. When you manage, you need to do so as a united process, not as fragmented parts.

A cohesive organization will work better together. The need to have cross-functional teams is important when a process involve the inputs, activities and outputs of other departments.

According to Larson and LaFasto ("Teamwork: What Must Go Right/ What Can Go Wrong," Sage Publications Inc., 1989), there are three types of team task requirements, which all require slightly different members.

1) Analytical problem solvers, who can address issues without getting caught up in administrative minutiae or emotional matters.

2) Creative, cerebral members, able to explore possibilities and to talk in terms of "what if" rather than "yes but."

3) Tactical implementers, who are highly responsive to deadlines and team needs. They work with small margins of error, are action-oriented, and possess a sense of urgency.

Because most processes have tasks that will fall into these categories, it is important to have a cross functional team in place to effectively address the issues.

Companies like SteelCase utilize cross-functional teams to achieve a closer link between their employees and their customers. The company has a team-oriented culture and was able to use these teams to help reduce cycle time by roughly 80 percent and reduce Work in Process inventory by approximately 50 percent.

Keep process-based performance measures

We've already discussed performance measures but it is important to briefly mention them in our list of business process attributes of excellence. The old adage, "you only manage what you measure," is very true. The right performance measures are essential to any improvement program.

The ideal scenario is a small, well-balanced family of measures. Recall our discussion where we stated that your system should focus on cost, quality, time, productivity, and customer orientation. Review your existing performance measures and ensure they are balanced.

The purpose of performance measures is not only to manage and monitor your process, but also to have as a record for goal setting. Performance measures should be challenging yet attainable. Use them as motivating factors to strive to be the best you can be. The quantification of these measures result in their being the most observable way of showcasing performance compared to goals.

Although we have identified cost, quality, time, productivity, and customer orientation, also consider the following types of measures to further round out your process-based performance measurement system.

- Accuracy
- Degree of automation
- Compliance with laws and regulations
- Compliance with internal policy

Keep an eye on time management

Time is always a factor because the clock never stops ticking. Just look at sports. I just watched a football game yesterday. The visiting team dominated the first half. The second half saw a resurgence in the home team but time ran out and they lost the game.

As a new manager, understanding cycle time is important. How long it takes to accomplish a task can help you identify the weak links in the chain. It can also help you communicate better to your suppliers and your customers because you will have a better grasp on lead times.

Strive to reduce cycle time wherever possible. At Gates Rubber, a team discovered that a shipment from their Mexico plant to the United States went through seven handoffs. By streamlining the handoffs and implementing process changes, they reduced the cycle time from 21 to 5 days.

Use adequate internal controls

Being a former auditor I know first-hand the value in this tip. Internal controls are the actions you take to mitigate a business risk in your process. For example, you may have an internal control that separates the duties between the people who deposit cash receipts and those who open the mail. The reason is to ensure that the same person does not do both because the risk is higher that funds could be misappropriated.

Sound internal controls must be embedded in every process. You should identify all areas where your process might encounter a business risk. Then build adequate and sound internal controls to ensure that your risk is mitigated as much as possible.

For more information on business risk management and how to adequately design the appropriate internal control structure for your process, it is best to consult with your organization's internal auditors. If you don't have internal auditors, talk to your external auditors or even your accountant. They are excellent starting points and can probably suggest additional resources for you to look at. A great resource I suggest is the Institute of Internal Auditors (the IIA). You can find out more about them at their website, http://www.theiia.org/.

Finally, an excellent resource that discusses an organizational approach to risk management can be found in the executive briefing Enterprise-Wide Risk Management: Strategies for Linking Risk and Opportunity by James W. DeLoach. It is a Financial Times/Pearson Education publication from September 2000. This briefing will walk the reader through how to design and implement an integrated enterprise wide risk management system.

Minimize rework loops

The goal of this tip is to reduce the amount of scrap and rework as much as possible. Rework means you are doing something again because it was not done right the first time. This means you are not only wasting time and money making up for past mistakes but you are creating a bottleneck because your current and future work load is not being addressed.

As a manager it is important to understand where the errors are taking place and to instill a sense of quality controls to mitigate the risk of those errors causing significant delays in your deliverables.

The goals of programs like Six Sigma are to root out errors. While you might not ever get your process to be at 99.9997% error free, the rigor of a continuous improvement program like Six Sigma may provide you with the sense of urgency and formality that your team needs to keep quality and high first pass yield rates top of mind.

Build quality into the process

Organizations who have heavy reliance on inspections and reviews after the majority of the work has been done expose themselves to significant risk. If there are problems with the work at this point, rework (discussed above) is inevitable. If the process is complex or is a critical set of steps in your customer deliverables you should strive to build quality into the design of those steps themselves rather than to structure it outside of them.

Think of it from a cost of quality viewpoint. It costs a $1 for prevention, $10 for inspection and $100 for correction. With these costs it seems like a no brainer not to build quality into the design of your processes. Yet surprisingly many organizations fail to do so and they are doomed for failure.

TRW Canada Ltd., was one of the 10 recipients of IndustryWeek's 1998 America's Best Plants Award.   TRW's total productive maintenance (TPM) program is a total partnership of manufacturing, engineering, and maintenance to predict failure, reduce downtime, and increase productivity. In addition, teams operate as their own small businesses with responsibilities for production scheduling, skills certification, daily job assignments, team-member hiring, materials management, and training scheduling.   This attention to quality has resulted in an increase in sales per employee by 179%, a low customer reject rate of only 3.21 parts per million, a reduction in scrap as a percent of sales by 46% and the flexibility to no longer inspect 99.7% of purchased materials.

Cultivate cohesive supplier relationships

If you think about it your suppliers be it internal or external can often be your lifeline to success or failure. If you don't receive the right inputs at the right time you can't create the outputs your customers need.

To this end, your ability to cultivate cohesive relationships with suppliers becomes very important in your role as a manager continuously improving his/her process.

The first important point is that your lowest purchase price is not always the best choice for a supplier. Other important factors to consider include:

- Product and service quality
- Lead time and flexibility with timing
- Ability to customize your requests
- Joint marketing and sales efforts
- Ability to purchase via multiple methods (EDI, phone, fax, online etc)
- Geographic distance from supplier
- Service and support from supplier

In addition, for the suppliers who are critical to your success you'll want to evaluate them carefully be for selecting them as a strategic supplier. Methods used to evaluate suppliers include the following:

- Review financial statements
- Review credit histories
- Interview references
- Tour facilities
- Review quality certifications
- Assess management ability and integrity

Finally, once you've chosen the right suppliers you'll want to periodically measure their performance and share your results with the supplier so they can continue to improve. To this end you'll want to track on-time delivery rates, error rates, quality of service levels and build these measures into your supplier contract so the supplier knows how their performance will be evaluated.

For more information on supplier management you may want to check out the Institute for Supply Management at http://www.napm.org.

Keep an eye on cost management

Cost is always a significant driver in continuous improvement initiatives. It is important to ensure your revisions help you create a process that is cost effective.

The key to cost effectiveness is understanding the cost components of a process inside and out. Although the costs may not be directly evident you need to get in the habit of identifying these costs so they can be measured and managed.

Cost management is a factor in manufacturing operations. Most manufacturing operations will track the direct labor, direct materials and overhead components to understand the costs of manufacturing.

For processes that need improvement you want to come up with cost components as well. Processes like purchasing, sales force, marketing, information technology and other common functions within an organization try and come up with a common template for tracking and managing costs.

Exhibit 7-1 is a job aide for identifying and calculating the cost components of a process. Use a tool like this to help you identify, track and manage costs.

Exhibit 7-1 Cost Management Job Aide

Direct Labor – wages, overtime and benefits of the employees who perform the activities of the process (base this on a 40 hour work week so if an employee only performs the activities of your process for 20 hours than half of their direct labor is placed here)
Contracted Services –temporary and contract employee labor, including outsourced servicing fees
Operating Expenses – supplies, training, rent, allocated overheads, license and royalties paid on software, locally controllable expenses
Capitalized Costs - depreciation on capitalized costs such as computer equipment and office equipment

Learn from the best

Learning from the best is the process of identifying both internally and externally that the top performers are and understanding how you can adapt what they do as a part of your process.

The key to doing this is to benchmark against these world-class organizations. A great resource for benchmarking is the Houston-based not-for-profit American Productivity and Quality Center (APQC). The APQC has a methodology to aide in benchmarking against world-class organizations as well as a benchmarking Code of Conduct. The APQC can help you find the right benchmark partners and facilitate a meeting. For more information about the APQC go to their website at www.apqc.org.

The APQC defines benchmarking as "the practice of being humble enough to admit that someone else is better at something and wise enough to try and learn how to match and even surpass them at it."

The APQC approach to benchmarking is accomplished in four steps: plan, collect, analyze and adapt. Let's look at each of these steps.

The key steps, per the APQC, when you plan a benchmark project start with understanding what you want to benchmark and developing a benchmark team to execute the benchmarking effort.

Once you have determined if benchmarking is right you research what other companies are doing and use your networks to identify the right benchmark partners. Once that is done you'll want to screen the potential benchmark partners to see if a true fit exists between what they do well and what you want to improve.

The next step in the APQC methodology is to collect data. This involves the collection of qualitative and quantitative data. Once done you'll want to verify the data to ensure it is reasonable.

Thirdly, the APQC suggests analyzing the data you collected. This is when you do a gap analysis to understand how what you do differs from the benchmark partner. You do this at both a quantitative and qualitative level.

The final step in the APQC process is adapting best practices. This is where you report your findings. You also might go back to the benchmark partners for tips on "how to" implement the practices. Open, structured, collaborative discussion groups are used to create implementation plans.

The APQC benchmarking methodology sounds a lot like our continuous improvement methodology. It should because benchmarking is a significant component of continuous improvement. You cannot improve a process unless you have the right ideas from the best that do it and benchmarking is a tool to help you do that.

We also discussed how the APQC has a Benchmarking Code of Conduct. It is very important that you act in an ethical and professional way when benchmarking. This maintains your credibility and builds trusting relationships with benchmark partners.

Please see exhibit 7-2 for the Benchmarking Code of Conduct. The APQC's International Benchmarking Clearinghouse created the Code of Conduct,

Exhibit 7-2 International Benchmarking Clearinghouse Code of Conduct

Preamble

Benchmarking--the process of identifying and learning from the best practices anywhere in the world--is a powerful tool in the quest for continuous improvement.

To guide benchmarking encounters and to advance the professionalism and effectiveness of benchmarking, the International Benchmarking Clearinghouse, a service of the American Productivity & Quality Center, and the Strategic Planning Institute Council on Benchmarking have adopted this common Code of Conduct. We encourage all organizations and individuals involved in benchmarking to abide by this Code of Conduct. Adherence to these principles will contribute to efficient, effective, and ethical benchmarking. This edition of the Code of Conduct has been expanded to provide greater guidance on the protocol of benchmarking for beginners.

Benchmarking Code of Conduct

Individuals agree for themselves and their company to abide by the following principles for benchmarking with other organizations.

1. Principle of Legality

1.1   If there is any potential question on the legality of an activity, don't do it.

1.2   Avoid discussions or actions that could lead to or imply an interest in restraint of trade, market and/or customer allocation schemes, price fixing, dealing arrangements, bid rigging, or bribery. Don't discuss costs with competitors if costs are as element of pricing.

1.3   Refrain from the acquisition of trade secrets from any means that could be interpreted as improper, including the breach or inducement of a breach of any duty to maintain secrecy. Do not disclose or use any trade secret that may have been obtained through improper means or that was disclosed by another in violation of a duty to maintain its secrecy or limit its use.

1.4   Do not, as a consultant or client, extend one benchmarking study's findings to another company without first obtaining the permission of the parties to the first study.

2. Principle of Exchange

2.1   Be willing to provide the same type and level of information that you request from your benchmarking partner to your benchmarking partner.

2.2   Communicate fully and early in the relationship to clarify expectations, avoid misunderstanding and establish mutual interest in the benchmarking exchange.

2.3   Be honest and complete.

3. Principle of Confidentiality

3.1   Treat benchmarking interchange as confidential to the individuals and companies involved. Information must not be communicated outside the partnering organizations without the prior consent of the benchmarking partner who shared the information.

3.2   A company's participation in a study is confidential and should not be communicated externally without their prior permission.

4. Principle of Use

4.1   Use information obtained through benchmarking only for purposes of formulating improvement of operations or processes within the companies participating in the benchmarking study.

4.2   The use or communication of a benchmarking partner's name with the data obtained or practices observed requires the prior permission of that partner.

4.3   Do not use benchmarking information or any information resulting from a benchmarking exchange, or benchmarking related networking as a means to market or sell.

4.4   Contact lists or other contact information provided by the International Benchmarking Clearinghouse in any form may not be used for marketing in any way.

5. Principle of First Party Contact

5.1   Initiate benchmarking contacts, whenever possible, through a benchmarking contact designated by the partner company.

5.2   Respect the corporate culture of partner companies and work within mutually agreed procedures.

5.3   Obtain mutual agreement with the designated benchmarking contact on any hand-off of communication or responsibility to other parties.

6. Principle of Third Party Contact

6.1   Obtain an individual's permission before providing his or her name in response to a contact request.

6.2   Avoid communicating a contact's name in an open forum without the contact's prior permission.

7. Principle of Preparation

7.1 Demonstrate commitment to the efficiency and effectiveness of benchmarking by being prepared prior to making an initial benchmarking contact.

7.2 Make the most of your benchmarking partner's time by being fully prepared for each exchange.

7.3 Help your benchmarking partners prepare by providing them with a questionnaire and agenda prior to benchmarking visits.

8. Principle of Completion

8.1 Follow through with each commitment made to your benchmarking partner in a timely manner.

8.2 Complete each benchmarking study to the satisfaction of all benchmarking partners as mutually agreed.

9. Principle of the Understanding and Action

9.1 Understand how your benchmarking partner would like to be treated.

9.2 Treat your benchmarking partner in the way that your benchmarking partner would want treated.

9.3 Understand how your benchmarking partner would like to have the information he or she provides handled and used, and handle and use it in that manner.

Leverage automation and technology

Today's world is rapidly changing the way we do business in thanks to technology. As a manager you need to assess the degree of technology leverage you can exert in your process.

Your needs assessments need to take into account how your process leverages technology. Isolate tasks that are automated versus manual. In a perfect world all non-value added tasks that are merely transaction processing in nature should be done through the use of technology.

Continuously seek out where potential technologies can be used to enhance your existing process. In your evaluation of technology, always talk to other folks who have used a technology you are considering and get their opinion on its flexibility and scalability.

Create a learning organization

A learning organization is one that facilitates the acquisition and dissemination of knowledge and skills within the workforce. This involves a combination of training programs, certification programs, and a robust knowledge management system.

Training programs need to be formalized and should be customized for each of the employees that serve you. They should also be tied to your department and overall corporate objectives. As a manager you'll want to evaluate the usefulness of that training by ensuring it is taken at the right time and is impacting the job in a positive manner.

Certification programs are a way to build skill sets, provide proof of learning, and add value to the employee's credentials. For example, becoming certified in Microsoft technologies or becoming certified as a Six Sigma Black Belt are great ways to motivate your employees while enhancing their skill set to apply to their jobs.

Knowledge management programs, which we'll discuss later in this book, is the way to ensure that knowledge gained by your employee's stays within the organization even if the individual departs. With the advent of intranets and groupware, it has become commonplace to allow employees to share information with each other.

As a manager you can make it easier by formalizing and standardizing the knowledge management process. First, you can champion the cause. Reverse the mindset that information hoarding is good and let it be known that sharing information is the right way to be successful. Second, place your knowledge into an organized classification matrix that helps people contribute to it and take from it. Finally, encourage use of the knowledge management system. Track the hit rates, understand how people have used it and what can be done to make it better.

Focus on employee morale

The morale of your employees is very important. If you don't have the respect and commitment of your people being a leader is nearly impossible.

As a new manager, it is your responsibility to motivate your employees. Take the appropriate steps to retain them. Motivation starts with providing your employees with salaries that are internally equitable and externally competitive. Also provide appropriate benefits to entice employees to join and stay at your organization. Beyond the basics like medical benefits, flexible work options, sabbaticals, childcare, employee assistance programs, flexible spending accounts, and even casual dress codes are a few.

Did you know that one of the main reasons employees' leave an organization is because they are no longer challenged? To prevent this, empower your employees and make them accountable for their actions. Empowerment and accountability give employees more control over their destiny and lead to more challenging tasks.

Build effective teams

Teamwork is essential when large tasks need to be accomplished. As a new manager you'll want to encourage good team working skills within your group.

The keys to creating effective teams evolve around some key points:

- Establish a specific goal and ensure that a team as opposed to an individual is the appropriate response to meet this goal
- Ensure team dynamics leverage unique skill sets of individuals that can come together to accomplish a task
- Train your employees in how to work in a team environment
- Give the team and its leader enough flexibility and empowerment so they can feel in control of their responsibilities and duties
- Support the team culture with appropriate mission statements, rules and agendas

The Internal Revenue Service (IRS) has been successful at using teams effectively. The IRS has developed hundreds of teams across several regions, service centers and district offices. Some of their achievements have included:

- An employee handbook for preparing tax adjustments. Because of the step-by-step guidance this gave to employees, errors and processing time were greatly reduced.

- Changes in the U.S Partnership Return of Income (1065) form in the Laguna Niguel, California area reduced the time taken to prepare an average return by 40%.

The IRS project teams not only realized tangible improvements such as those mentioned above, but also improved the internal communication processes within the IRS.

The IRS set strategic objectives for the teams to exceed customer expectations and to move from problem-solving to continuous improvement.

Chapter Eight: Manage Business Risk

In the last chapter we touched upon the success factors for achieving excellence in your business processes. For the most part, when people improve performance in business processes they often think about reducing cycle time, eliminating errors, and cutting costs.

In fact, many reengineering efforts have the focus of improving the operational efficiency and effectiveness of business processes. For example, if I am reducing the cycle time to close my accounting ledger each fiscal year that is often perceived as a positive step because you are consolidating, streamlining, and cutting steps out of the process. But, what if the steps you cut now leave gaping holes in your process and expose you to significant business risk? For example, if you eliminate a review check point that seemed like a duplication of tasks at the time but now is the cause of data discrepancies you have created a business risk that is going unmitigated.

The point is this, never improve processes for the sake of efficiency and effectiveness without considering the impact it has on the internal controls surrounding the process and the business risk exposures you might open yourself up to.

Business risk was once defined as "the threat that an event or action will adversely affect an organization's ability to achieve its business objectives and execute its strategies successfully." Business risks can impact virtually any business process, large or small, and expose the organization to unnecessary problems.

To the manager in charge of performance improvement, business risk is a critical consideration in everything he/she does. The ability to maintain the delicate balance between 'best practices' meant to improve efficiency and effectiveness and 'best control practices' meant to mitigate business risk is what will set the successful change agents apart from those that crash and burn.

So how do you do it? If you don't know much about business risk management what should you know? Who can you turn to for help? I'll answer the second question first. Typically, business risk management is a senior management cause that is led by the finance and accounting group but as we'll see effective risk management encompasses much more than just the accounting folks. Companies seeking advice on this subject should contact their internal audit departments or their external auditors and accountants who should have a decent skill set in working with the organization to identify, prioritize and manage business risk.

Second, what should you know? At a minimum try and cover the following key points in some shape or form:

- Set the tone for business risk management within your organization

- Create a common risk management language
- Identify and prioritize business risks
- Monitor and manage external risks
- Maintain adequate resources to support a risk management infrastructure

Set the tone for business risk management within your organization

The key here is to involve senior management (the C-level executives) in supporting risk management policies. Without their support and buy-in, risk management can pass as simply the flavor of the month and you'll have a lot of polices without teeth that never function as they were designed.

The right tone involves formality. This means documentation of the risk management policy and procedures. These should be clear, articulate, and actionable.

Additionally, communication is critical. Reinforcing the existence and seriousness of risk management policies on a regular basis will help build the perception and ultimately the reality of the organization's commitment to business risk management. Think about the large organizations that went bankrupt in recent years. Ethical misconduct, lack of oversight, too much authority in the hands of a few were just some of the business risks those companies left uncontrolled. If only they had created polices and regularly communicated them, at least the perception of risk management would have been created. In many instances perception is a very strong deterrent.

A key to communication is employee education and training. Ensure that managers and employees receive the training they need and the supporting tools and coaching back on the job to effectively manage business risk.

Going beyond perception and translating it into reality is the next way to set the appropriate tone for risk management. This is done in the way management monitors the adherence to its risk management policies. Routine audits done by managers, internal auditors and external auditors must be done to ensure effectively designed policies and procedures are functioning as intended.

Create a common risk management language

When thinking through business risk you need to ensure you look at all the possibilities, leaving no stone unturned. To do this, identify the major categories of business risk that could impact your organization. This could be done by functional process such as Finance, Supply Chain, IT, HR, Marketing, Customer Service, and Sales. It could be a business unit categorization, or a business process categorization.

In addition, you might ask your accountants or auditors if they have risk management categories they look to when assessing business risk. At a minimum it gives you more coverage and ensures you are addressing risk management in a complete and holistic manner.

The logical groupings of risks begin to create your risk management map by which your communications of business risk are made easier.

In Exhibit 8-1 you will see an example of a business risk map. This map categorizes business risks into 3 main categories and multiple subcategories. Table 8-1 then defines the major categories on the map.

The key is to categorize risks relative to your business and ensure they are properly mitigated. Ensure that the map you create can be easily mapped back and is all inclusive of your business, its external threats and internal processes.

Identify and prioritize risks

This is where the rubber meets the road. Conduct a risk assessment. Use the risks on your risk management map that you've hopefully created to probe a little deeper into each identified risk.

Understand the risks in each business process and determine the appropriate control objectives and related internal controls to mitigate business risk. Consider creating summary documents for every major business process that identifies these elements.

In Exhibit 8-2 we illustrate an example of a business risk summary document for the Procurement Process. In reviewing that document, you can see that an identification of the control objectives is documented for this process. Control objectives are the major business risk themes that require attention as they pose potential risk to the company if left uncontrolled.

You will also observe in Exhibit 8-2 that the business risks are formally listed. This is done relative to the control objectives. Basically the risk essentially communicates what can happen if the control objective goes unchecked.

Finally, you see an area on the Summary Risk Management Document for the internal controls. Again, these are stated relative to the control objective and the risks and articulate what the action steps are that need to take place to mitigate the stated business risk.

Documents such as those in 8-2 are no small task to create let alone execute and enforce. So it is important to prioritize the most sensitive risks and build adequate controls around them to limit exposure to those risks. For example, if you analyzing the cash management function, if you use lock boxes to receive cash there is less risk it could be stolen. But, if you have a junior accountant managing the idle cash accounts and investing that cash in derivatives or risky hedge funds you could easily lose significant amounts of cash in that manner. My point is that risk management is not just about unethical behavior, it is about detrimental business impacts from poorly designed processes.

Finally, when you conduct a risk assessment to identify and prioritize your risks, have a sense of the warning signs of business risk. Warning signs are those factors that will indicate if your process or your organization as a whole is at risk.

Examples of warning signs to look out for in your business risk identification and prioritization process include but is not limited to the following:

- No linkage of risk to value. The company does not equate business risk to financial loss.
- No effort to anticipate risk. The company does not routinely scan its internal and external environment for risk exposures.
- No business risk policy. The company lacks formal risk management policies and procedures.
- No risk management ownership. The company does not make its employees accountable for risk management and identify parties responsible for risk management.
- Risk management is not a priority. Management and employees place little emphasis on risk management.
- No common risk language. Risk management has no common lexicon or definitions within the organization.
- Organizational distrust. Employees have little faith in management and the business.
- Fragmented management style. Managers are more likely to act on their own with little oversight or supervision.
- Lack of separation of duties. Incompatible duties that should be segregated are not. (ex. the person who receives the cash, deposits the cash and records the cash in the accounting records)
- Poor risk communications. Risk management is not appropriately discussed with employees.

Monitor and manage external risks

As a person managing a business process the focus tends to be internal. However, do not neglect the externalities that can expose your organization to serious harm. The unfortunate events of September 11, 2001 could not have been prevented nor predicted but could have been mitigated as much as possible through the use of disaster recovery plans meant to keep a business up and running even in the most serious of disasters.

Always keep a close eye on the following items:
- Changes in customer behaviors and buying patterns
- Actions of competitors
- Supplier sources
- Economic conditions
- Changes in demographic patterns
- Technology changes
- Creditor's demands

- Regulations and legal requirements
- Political climate

An interesting point on external risk is that it is often folks outside of accounting or finance keeping an eye on these risks. For example, the procurement group should be the team responsible for supplier risk. The marketing or sales teams are responsible for keeping an eye on the competition and buying patterns. The Information technology group is the obvious party responsible for ensuring that the organization is keeping up with the swift pace of change taking place in technology. The legal department is typically responsible for ensuring the company complies with laws and regulations. So, if managers outside the accounting department think risk management is not their problem, they should think again.

Maintain resources to support risk management processes

Like any performance improvement initiative it is futile to make suggestions for change without appropriate resources to support that change. Risk management is no different. Ensure you are covered by maintaining appropriate financial, physical, and human resources to design, implement, and maintain the appropriate risk management processes for your organization.

Specifically, look at resources from a people, process, technology and culture perspective.

From a people perspective, ask yourself if you have the right skills set to design, implement and maintain risk management. Are these individuals qualified and trusted?

From a process perspective, ask yourself if your existing process can support new policies and procedures that address risk management. If the process is currently inefficient and ineffective or not properly documented, implementing risk management can be very difficult.

From a technology perspective, ask yourself if you can leverage automation and technology to reduce manual risk management procedures. For example, in accounts payable departments the term '3 way match' describes an internal control to ensure validity of information and prevent inappropriate payments being made. To do so, purchase orders are matched against bills of lading and invoices prior to checks being cut for payment. Rather than do that manually, most payables systems will perform such matching exercises in an automated fashion and produce exception reports when the 3 way match does not occur.

Finally, culture is important. Ensure the right culture has been created to transition the change to a risk sensitive business. Dedicate resources to ensuring that training and support exist to create the appropriate culture.

Appendix A to Chapter 8: Business Ethics

A significant business risk that is often overlooked is business ethics. With the collapse of large multi-billion dollar organizations, the risk of unethical behavior has grown increasingly obvious. As a person conducting performance improvement projects it is absolutely essential to carryout that mission in a professional and ethical manner.

However, you may be asked to help the organization clarify and define the company's ethical processes. The purpose of this appendix is to discuss some helpful hints around business ethics.

Why is business ethics even important? It mitigates reputation and legal risk. Those are some pretty important risk areas you'll want to ensure are controlled.

If you are asked to help create a business ethics program, ensure it has the following components:

- Code of conduct
- Business ethics training
- Reporting/advice channels
- Feedback gathering mechanisms
- Periodic declarations of compliance
- Value and mission statements
- Consideration of needs of stakeholders
- Departments with business ethics responsibilities
- Ethical criteria included in employee, customer and supplier reward systems
- Assessment of business ethics by an external body

Ensure that you work with groups such as the internal audit department, line management, legal department, human resources, public relations, board of directors, senior management, and external consultants. This diverse group can add value and relevant feedback into an ethics program.

As a performance improvement person you know to seek the help of external experts as well. Go to your personal network, attend conferences, industry working groups, and just read up on the topic in the media to acquaint yourself with the current state of ethics in business.

Appendix B to Chapter 8: Designing Policies and Procedures

We have discussed the importance of controls to mitigate risk. A starting point to doing this is to create policies and procedures to clearly and formally document the internal control structure. Policies and procedures are also an effective way to communicate the importance management places on the tasks contained in those documents.

The following brief outline helps you think through the main structure within a policy and procedure document.

1) **Statement of Purpose.** This area introduces the document and explains that the document represents the obligations and responsibilities of the process.
2) **Procedure #.** A separate number should be assigned to each procedure within the policy document.
3) **Policy Statement.** A specific statement related to a specific guideline or principle for which there will be accompanying procedures.
4) **Scope.** Describes the areas, functions, individuals, or departments affected by the policy and procedure.
5) **Procedures.** These are the specific action steps that must be taken to achieve the objectives mentioned in the policy statement.
6) **Accountable Parties.** Specific assignment of accountable for the procedures from both a supervisory and staff perspective.
7) **Attachments.** Examples of standard forms, templates, illustrations, etc. that are required to be used in executing the procedures.
8) **Exceptions.** Document when exceptions to the general policy are allowable and the corresponding procedures for handling the exceptions.
9) **Effective Date.** The original date the policy become active.
10) **Revision Date.** The date of the most recent revision.
11) **Preparer Name(s) and Title(s).** Lists the specific personnel and their job titles that authored the document. This helps when questions need to be answered about the document.
12) **Approval Name(s) and Title(s).** Lists the specific personnel and their job titles that authorized the document for use.
13) **Definitions.** If any terms are unclear or require clarification, cite those in a definitions area.

Exhibit 8-1 Risk Management Map

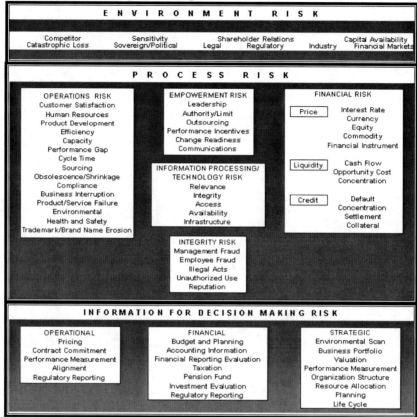

Enterprise-wide Risk Management: Strategies for Linking Risk and Opportunity by James Deloach and Nick Temple, December 2000, Arthur Andersen, Business Risk Model, 1997

Table 8-1 – Major Risk Categories

Business Risk Category	Description
Environment Risk	The risk that external forces such as political, economic, competitive, and industry forces could adversely impact the business
Process Risk	Risk that internal processes are not defined, lack structure, lack policy and procedure, or are inefficient and ineffective
Operational Risk	Risk that customers needs and expectations in terms of cost, quality, and time objectives will not be met
Financial Risk	Risk that the company will not be liquid enough; that currency, credit and other financial risks will not be controlled
Empowerment Risk	Risk that managers and employees are not properly led, don't have appropriate boundaries of authority
Information Technology Risk	Risk that IT is not supporting the current and future business needs; IT assets are misused
Integrity Risk	Risk of management or employee fraud; illegal acts
Information for Decision-Making Risk	Information to support decisions is not relevant or reliable

Exhibit 8-2 Summary Risk Management Document – Procurement Process
PROCUREMENT PROCESS BUSINESS RISKS AND CONTROLS

CONTROL OBJECTIVES

Reliability of Information
- Purchase orders are properly authorized.
- Purchase orders are accurately and completely prepared and recorded on a timely basis.
- All purchase order transactions are reliably processed and reported.
- Receipts of materials and supplies are recorded accurately and completely on the timely basis.
- Receipts of materials and supplies are recorded accurately and completely on a timely basis.
- All material/supply receipt transactions are reliably processed and reported.
- Performance measurements used to control and improve the process are reliable.

Relevance of Information
- Employees and management are provided the information they need to control the process of obtaining materials and supplies.

Operational Effectiveness and Efficiency
- Materials purchased satisfy the company's requirements and needs.
- Materials are purchased at an appropriate price.
- Orders are placed on a timely basis.
- Materials are received on a timely basis.
- The receiving are process is efficient and cost-effective.
- Materials received are processed on a timely basis.
- Materials received meet required quality standards.
- Physical safe guards are adequate.
- The receiving process is safe.

Compliance With Laws and Regulations
- Materials are obtained in compliance with applicable laws and regulations.

Management Control
- Management develops strategic business alliances with suppliers.

BUSINESS RISKS

Reliability of Information
Purchase Orders Are Properly Authorized
Risks:
- The company will make unauthorized orders for materials and supplies.

- The company will order materials and supplies from unauthorized vendors, or at the wrong prices or terms.
- Goods purchased will not meet quality standards.
- Unauthorized individuals will order and receive materials and supplies.

Purchase Orders Are Accurately And Completely Prepared And Recorded On A Timely Basis
Risks:
- Receiving will reject deliveries because there is no valid purchase order.
- The company will receive incorrect materials and supplies, or quantities of materials and supplies, and incur additional costs to return or store these goods.
- The company will obtain an inadequate supply of materials and supplies.
- The company will lose purchase orders. This will result in incomplete records of materials and supplies to be received.
- Management will be unable to determine unfulfilled purchase commitments.

All Purchase Order Transactions Are Reliably Processed And Reported
Risks:
- Unauthorized changes will be made to programs. This will cause unauthorized processing results.
- Unauthorized versions of files and/or programs will be used to process transactions. This will result in unauthorized or incorrect business transactions.
- Files (transaction, reference or master) will be lost, altered or damaged. This will result in inefficiencies, lost assets, or incorrect processing of transactions.

Receipts Of Materials And Supplies Are Properly Authorized
Risks:
- The company will accept materials and supplies for which no authorized order has been placed.
- The company will accept incorrect, or excessive quantities of, materials and supplies, and materials and supplies, which do not meet company specifications.
- Unauthorized individuals will order and receive materials and supplies.
- The company will receive and pay for, rather than return or refuse:
  - Unordered materials and supplies,
  - Excessive quantities or incorrect items, and
  - Canceled or duplicated orders.

Receipts Of Materials And Supplies Are Recorded Accurately And Completely On A Timely Basis
Risks:
- The company will not record, or inaccurately record, receipts of materials and supplies. Liabilities will not be recorded and inventory and cost of goods sold will be misstated.
- The company will lose the records of materials and supplies received.

All Material/Supply Receipt Transactions Are Reliably Processed And Reported
Risks:
- Unauthorized changes will be made to programs. This will cause unauthorized processing results.
- Unauthorized versions of files and/or programs will be used to process transactions. This will result in unauthorized or incorrect business transactions.
- Files (transaction, reference or master) will be lost, altered or damaged. This will result in inefficiencies, lost assets, or incorrect processing of transactions.

Performance Measurements Used To Control And Improve The Process Are Reliable
Risks:
- Inaccurate measurements will result in erroneous perceptions about process performance. This will result in inappropriate decisions.

Relevance of Information
Employees And Management Are Provided The Information They Need To Control The Process Of Obtaining Materials And Supplies
Risks:
- Employees and management will not be able to accurately determine whether the process is in control (i.e., that it is operating as planned).
- Employees will not be able to improve the process on a timely basis.
- Information provided to employees and management about the process will conflict with the company's objectives.

144 Champions of Change

- Plans to improve the process will be based on incorrect perceptions of process performance.

<u>Operational Effectiveness and Efficiency</u>
Materials Purchased Satisfy The Company's Requirements And Needs
Risks:
- Products ordered will not meet the necessary technical specifications or quality standards.
- Materials will be received too early or too late. This will result in business interruptions and/or excessive levels of inventory.
- Vendors are not aware of the company's needs or are not able to supply the necessary materials.

Materials Are Purchased At An Appropriate Price
Risks:
- Product costs will be higher than anticipated.
- Products will not be profitable or able to compete in the market at a reasonable price.

Orders Are Placed On A Timely Basis
Risks:
- Excessive inventory levels will increase costs.
- Insufficient quantities of materials will cause production delays.
- Orders will not be placed in sufficient time to account for vendor lead times.
- Late deliveries will result in business interruptions.

Materials Are Received On A Timely Basis
Risks:
- The company will not receive goods in time for production needs.
- The company will receive goods prior to production needs. Storage space will not be available.

The Receiving Process Is Efficient And Cost-Effective
Risks:
- The receiving process will incur higher labor costs than necessary.
- The organization of the receiving area does not allow for optimum storage of goods, or for the efficient movement of goods from receiving into warehousing or production.

Materials Received Are Processed On A Timely Basis
Risks:
- Materials required for production will arrive, but end users will remain unaware of the receipt.
- Plans and schedules for goods to be received are not communicated to the receiving department.

Materials Received Meet Required Quality Standards
Risks:
- The company will encounter production problems because materials received do not meet quality standards and specifications.
- Production will be delayed if accepted materials are later found to be unusable.
- The company will incur additional costs of returning unacceptable goods at a later date.

Physical Safeguards Are Adequate
Risks:
- Materials and supplies will be lost, stolen, damaged, destroyed, used for unauthorized purposes, or temporarily diverted.

The Receiving Process Is Safe
Risks
- Accidents will occur in which employees are injured or facilities are damaged.
- The company will not comply with regulatory requirements.

Compliance With Laws and Regulations
Materials Are Obtained In Compliance With Applicable Laws And Regulations
Risks:
- The company will incur fines or other penalties.
- The company will make sensitive payments, violate export controls, and/or incur conflict of interest situations.
- The company will incur bad publicity and loss of reputation.

Management Control
Management Develops Strategic Business Alliances With Suppliers
Risks:
- The process will not achieve optimal results.
- The company will lose competitive advantage to those competitors that are able to increase efficiencies with their suppliers through technology links and joint cooperation.
- Adversarial approaches will lead to sub-optimal results for both parties.

INTERNAL CONTROLS

Reliability of information
Purchase orders are properly authorized.
- The requesting department is required to prepare the purchase requisition for all materials and supplies purchased.
- Requisitions are approved before purchase commitments are made. Vendors, prices, quality, quantities, and terms are approved.
- Computer system input screens and routines are used to generate purchase order documents/transactions.

- Computer system routines have been designed to automatically verify that purchase orders are created only for authorized vendors (e.g., the system automatically verifies the vendor against the vendor master file during purchase order entry).
- Purchasing personnel are provided with current prices, vendors, specifications, and terms (e.g., a supplier extranet site or computer inquiry terminals that have direct access to vendor product and inventory record files are used) to ensure that only authorized terms are used to create purchase orders.
- All purchasing responsibilities are segregated (including supplier selection) from disbursement and accounting activities.
- Purchasing agents or buyers are periodically rotated among purchasing responsibilities to ensure independence. If business conditions make it impractical to rotate agents or buyers, other compensating controls are implemented.
- An approved vendor master file is used by the system for verifying approved vendors during purchase order creation.
- New suppliers are added to the established master file only if they meet the criteria established by management.
- Suppliers are investigated prior to approval. Such factors as price competitiveness, reputation, product quality, delivery abilities, and financial solvency are considered.
- Competitive bids are obtained for all purchases over amounts specified by management.
- Justification and management approval are required for the absence of competitive bids or for the acceptance of a price other than a lowest bid.
- Computer system controls, such as access control software, are installed to preclude unauthorized purchase transactions.

Purchase orders are accurately and completely prepared and recorded on a timely basis.
- Computer system routines or pre-numbered purchase order forms are used to assign purchase order numbers to order requests.
- Pre-numbered forms are safeguarded from unauthorized use.
- Appropriate personnel (e.g., the original requestor) review generated purchase orders to ensure that items ordered are correct.
- Computer system routines are used to generate exception reports to identify purchase orders that have been outstanding for excessive lengths of time.

All purchase order transactions are reliably processed and reported.
- Authorization is required for all changes to program routines.
- User approval is required for program change test results.
- Tape and/or disk management systems are used to ensure that appropriate versions of transaction files, master files, and programs are used for processing.
- Computer system controls, such as access control software, have been installed to preclude unauthorized changes in the versions of files and programs used to process transactions.

- Computer system controls, such as access control software, have been installed to protect files and programs from unauthorized use, modification, or deletion.

Receipts of materials and supplies are properly authorized.
- Only materials supported with an authorized purchase order or its equivalent are accepted.
- All other receipts are returned to the supplier, or they are investigated for propriety in a timely manner.
- Computer system routines are used to verify that the material orders received are for legitimate outstanding purchase orders (e.g., match the purchase order number entered as part of the receiving transaction with records contained on the purchase order master file).
- The computer application is used to generate exception reports for any material receipts for which there is no outstanding purchase order on file.
- Computer system controls, such as access control software, have been installed to preclude unauthorized entry of receiving transactions into the system.
- Receiving reports are safeguarded from theft, destruction, and unauthorized use.
- Authorized personnel are designated to correct errors in original receiving reports and reenter them into the system.

Receipts of materials and supplies are recorded accurately and completely on a timely basis.
- Incoming goods are test counted, weighed, or measured on a sample basis to determine the accuracy of the suppliers' shipments.
- All discrepancies are noted on the receiving reports, and these discrepancies are resolved with the supplier.
- Incoming goods are inspected for damage, quality characteristics, product specifications, and so on.
- Receiving documents or online computer input routines are used to record the actual receipt of materials and supplies.
- Reconciliation controls have been implemented to ensure that all receiving transactions are entered into the system if receiving documents are initially used to record receipts of materials and suppliers.
- Computer system routines are used to match each line item of the receiving transaction with the line items of the corresponding purchase order record.
- Computer controls have been installed that are designed to highlight discrepancies on exception reports and denote purchase orders on file with partial receipt indicators.
- Computer procedures have been designed to close purchase order records when all line items match and have been received.

All material/supply receipt transactions are reliably processed and reported.
- Authorization of all changes to program routines is required.
- User approval is required for program change test results.

- Tape and/or disk management systems are used to ensure that appropriate versions of transaction files, master files, and programs are used for processing.
- Computer system controls, such as access control software, are used to preclude unauthorized changes in the versions of files and programs used to process transactions.
- Computer system controls, such as access control software, are implemented to protect files and programs from unauthorized use, modification, or deletion.

Performance measures used to control and improve the process are reliable.
- Controls have been implemented to automatically calculate and process the performance measures based on data captured at the transaction source (e.g., processing time, number of defects, and on-time delivery).
- The measures are periodically reviewed to ensure that they reflect actual process performance.
- Quality reports and customer surveys are used to capture relevant information about process performance.
- The information captured is communicated to employees responsible for vendor relations and improving the procurement and receiving process.
- Management and employees understand the linkage between the measures and customer satisfaction.
- Management and employees buy in to the use of these measures as tools to improve process performance.
- The performance measures are linked with employees' performance evaluations.

<u>Relevance of information</u>
Employees and management are provided the information they need to control the process of obtaining materials and supplies.
- Approved suppliers are periodically and systematically monitored to ensure that their actual performance meets expectations. Performance measures may include percent of on-time delivery, accuracy of shipments, product quality, and actual cost performance compared with original cost projections.
- Purchasing agents, buyers, and cross-functional teams are evaluated in a manner consistent with management's objectives of reduced inventories, improved quality, lower costs, and frequent reliable deliveries.
- Appropriate performance measures are selected to ensure that the procurement and receiving processes are properly controlled.
- Quantifiable and controllable measures are selected that (a) link the process to the company's goals and to customer expectations and (b) will stimulate continuous improvement.
- The process used to collect the required data and calculate the measures is defined (e.g., define whether data collection is an integral part of the operating process or a separate process, and whether it is cost effective).
- Management understands how the procurement and receiving processes contribute to customer satisfaction and the overall company objectives.

- Selected performance measures support the creation of value and customer service by reflecting quality and time as well as costs.

Operational effectiveness and efficiency

Materials purchased satisfy the company's requirements and needs.
- The company investigates and periodically updates vendor capabilities regarding product line and product specifications, product quality, and capacity and order lead times.
- Procedures are specified for notifying vendors of potential performance problems and for appropriate Investigation and follow through.
- Data is developed on alternative vendors, and the vendor selection decision is periodically reevaluated.
- Purchasing agents, buyers, and cross-functional teams are evaluated consistently with management's objectives of reduced inventories, improved quality, lower costs, and frequent reliable deliveries.
- Other measures are used to address issues such as supplier relationships, frequency of returned purchases, production problems related to out of stock materials, and quality problems.
- Vendor representatives are involved in product design and development.
- The approved suppliers are periodically and systematically monitored for just-in-time purchasing to ensure that their actual performance meets expectations. Performance reporting includes: percentage of on-time delivery, accuracy of shipments, product quality, and actual cost performance compared with original cost projections.

Materials are purchased at an appropriate price.
- A mechanism has been developed for determining the total cost of major purchases from particular vendors. Considerations should include: percentage of on-time delivery, accuracy of shipments, product quality, and actual cost performance compared with original cost projections.
- Purchasing is centralized within the company.
- Materials and supplies are ordered from one or a few vendors to maximize the benefits of volume purchases.
- Appropriate performance measures are used to monitor process performance, such as percentage of purchases made under a bid process, amount of volume discounts obtained, and actual cost performance compared to original cost projections.
- The performance of winning vendors and whether their pricing structures remain at competitive market rates is periodically evaluated.

Orders are placed on a timely basis.
- Communication channels are established between the marketing, production, and purchasing functions.
- Production schedules and material requirements are documented.
- Production needs are periodically reconciled with purchase orders and inventory levels to ensure they are adequately aligned.
- Long-term needs are analyzed and forward contracts are established with standing orders.

- The production scheduling system is integrated with the purchasing system.
- The computer system is used to generate purchasing requirements based on production schedules recorded in the purchasing system and on standard bills of material master files.
- The computer automatically generate purchase orders based on these material requirements, current stock levels and previously specified desired minimum stock levels.
- The company has at least considered using electronic data interchange (EDI) to place orders directly into the suppliers order entry system.

Materials are received on a timely basis.
- Just-in-time inventory techniques have been implemented.
- Supplier performance ratings have been developed, applied, and monitored.

The receiving process is efficient and cost-effective.
- The physical activities of the receiving process are reviewed.
- The receiving area and procedures are designed to reduce the number of activities and the time required to complete activities.
- Employees are trained in the process of materials handling.
- Employees are encouraged to share ideas and suggestions on ways to improve the process.
- Only limited storage space is allowed for within the receiving area to enforce the efficient distribution of goods away from receiving.

Materials received are processed on a timely basis.
- Production is notified when materials and supplies are received.
- Communication channels have been established between purchasing, production, and receiving to ensure all parties are aware of material needs and the timing of these needs.

Materials received meet required quality standards.
- Receiving personnel are trained in inspecting the quality of materials received, or materials are sent to trained personnel to ensure the materials meet the company's minimum standards for production use.
- Strategic alliances or partnerships have been developed with suppliers to ensure quality is built in by the supplier.
- The number of suppliers is optimized to achieve total delivered cost targets and meet specific customer needs.
- Strategic business alliances have been developed with suppliers.
- Suppliers are involved in the new product development and value analysis process.

Physical safeguards are adequate.
- Access to receiving and storage areas is restricted to authorized personnel.
- Receiving gates or loading docks are kept closed when no delivery is in process.
- Entry to facilities is checked, appropriate visiting documents are issued, and random checks of person are on the premises are performed.

- The receiving function is physically segregated from production facilities and shipping, unless good business practice dictates otherwise.
- Incoming goods are secured and safeguarded upon receipt.
- Appropriate handling and storage practices are communicated to employees to prevent damage to materials.

The receiving process is safe.
- Employees are fully trained in the safe handling and storage of non-hazardous materials.
- Procedures have been established for reporting and addressing safety concerns.
- Procedures and policies, which comply with relevant rules and regulations concerning safety, are maintained.
- Employees are fully trained in the safe handling and storage of hazardous materials.
- Hazardous materials are stored in appropriate containers.
- Hazardous materials are segregated from the main facilities used by employees.
- The handling and storage procedures and facilities are regularly inspected.

Compliance with laws and regulations
Materials are obtained in compliance with applicable laws and regulations.
- Legal review of all relevant laws and regulations is required.
- Procedures have been developed that comply with these laws and regulations.
- Industry organizations or regulatory bodies are consulted about compliance with laws and regulations and possible future requirements.
- The political, law making, and regulatory environment is monitored to ensure that the company's procedures remain in accordance with any industry standards and applicable laws and regulations.
- The company's policies and procedures concerning compliance with laws and regulations are documented.
- This information is distributed to appropriate personnel.
- A legal officer has been designated and is generally responsible for compliance with laws and regulations and is available to advise management.

Management control
Management develops strategic business alliances with suppliers.
- Strategic business alliances have been developed with suppliers. These suppliers are involved in developing better ways to process accounts payable.
- Vendor relations are continuously improved upon.
- Objectives have been developed to use in identifying potential candidates with whom the creation of strategic alliances makes sense.
- Due diligence reviews of potential vendors are performed .
- Partnership relationships are formalized and documented.

- In cooperation with strategic partners, the purchasing and accounts payable processes have been reengineered to eliminate redundancies.
- Integrated system technologies, such as EDI or web links are used to streamline the accounts payable process and to build linkages with strategic partners.

Exhibit 8-3 – Sample of an Ethical Code of Conduct
Source: Example of a Code of Conduct, PACE Business Ethics, July 15, 1999, St. Edwards University, Austin Texas (note, slight revisions have been made to preserve anonymity)

Preamble

At Company A, our dealings with others – inside and outside the company – are based on unquestioned integrity, open communications, social responsibility and proactive safety conscientiousness, in addition to a commitment to high productivity, total quality, continuing improvement and maximization of profits.

Doing business is a privilege bestowed upon us by our fellow citizens. They have the right to expect our behavior to be in full and complete compliance with all applicable laws and regulations of every state and country with which we conduct business

Our dealings with others must extend beyond mere compliance with the law. They must be based on complete candor, cooperation, honesty and mutual respect. A genuine feeling of decency, warmth and openness is a trait of Company A that everyone works to preserve.

We earn the credibility and respect of our owners/investors, employees, customers, suppliers, competitors and community by dealing with them in a fair and honest manner (88). We encourage personal commitment and dedication by empowerment and open communications. We strive to do what we say we will do, not to over- promise or under-perform. We accept accountability for our actions and strive to quickly correct any shortcomings.

General Principles

Integrity

Our Company is committed to providing a standard of values for our business that all employees and customers can appreciate.

Open Communication

COMPANY A fosters an environment of open and honest communication with the intent of upholding our responsibility to all of our stakeholders.

Social Responsibility

Reflecting society itself, COMPANY A has a vested interest not just in rapid economic growth, but also for the quality of life in its community and for the preservation of the environment.

Use of Resources – Company owned or issued property shall not be used or applied in order to obtain personal benefit or to harm another person. This ethics policy prohibits employee theft, fraud, embezzlement or misappropriation of property belonging to the company, another employee or any associate of the company.

Charity – COMPANY A allocates a portion of its profits for various community charities.

Environmental – COMPANY A respects the integrity of the world in which we live and recognizes the right to a livable environment. Sensitive to the impacts of intrusions on the physical environment, COMPANY A is committed to minimizing the impacts or eliminating the intrusions whenever possible.

Product Liability

All products assembled or produced by COMPANY A will be assembled in an effort to create the best value in the marketplace.

Retention of permanent employees is critical to maintain production quotas and standards.

Stakeholder Principles

While all of our business activities are governed by these general principles, the following are some of the principal relationships where upholding these values is particularly critical.

Customers/Consumers

The Company will treat all customers with dignity and respect while providing the customer with exceptional service. COMPANY A is committed to providing their customers with clear and relevant information regarding the products that they offer. Customers will not be intentionally misled by advertising concerning the quality or nature of products produced by COMPANY A.

Meeting or exceeding customer (both internal and external) expectations is fundamental to the success of COMPANY A and is a basic responsibility of all employees. By satisfying our customers, we create economic advantages for them and provide incentives for them to do business with us. Customer satisfaction requires a commitment to total quality, continuing improvement across all phases of our operation.

The company will do its best to meet customers expectations to protect the safety of our environment. The company will properly dispose of wastes and recycle when possible. Our company guarantees consumers the safest product possible. Because consumers are not in a position of technical expertise to judge the sophisticated products that are necessary for contemporary life, they must rely primarily on the conscientious efforts of business to ensure consumer safety.

COMPANY A will investigate customer complaints, deal fairly with consumers, and use the most effective source of product improvement: the opinions of those who use the product.

Employees

COMPANY A encourages open communication amongst employees at all levels. This is accomplished through regular staff meetings, company-wide meetings in which top officials are available to answer employee questions and an employee hotline for those who wish to remain anonymous.

Employees in the company are encouraged to exhibit a respectful behavior in the workplace. Likewise COMPANY A respects the rights and dignity of our employees, in particular by acknowledging their civil liberties and guaranteeing them due process. Employees will be treated fairly when considered for all activities.

It is the policy of COMPANY A to provide equal employment opportunity to qualified individuals regardless of race, religion, _gender, national origin, age, or their status as Ste veterans, disabled veterans or as disabled individuals. We will meet or exceed all laws regarding non-d non-discrimination nation and affirmative action. All employees are entitled to work in an environment free of discrimination and harassment. Misconduct and harassment are unacceptable behaviors.

Every COMPANY A employee has a responsibility to protect the physical and intellectual property of the company. Employee work time is a resource belonging to the Company. Employees may not misapply work time to personal issues.

COMPANY A recognizes that its success depends on benefiting from the unique and diverse talents and experiences of individuals from every facet of society.

Employees are encouraged to exhibit good safety habits at all times. When a situation creates a hazard, employees will inform the appropriate personnel at once (supervisor, law enforcement, etc.).

An employee's conduct in his/her professional life will be consistent with the responsible image that the company wants to project to the customers, suppliers, competitors, and community.

Owners/Investors

The Company will operate in a manner, which will increase profits responsibly. Our company will remain fair and profitable to encourage new and existing investors to invest in our company.

Financial results of COMPANY A will be reported in accordance with generally accepted accounting principles. Those reports will fairly present the Company's financial position and operating results.

The owners will provide a workplace free from recognized hazards that are likely cause death or serious injury.

Our Company will purchase supplies from reputable suppliers who will treat our company and employees with respect.

COMPANY A shall interact with their suppliers in an open, honest, and timely manner. Such communication will create a partnership that will in turn benefit the company's stakeholders.

Suppliers of goods and services to COMPANY A will be selected on the basis of value, quality and service only. In selecting suppliers, we also will be mindful of our commitment to supporting minority business enterprises. No employee may profit it personally from a relationship with a supplier.

The company will purchase supplies from suppliers who strive to be environmentally conscious.

Competition

COMPANY A shall provide information to its competitors as the need arises and as required by law but without jeopardizing their competitive position.

Competition is good to keep business growing and profitable, but we will run our company in a manner, which will encourage healthy competition within and without the organization.

COMPANY A sells premium quality products at a fair and competitive price.

The safe environment that exists at COMPANY A will promote the manufacture of quality products in an efficient manner. This will allow the company to be competitive in its industry.

Communities

COMPANY A shall provide to the communities in which it does business any information relevant to the community's interest.

The Company will strive to be a respectful citizen in the community. To achieve this status our company will participate in activities within the community and support local charities. Participating in community activities enables our company to provide for the citizens and to uphold our considerate reputation.

COMPANY A will maintain open and honest relationships with the public at all times, and will operate its business mindful of the health, safety and welfare for the general benefit of the public.

The company's human, financial and technological resources will be used for the benefit of its communities and the public at large. COMPANY A encourages its employees to become involved as leaders in civic and cultural affairs and, as a company, is actively involved in public policy issues that affect its businesses or the fundamentals of competitiveness.

The COMPANY A Business Ethics Committee determines and governs all charitable contributions on behalf of the Company. All requests for company donations must be submitted to the committee for consideration. COMPANY A encourages employees to contribute their own time and money to the charities of their choice.

The 1970 Occupational Safety and Health Act ensures so far as possible every working man and woman in the notion safe and healthful working conditions. The company will endeavor to be a leader in the community to ensure safe conditions for all employees. By consciously preventing pollution, the company will help to provide a clean environment for the citizens living in its community. The company will take action against vandals in order to protect the professional image of the facility and maintain the reputation of the Company.

Compliance Policies

COMPANY A requires ethical and legal behavior by anyone working for or on behalf of the Company. All employees or agents of the Company are required to comply with all applicable laws. The Company will take reasonable steps to communicate with and train individuals employed by COMPANY A about the Company's expectations, requirements and how to deal with ethical issues.

An employee who becomes aware of possible business abuse or illegal activity may bring it to the attention of the Company in the following manner:

The issue will first be discussed with the employee's immediate supervisor, if possible and appropriate.

If circumstances preclude such a discussion, the issue will be discussed with senior management or Human Resources.

The issue may be brought to the attention of the General Auditor of COMPANY A.

Employees may contact an organization called "The Network". The Network is a national firm retained by COMPANY A to act as a liaison between employees and Company management. To report real or suspected abuse, the employee should call the Network's toll free number, and provide pertinent information. Anonymous reports may be made.

Chapter Nine: Creating Action Plans

Transform ideas into action

Action steps are the ideas that result from a continuous improvement exercise. The action plan is the organized framework to manage the tasks of implementing ideas.

Action plans are used all the time as companies to help organizations turn ideas into reality. For example, Sears management spent nearly three years gathering information to improve its business model. To implement the changes it felt it needed to make, a series of town hall meetings were held to communicate the changes to employees and detailed action plans were used to implement the changes.

GTE adopted a quality-improvement methodology for its business units. It researches a process and then drafts a "killer gap table" to showcase how business was lost and root causes. A two-day gap-closing process hammers out a strategy for narrowing the gap. The outcome of the process is a detailed action plan.

Meyer Tool, adopted a TQM program in 1994. They utilize Six Sigma philosophies and tools to improve their processes. Their TQM methodology begins with standard measurements to establish baselines, proceeds to an analysis phase where key variable of the process are identified and studied, and conclude with improvements that are comprised of action plans to help reduce defects found from the 6 Sigma studies.

As a result of a survey process, Allstate Insurance developed action plans and goals for improving diversity in its workforce. These techniques helped the organization capture the 1997 Catalyst Award for women's advancement.

To create the most complete action plans, you should confirm that the proposed idea will resolve a significant business problem. Your ideas should be bounced off of key stakeholders to make sure they don't shift the problem elsewhere in the organization.

You'll also want to do an inventory of all the key people who will need to be involved in implementing your idea to transform it into action. Understand whom the managers are that need to support and champion the idea and who the staff are that can be leveraged to help change the process. Create a team out of the key staff members who will be involved. Use the team to help define steps and prioritize work time.

When you are trying to transform your ideas into actions, you'll want to ensure you have thought through some key elements that may facilitate or curtail successful implementation. These elements include the following:
- Human resources issues

- Technology requirements
- Training
- Performance measures/hurdle rates
- Regulatory, environmental, and legal considerations
- Business risks and controls
- Cost, quality, time and productivity issues
- Communications strategy
- Methods of monitoring progress

Action Plan Template

The action plan template is a document used for each idea to help in the implementation of the idea. The following fields are typically used in the action plan template:
- Statement of the problem
- Statement of the recommendation
- Key parties responsible for implementation
- Key action steps needed to implement change
- Timing for the action plan to be conducted
- Reward if successfully implemented
- Performance measures in place to monitor progress

Refer to Exhibit 9-1 for an example of a blank template.

Exhibit 9-1 Action Plan Template

PROCESS NAME
ACTION FORM N° 01

DEPARTMENT NAME: the entity to which the action is applied

RECOMMENDATION: a brief description of the suggested improvement step, and the benefits that may accrue

IDENTIFIED PROBLEMS: a brief description of the problems that action step is meant to resolve

PERSON IN CHARGE: name of the person in charge of implementing the action

ACTION STEP: high level descriptions of the actions that need to be done to implement the recommendation, if possible try and identify a time and team member accountable for each action step

TIMING: state the begin and end dates for actions to occur

REWARDS: incentive plan if actions implemented on time and correctly

PERFORMANCE MEASURES: track progress of the actions after they have been implemented so the process does not get off track again

Next is an example of a completed action plan template. It is for the Human resources department.   The suggestion was to use training to improve performance.

Human Resources
ACTION FORM N° 01

DEPARTMENT NAME : Human Resources

RECOMMENDATION : Invest in a formalized system of training to help improve employee performance. The benefits of implementing this action may be: improved productivity, greater employee satisfaction, increased quality in products and services, and enhanced customer satisfaction.

IDENTIFIED PROBLEMS : Currently each department in the company has its own policies on training. In many instances employees are not receiving the training they need to grow and advance in the company or to stay abreast of changes impacting their current jobs.

PERSON IN CHARGE : John Smith, Vice President of Human Resources

ACTION STEP :
1. Conduct a needs assessment before providing training. (February - - Jason is in charge of this)
2. Ensure training goals fit the goals and objectives of the organization. (March - - Mary is in charge)
3. Identify department heads to be a liaison to HR on building standard training programs. (April - - Phil)
4. Develop a standard set of policies and procedures for the department liaison to use as guidance. (May-Aug - - Mary, Phil, and Jason)
5. Review the training programs developed by each department liaison to ensure consistency and compliance with overall HR training objectives. (December - - John Smith)
6. Measure the impact of training. For example hours per person, employee retention, survey post-training. (done quarterly beginning the next year- - Jason will conduct the reviews)

TIMING : This recommendation is to begin implementation in February and should be completed by December. Completion means that HR has effectively created a standard set of training policies and procedures that each department liaison has followed to create their own training program specific to their departments. The department training programs have been reviewed by HR and are currently being implemented by the departments.

REWARDS : If each individual HR team member completes their assigned task on time and effectively, then they will receive a half day of paid vacation. If the entire team completes this implementation on time and effectively, then they will receive a team outing (e.g., a baseball game, going to the theatre etc.)

PERFORMANE MEASURES:
Percent of all departments submitting training plans to HR on time and complete.
Percent of all departments who execute their training plans completely.
Average number of hours of training each employee had in a year.
Average training budget each employee had allocated and actually used in a year.
Employee turnover in each department.

Monitor Results

A critical step in using action plan templates is to monitor results. This means that as the new manager in charge of implementing these actions you should ensure that the timing of implementation is challenging yet attainable. Once established, you'll want to ensure that you monitor adherence to the deadlines you have set. If you don't do this you might lose credibility so it is important to ensure deadlines are met.

In addition, part of monitoring results is the use of performance measures to monitor improvement. Performance measures will help ensure that the action step is working as designed, once it is implemented.

Finally, part of monitoring the results both during implementation and afterwards is to ensure appropriate communications are made to key stakeholders. This means communicating progress of implementation to management who supported and championed the idea.

Chapter Ten: Change Management Principles

Guiding Principles on Change Management

Jean-Jacques Rousseau summed it up best by stating "There is nothing more difficult to take in hand, more perilous to conduct, or more uncertain in its success than to take the lead in the introduction of a new order of things."

What are we doing and why? How does change relate to our strategies and objectives? Is management really committed? What is the change plan, is it doable? These are some central questions you'll want to ask as you begin to migrate your action steps into implementation.

Organizational change needs to be recognized and dealt with head on by the new manager looking to improve a process. Examples of organizational change include the following: change in mission, restructuring, new technologies, mergers, major collaborations, new programs like Total Quality Management, and re-engineering initiatives just to name a few.

Change management is one of the most overlooked steps in the continuous improvement process. Yet if not properly addressed, it can spoil your entire improvement effort. Resistance to forced change can have that power. To help create a successful change, let's look at common reasons why change fails, as suggested by Mark Sanborn, in his paper "Mastering Change: Why Organizational Change Fails."

- Misstarts: ill advised, hastily attempted change
- Making change an option: if people have the option not to change they probably won't
- A focus only on process: to much attention on the details and lose sight of results
- A focus only on results: ignore the human elements of change
- Not involving those expected to implement the change: not soliciting inputs from those affected by change
- Delegated to "outsiders": using consultants in a way that appears to be passing it off to somebody else
- No change in reward system: failure to adjust employees recognition and compensation for reaching desired change
- Leadership doesn't walk the talk: leaders don't commit to the change they force on others
- Wrong size: change is either too massive to be achievable or too small to be significant
- No follow-through: lack of clearly defined responsibilities for executing change

Philip Diehl, was a director of the U.S. Mint and oversaw an enterprise wide systems project with major change ramifications. The Mint was dramatic declines in its performance measures after systems changes. According to Diehl, "If I could do it all over again, I'd spend more money educating the organization on what life was going to be like after the implementation. We invested a lot in training, but we probably should have spent twice as much time and money. To other executives sponsoring similar projects I would say this: The organization needs to understand that it will be painful and expensive. The most critical thing is to start with a business requirement. What does your business lack that such a solution will provide? If the business requirement doesn't justify the pain, don't do it. But if the business case is clear, the returns are excellent."

According to the white paper "Organizational Change: Managing the Human Side," several key factors contribute to successful change management. These include leadership, communication, and education. Leaders will motivate the troops in times of turbulence. Education and communication are also vital to change management. These actions help management articulate changes and expectations and can ease tensions.

Organizations like Corning developed and implemented a tool kit to help managers assist their employees with organizational change. Self-assessment tools help focus on employee and company relationships. A Post-change revitalization plan maximizes positive aspects of the change, reduces trauma, motivates employees, and provides a tool to cope with change.

At the employee level you'll want to have answers to the following questions because the employees will probably be asking these questions of you and your team:

- What are we doing and why?
- How will the change work and how will if affect me?
- Can I influence the change?
- Will I have a job when this is over?
- Can we have a dry run first so I can learn to do it without failure?
- Can we make modifications to make it work better?

Human beings react to change? Exhibit 10-1 presents an interesting graph of the lifecycle of human reaction to change. Below are the major points of the human reaction to change. These reactions to change are adapted from Managing At The Speed Of Change, Daryl Conner, Villard, New York, 1992. Conner studied the clinical research of Elizabeth Kubler-Ross who wrote the book On Death and Dying in 1969 and researched how her clinical model applied to dramatic organizational shifts.

- Uninformed optimism
- Immobilization and denial
- Anger
- Bargaining
- Informed pessimism
- Despair
- Testing
- Hopeful realism

- Acceptance
- Informed optimism
- Initiative completion
- Continuous improvement

As a manager you need to be prepared to deal with this human reaction. There tends to be a predictable drop-off in performance due to the implementation of new processes and systems. Performance can be reached if you properly manage the change.

So how will your employees react to the changes you try and implement? Let's think it through in how a typical group of employees may react to a change.

First there may be rumors of change coming and uninformed optimism amongst the ranks can begin to set in. Second, employees may begin chatting amongst themselves and speculating on how the change will affect them. Once the change is sprung on employees they may react in anger, if the change is forced upon them. They reach their low point of despair if they feel they have no control over the changes being implemented. At this point they may want to quit or feel far less motivated to work through these changes.

So how do you avoid this problem? What are the keys to effective change management?

First, you'll want to create the case for effective change management. This is when you plead your argument that a change is necessary and if it is not made it could mean a worse set of alternative outcomes. Your argument as a new manager must be persuasive and supported by direct evidence in order for it to be credible.

In addition, to support your case for change, you'll want to paint the picture of what the future, after the change will be like. This is the idealized picture of what the organization and the employee can become as a result of the change. This is your guiding light of goals and objectives.

If necessary, you may want to have employees and management complete a change readiness assessment. This is a workshop or a survey that helps you determine if the organization is ready for change. See Exhibit 10-2 for a sample change manage readiness survey.

It can be argued that change management is so important to a successful continuous improvement project, that you should identify project team members responsible for handling this aspect of the project. This team should begin by identifying and meeting with people that would be most effected by the change. This meeting should take place as early as possible. If these folks can help in the project than accepting changes will be easier.

A proper mix of skills is also required for change management to work. First, political skills are needed. Change agents will need to maneuver their way through senior, middle and lower level ranks. Discussions can get heated so the change agent must be politically savvy. Next, the change agent needs analytical skills. Arguments for change need to be well argued. Thus, the change agent needs to do the appropriate analysis to ensure that the business case for change is rational, defensible and coherent. Finally, and obviously, the change agent needs to possess excellent people skills. In times of change the change agent will interact with people from all walks of life with personalities that span the spectrum. If the agent is not a people person it will be very difficult to orchestrate change.

In addition to the political, analytical and people skills, there are some additional skills a change leader should have in his or her toolbox. For example, the leader needs to be tuned into the environment. They need to know what is going on so they can anticipate and react to change. They also need to be willing to challenge existing paradigms. Leaders of change recognize that there are many ways to solve problems and their ability to look at problems in different lights is critical. Thirdly, the leader of successful change will have conviction. They need to sell change and get people on board. In addition just like a good politician, change agents build coalitions. They get buy-in from anyone that might otherwise circumvent the change. Finally, the greatest leaders of change rarely take credit for it. Instead, they make heroes out of their followers. They recognize and reward the accomplishments of their disciples to build an even larger following and keep momentum strong.

Remember that inherent in change is the ability to think differently. Just a moment ago we talked about the change agent needing to challenge existing paradigms. They must be able to suggest creative and innovative solutions to ease change. For example, as a change agent you'll want to investigate insightful HR practices to compensate employees for change concessions. Look at tactics such as flexible work options including telecommuting, flex-time, job sharing, and compressed work weeks as new rules when change is needed.

The keys to a successful change management can be summed up in the following bullets:

- Visible participation and support by the project team, managers, and those effected by the change
- Building a shared vision articulated by the project team and management and bought into by those effected by the change
- Frequent positive direction and reinforcement whereby the project team continues to be visible in helping those affected by the change deal with the change
- Create "champions" whereby someone affected by the change champions it and serves as a role model to the others
- Emphasize support, continued training, and education
- Consider using a consultant experienced in change management to facilitate the process
- Don't do change for the sake of change. Ensure there is a clear business case for change.

- Plan the change. Ensure there are goals and action plans to support your business case for change.
- Involve employees in decisions as much as possible to make them a part of the change.
- Keep perspective. Stay focused on the reasons for the change during the midst of difficult change implementations.
- Try not to control change. Just try and understand it and manage it.
- Create closure for the change. Reward success and acknowledge accomplishments

Change Management in Practice:

Although I could write significantly more on the topic of change management, I'd rather illustrate the importance of change management with an example of a company that excelled at change management during a major system implementation that would significantly change the way their employees worked.

Consulting Company XYZ's New Cost Allocation System

A few years ago, Consulting Company XYZ implemented a new system to better track cost allocations in order to more accurately invoice clients. The new system was a significantly different approach to tracking costs than the previous method of doing so. It would require a great deal of knowledge of the details of the new process. Consulting Company XYZ has thousands of consultants and getting them all to learn this new process would not be an easy task. The team rolling out the new system knew this and built a change management approach into their implementation process.

The major tenants of change management the team followed included:

- Integration of all change management activities within the other aspects of the project rollout
- Ownership of change management initiatives by the project management and team leaders
- Coordination of the delivery of different components of the change management strategy
- Visibility of managers in promoting and supporting the change
- Significant levels of user involvement in the different phases of planning and delivery
- Building on the work that current cost allocation methods use to facilitate the change

Within the project there were four critical change management components:

Change Navigation: The management and direction of the project, coordination of components, the planning and management of interdependencies between all the different elements, the integration of change resources within the total project team, the measurement and monitoring of outcomes to ensure that all the potential benefits of the project were achieved.

Change Enablement: Ensuring the right change interventions were undertaken at the right time. These included:

- Organizational and job design – ensuring the organizational structure and jobs were aligned with the process changes implied by the new cost allocation solution
- Training and user support – ensuring the training and user support needs of the organization were identified and appropriate solutions were developed and delivered
- Communication – ensuring the most appropriate forms of communication for each group of people were identified for each stage of the change, and that communication flowed in both directions

Change Leadership ensuring senior management of the Cost Management Group (the team that managed the existing and new cost allocation process) were visible in supporting the project's goals, identifying appropriate champions for the project who were able to promote the project through its lifespan and create the 'pull' for people to change.

Business Ownership the involvement of the Cost Management Group staff particularly end users, at all stages of the project, creating ownership of the new business processes and associated software and organization, selling the benefits of the solution to all levels of staff within the Cost Management Group, and ensuring key users within the Cost Management Group were prepared before training began.

The management of change within the project was a continuous process throughout the life of implementation. Therefore, the success of the change effort needed to be measured at appropriate agreed milestones during the project to enable continuing process improvement. The effectiveness of the program was measured in two ways:

1) The degree of commitment to the project by people impacted was measured using a Commitment Curve. By using this approach it was evidenced that the people impacted by the implementation of the new cost allocation method moved up the Commitment Curve throughout the project lifecycle as they began to feel more involved in design, development, and implementation and therefore more committed to the success of the project.

2) The success of the change management effort was also measured by focusing on the business performance measures used by the Cost Management Group. The appropriate performance measures were identified during the Design Phase. As part of the change effort, performance in key indicators was monitored before and after the implementation of the new process. During the implementation and initial post 'go-live' period performance dipped but consistently rebounded and even exceeded pre-implementation performance levels.

Change Management Scope:

The change management scope included the following activities:

- Organizational change support
- Communication and sponsorship
- Training and performance support

Organizational Change Support:

The implementation of the new cost allocation model was going to have a major impact on the way people work. Anticipating and preparing for this change minimized this impact. A key outcome of the work in the design phase was the identification of the impacts that the changes to business processes and the introduction of the new software would have on personnel. Many aspects of these impacts were supported through the training, performance support, sponsorship, and communication.

Supporting organizational change was focused on confirming organizational impacts with managers and the agreement of appropriate strategies to ensure organizational changes were successfully managed. This ensured managers understood the changes that would impact their area and that the changes were well planned and monitored. In summary, the main objectives in working with managers was to encourage the alignment of the organizational structure processes and jobs with the cost allocation model, ensure employees and supervisors understood what changes were made and how this affected them, ensure new jobs adequately documented with roles and responsibilities clearly defined, and to identify skills required and provide the necessary training.

The key tasks in this area of effort included:

Assessing the current organization:
Management established the current roles and responsibilities of the Cost Management Group personnel in the current organization to prepare an initial view of the roles affected by the implementation of the new cost allocation method.

Assessing the impact of the 'to be' processes
The impact of the cost allocation method on user groups was determined. Analysis was conducted for primary users whose work was to be driven by the system and for secondary users who would use the system for inquiry and reporting. Impact assessments were developed which reflected the overall magnitude of change on the members of the target audience. This information was then used to communicate changes to stakeholder groups and was provided input into determining training needs.

Role Mapping
As new business processes were identified, these were reviewed to identify new roles. An individual's job may be made up of one or more cost allocation roles along with other responsibilities that may not be related to the cost allocation

model. Once defined, these roles were then mapped to specific people and jobs in the current organization. The manger conducted this process with assistance from the Cost Management Group.

Determine Organization Structure and Job Design Changes
An approach was developed with the manager to implement the new work processes. This involved supporting management so that they could decide on any adjustments required to organizational structure, job responsibilities, and reporting relationships. Support was given to integrate descriptions of new roles and responsibilities into existing job descriptions.

Determine Employee Security Access Levels
Prior to implementation, support was given to management to determine the level of access individuals should have to the system. This information was then relayed to the deployment team for set-up.

Communication and Sponsorship

The key objectives of the change management effort for the communication and sponsorship initiatives included obtaining the commitment and the support for the change by working with the executive leadership; building an awareness of the project, its objectives, and proposed time frame; providing staff with an understanding of how the changes would impact them and how they would be supported through those changes; encouraging business ownership to create acceptance towards the change in the organization; providing regular updates on progress to ally any 'fears of the unknown' which existed in the user community; and acknowledging the concerns of the users and encouraging participation in the planning and implementation of change.

The key tasks in this area of effort included:

Develop Communications and Sponsorship Strategy
The communication and sponsorship strategy detailed the approach for planning sponsorship, business ownership, and communication activities. Elements of the communication strategy included identifying the audience groups and their communication roles, assessing the most effective communication channels/media, and determining the methods for evaluating communication effectiveness.

Build Sponsorship and Business Ownership
The sponsorship effort focused on developing and supporting the project's overall change strategy. Activities focused on building a network of sponsors, advocates, and agents and identifying their roles for a successful implementation.

Develop a Communication and Sponsorship Plan
A communication and sponsorship plan was developed in line with the communication strategy, which outlined specific tasks, dates, and responsibilities for activities during the design and prototype phase.

Executing and Evaluating the Communication and Sponsorship Plan
Activities were implemented as set out in the plan. The effectiveness of communications was evaluated on an ongoing basis and the plan adjusted according to feedback received.

Training and Performance Support

Training and performance support refers to the mechanisms the project team developed and delivered to enable impacted personnel to perform their job using the cost allocation system. Training focused predominantly on preparing staff through skills development prior to implementation of the new system. Performance support focused on supporting staff after the implementation. The training and support effort also focused on all system users were comfortable and confident in using the new system to perform their jobs from day one of the 'go live' date. Finally, it provided the structure and means for supporting users while they were on the job working on the new system and grew the Cost Management Group skills in order to support the training and the users after production.

Develop a Training Solution Plan
Based on the input from project team members, end users, and instructional design principles, the Cost Allocation Model team developed the solution plan. The plan developed during the course of the design phase included:

- Detailed analysis of the training audience and their training needs
- Structure of the training curriculum identifying user groups, numbers of users, and which users attend which courses
- Comprehensive description of the training approaches, to be used such as procedures development, training development, train the trainer, training database, and post production support
- Training delivery requirements and timeframe

Procedure development
The majority of systems and business procedures are maintained on-line as part of the new system help tool. This tool provides users with an integrated view of business processes and system functionality. End users can access the help site while they are working in the new system to view step-by-step instructions on how to complete tasks. The procedures development coordination effort included: developing the procedure standard templates, writing procedures, reviewing procedures as they were drafted, and coordinating and participating in testing help site procedures.

To ensure procedures were instructionally sound as well as contained the correct content, the team worked closely with the business experts to create, review and test all procedures.

Training development
Once the curriculum plan was confirmed and the training delivery method finalized, work began on designing and developing the training. The training

development coordination effort included; developing training standards and templates, designing training courses, writing training materials, reviewing training materials as they are drafted, and coordinating and participating in testing the integration of the training materials with the On-line help tool.

Throughout the training and development process, business experts provided training content and data and tested all walkthroughs and exercises. As a result of their involvement in the project, business experts gained the detailed understanding of both the business processes and the system and were able to deliver the training to all end users.

Because the business experts delivered the training, all training materials were in the form of high-level outlines. The materials did not include any content detail. The training materials used during training included: a Training Guide, an Activity Guide, and Job Aides.

In addition to the training materials, the on-line help tool was used throughout the training in order to provide participants with an understanding of the tool and its use. Wherever possible, training and on-line help materials were leveraged from any existing training. Feedback on required revisions to the training materials was collected. Materials were then revised based on the feedback and were prepared in their final form for the first implementation group training.

Ultimately, Consulting Company XYZ was proactive with the change management aspects of their new system implementation. The major success factor was the complete involvement of all staff members of the Cost Management Group during the design, development, and deployment of the tool. This made for a manageable change that smoothly transitioned the old system and process to the new one.

Exhibit 10-1 How Humans React to Change:

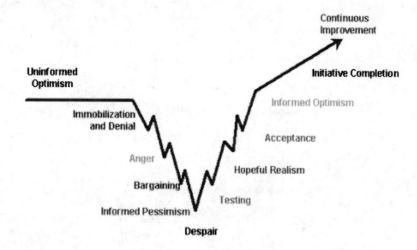

adapted from the following source: <u>Managing At The Speed Of Change</u>, Daryl Conner, Villard, New York, 1992

Exhibit 10-2 Change Readiness Survey

Strongly Agree	Tend to Agree	Hard to Decide	Tend to Disagree	Strongly Disagree
1	2	3	4	5

1. Communication between departments is very open.

2. Communication channels are very open here among employees.

3. Communication channels are very open here among management and workers.

4. Management actively solicits input from employees before major decisions are made.

5. I can trust our management and believe what it says.

6. Management seeks input from employees on major decisions.

7. Most projects designed to make things better in this organization have been successful

8. The number of changes that we go through here is "about right."

9. This organization is very supportive of change.

10. It is "easy" to get things done here.

11. Most management changes make my job easier.

12. Most people in this organization are encouraged to make suggestions for improvement.

13. Changes suggested by employees are usually implemented.

14. Employees agree with the Company's goals.

15. The department is free from "red tape."

16. The department values its people.

17. Compared to other companies that I know about, _____ is one of the best companies to work for.

18. My immediate supervisor respects me as an individual.

19. My supervisor is open to constructive criticism.

20. My immediate supervisor listens to what I have to say.

21. My supervisor deals fairly with me.

22. The department deals fairly with everyone--it doesn't play favorites.

23. My immediate supervisor encourages my suggestions for improvement.

24. My immediate supervisor has effective interpersonal skills.

25. People trust one another in this company.

26. Most managers here have effective interpersonal skills.

27. People work well together in this company.

28. The department is well respected for dealing fairly with employees.

29. The current management team is highly respected.

30. Everyone knows the goals of the department.

31. Our supervisors have done a good job of translating the organization's objectives into meaningful assignments and goals for their employees.

32. Employees are encouraged to take initiative and make decisions on their own.

33. Employee problems and complaints are effectively handled.

34. The department is open to suggestions.

35. I understand the goals and purpose for the continuous improvement project.

36. I fell there is a need for the continuous improvement project.

37. The continuous improvement project will make things better.

38. I feel that some positive changes may come out of this continuous improvement process.

Responses to the following questions will help us understand how major employee groups view things. These and all responses will be kept confidential. However, if you feel uncomfortable answering these questions, you don't have to.

Please indicate your current classification.
1. Management
2. Staff
3. Other

How long have you worked for the company?
1. 0-2 years
2. 3-5 years
3. 6-9 years
4. 10-14 years
5. More than 14 years

Thank you for your input. It will contribute tremendously to the success of this project.

Please use the space below to write additional comments about any topic, whether or not it was covered in the questionnaire. For example, you may want to discuss your department's major strengths or major problems or suggest some possible improvements. Or you may have suggestions for improving your work group's procedures, policies and other areas.

Chapter Eleven: Training, Training, Training

An essential element of performance improvement success is managing change. The prior chapter was dedicated to helping manage change appropriately. However, a key element when new policies and procedures or action plans move from the drawing board to the shop floor is training.

Training employees when implementing changes resulting from performance improvement initiatives helps ensure success of those initiatives. In addition, companies that invest in training and employee development realize the benefits of self-development by encouraging a work habit of learning--where learning is built around action rather than theory. The most effective training and employee development programs today:

- Are driven by the business strategy. Programs are developed and implemented to produce results identified as critical to the strategy.
- Maximize employee ability and potential. Best companies use self-directed training and encourage employees to identify their own needs and to seek learning opportunities.
- Are work-related--knowledge and skills acquired in training are relevant to the company and the individual's work requirements
- Focus on learning by doing, rather than on teaching theory and expecting employees to figure out how to apply it.
- Can be transferred to the job, and skills remain when training is completed.
- Have a positive cost-benefit ratio. Training today must show a return on investment--either long-term or short-term. Many training initiatives take years to meet their goals fully, and these timeframes are identified early on.
- Link to other departments. Training is often conducted by line managers, who also perform evaluations, set performance objectives, and draft compensation and promotion systems for the same employees. These programs respond also to individual needs as identified through appraisals, counseling meetings, assessments, and career development plans.

World-class organizations leverage training and development to improve performance within their business processes. General electric has used action learning to improve performance. (Action learning is a learning-by-doing approach to training, where real business problems are addressed by small project teams.) Initially, GE's action learning programs focused on customer service issues. The company's training challenge has been refocused to build the skills, self-confidence and experience base to enable it to compete globally. The training programs were therefore developed with a global perspective.

The Gillette Co. is an international producer of consumer products, headquartered in Boston, Massachusetts. It operates in over 50 countries. To establish and maintain a constant source of international managers with a westernized business approach, the company has, for the last several years, conducted an International Graduate Trainee Program. The program is the responsibility of the Gillette International division.

Known for its product innovation, Robert Bosch GmbH has an R&D staff that numbers in the thousands and was instrumental in developing fuel injection systems, anti-lock brakes, and air bags. Its commitment to quality is also evident in the way it prevents defects by adhering to the "rule of ten." In a manual for employees, the rule is described as follows: "Correcting a defect that is discovered in the final test in the factory costs $10. But if it is detected even earlier, in the initial inspection of a purchased part, for example, it can be corrected for only $1. And if the same defect can be avoided through preventative measures, it costs only $.10."

One of the foundations of Bosch's commitment to quality is its ongoing dedication to having the best trained employees throughout the firm. For example, candidates for production jobs at Bosch do not simply apply, take a test, interview and then receive a "yes" or "no." The first step for a prospective employee is to go through pre-employment training before being given a job. There is no guarantee that employment will be forthcoming, but the chances are very good if a candidate does well in the pre-employment training course. The pre-employment training program lasts three hours a night for 14 weeks, and students who miss more than two classes are out of the program. The curriculum of the program covers the history of the Bosch company, quality management techniques, technical subjects such as blueprint reading, as well as nine other topics. The rigorous schedule also tests a prospect's commitment to the job, and the absence of pay for the 14 weeks of pre-employment training truly separates the dedicated from the dilettante.

Bosch also strives to have the best journeymen on staff and finds that one way of getting the appropriate skills it needs is to train its own apprentices. Potential apprentices are sought out at local high schools, are given knowledge and skills tests, and are interviewed by Bosch's training and personnel staff. The interviewers look for a combination of academic skills and evidence of a sense of responsibility in a candidate. If accepted, the apprentices will go through a three-and-a-half-year program to become journeymen -- nearly three times the length of a typical apprenticeship program in the US. Bosch trainers also go to great lengths to help students complete the course by offering after-hours tutoring and other special assistance.

In addition to training their own employees, Bosch also offers programs for its distributors to upgrade their product knowledge and sales skills. Distributors say the all-day courses held in the field help to reduce errors in product recommendations and increase sales. Week-long courses are also offered at Bosch plants and product- specific training videotapes are viewed by thousands of distributor salespeople each year.

To approach training from a world-class perspective and truly integrate it into your performance improvement programs you need to be able to identify the right training delivery and design training effectively.

In Exhibit 11-1 a Learning Delivery Matrix is presented. The matrix is meant to help you think through all the ways you can deliver training to your employees. A tool like the matrix is a great organizational development tool because it presents a comprehensive list of ways individuals can learn structured in clearly defined categories based upon a mutually exclusive, collectively exhaustive approach.

In addition to defining your learning delivery to ensure you have the right way to train people for your performance improvement initiatives, development of the training is just as crucial.

A common methodology used in courseware development is the ADDIE Methodology. It is a systematic process heavily used in the field of instructional design. Exhibit 11-2 shows an instructional design (ISD) flowchart depicting the ADDI Methodology. Below is a brief overview of the ADDIE methodology.

ADDIE stands for the following:

- Analysis
- Design
- Development
- Implementation
- Evaluation

As we explain this methodology, consider its usefulness not only in instructional design, but also, like Six Sigma, ISO, and Baldrige, as yet another methodology that can help you in your performance improvement efforts.

Analysis:

The analysis phase is where you identify the business objectives for the training. Use brainstorming and process definitions to help structure your analysis phase. Focus on what the goal of the training should be. Understand what needs to be accomplished and the business case for training. The major points here are as follows:

- Identify the opportunity and target specific needs
- Define the process from beginning to end to understand it appropriately

Design:

This is where you take your business case for training and begin to make it more structured. The major points here are as follows:

- Design training solutions based on the analyzed business needs (type of delivery, outline of curriculum etc)
- Document the training objectives to meet the business objectives
- Define the performance measures to ensure a successful training program

Development:

This is where the rubber meets the road. This is where you get into the details. Actually developing the training content based on the training and business objectives takes place here. The major points here are as follows:

- Formulating the detailed content for implementing the approved training solution
- Build a project plan with key parties responsible and time frames for the development of the courseware

Implementation:

The implementation phase is when the training is rolled out to its intended recipients. The major points here are as follows:

- Conduct a pilot to 'test' the new training program
- Make revisions based on the pilot
- Execute the solution

Evaluation:

The evaluation phase is important because it helps training managers understand if training was a helpful tool to facilitate the implementation of performance improvement initiatives. A common set of evaluation tactics often used within the training and development industry is a set of 5 levels of learning. The first 4 levels were developed by Donald J. Kirkpatrick and the fifth was authored by Jack J. Phillips.

Level One-Reaction
Per Kirkpatrick, "evaluating reaction is the same thing as measuring customer satisfaction. If training is going to be effective, it is important that students react favorably to it."

The guidelines for Level One are as follows:

- Determine what you want to find out
- Design a form that will quantify the reactions
- Encourage written comments and suggestions
- Strive for 100% immediate response
- Get honest responses
- Develop acceptable standards
- Measure reactions against standards, and take appropriate action
- Communicate reactions as appropriate

The key to success for this Level is to not just use it as a "smile sheet" but as a true continuous improvement tool that will allow training managers and course developers to make proactive changes in a timely manner.

The benefits to conducting Level One Evaluations are:
- A proxy for customer satisfaction
- Immediate and real-time feedback to an investment
- A mechanism to measure and manage learning providers, instructors, courses, locations, and learning methodologies
- A way to control costs and strategically spend your budget dollars
- If done properly, a way to gauge a perceived return on learning investment

Level Two-Learning
Level Two is a 'test' to determine if the learning transfer occurred. Per Kirkpatrick, "It is important to measure learning because no change in behavior can be expected unless one or more of these learning objectives have been accomplished. Measuring learning means determining one or more of the following."

- What knowledge was learned?
- What skills were developed or improved?
- What attitudes were changed?

The Guidelines for Level Two are as follows:
- Use a control group, if practical
- Evaluate knowledge, skills, and or attitudes both before and after the program
- Use a 'test' to measure knowledge and attitudes
- Strive for 100% response
- Use the results to take corrective actions

The benefits to conducting Level Two Evaluations are:
- Learner must demonstrate the learning transfer
- Provides training managers with more conclusive evidence of training effectiveness

Excellent examples of Level Two evaluations occur commonly in the workplace.

- Passing the Certified Public Accountants exam
- Becoming a Six Sigma Black Belt by passing a certification exam
- Complying with appropriate legal and regulatory guidelines

Level Three-Behavior

Level Three evaluates the job impact of training. "What happens when trainees leave the classroom and return to their jobs? How much transfer of knowledge, skill, and attitudes occurs?" Kirkpatrick questions, "In other words, what change in job behavior occurred because people attended a training program?"

The Guidelines for Level Three are as follows:

- Use a control group, if practical
- Allow time for behavior change to take place
- Evaluate both before and after the program if practical
- Survey or interview trainees, supervisors, subordinates and others who observe their behavior
- Strive for 100% response
- Repeat the evaluation at appropriate times

The benefits to conducting Level Three evaluations are as follows:

- An indication of the 'time to job impact'
- An indication of the types of job impacts occurring (cost, quality, time, productivity)

Level Four-Results

Per Kirkpatrick, Level Four is "the most important step and perhaps the most difficult of all." Level Four attempts to look at the business results that accrued because of the training.

The Guidelines for Level Four are as follows:

- Use a control group if practical
- Allow time for results to be achieved
- Measure both before and after the program, if practical
- Repeat the measurement at appropriate time
- Consider costs versus benefits
- Be satisfied with evidence if proof not possible

World-class training organizations such as Capital One, NCR Corp., IBM, Hewlett-Packard, Lucent Technologies, International, TDIndustries, and Kinko's are at a Level Four in their training evaluation process.

The advantages to a Level Four evaluation are as follows:

- Determine bottom line impact of training
- Tie business objectives and goals to training

Level Five-ROI

Level Five is not a Kirkpatrick step. Kirkpatrick alluded to ROI when he created level Four linking training results to business results. However, over time the need to measure the dollar value impact of training became so important to corporations that a fifth level was added by Jack J. Phillips who has authored or edited over 30 books on the subject.

The Guidelines for Level Five are as follows:
- Use a control group, if practical
- Allow time for results to be achieved
- Determine the direct costs of the training
- Measure a productivity or performance before the training
- Measure productivity or performance after the training
- Measure the productivity or performance increase
- Translate the increase into a dollar value benefit
- Subtract the dollar value benefit from the cost of training
- Calculate the ROI

ROI calculations are being done by a few world-class training organizations. They help these organizations:

- Quantify the performance improvements
- Quantify the dollar value benefits
- Compute investment returns
- Make informed decisions based on quantified benefits, returns, and percent return comparisons between learning programs

Organizations such as Tennessee Valley Authority (TVA), Motorola, IBM, Synovus Financial Corp., and A.G. Edwards & Sons have reached level Five.

Ultimately training can make or break the successful rollout of a performance improvement initiative. Keep in mind the following best practices, when devising your training program.

- Always try and develop those affected by the performance improvement to their fullest potential. Empower them, through training with the right knowledge and skills to execute the new improvements they need to be successful.
- Constantly be identifying organizational initiatives and build training programs around those business needs.
- Develop training to the appropriate level of detail and deliver it at the time of need.

- Continuously evaluate training programs and enhance them on a regular basis.
- Provide employees with appropriate training and development opportunities within the confines of each performance improvement initiative.
- Build an organizational culture that champions and supports training as a key tool for implementing performance improvement initiatives

Exhibit 11-1 Learning Delivery Matrix

Source: KnowledgeAdvisors, 2001

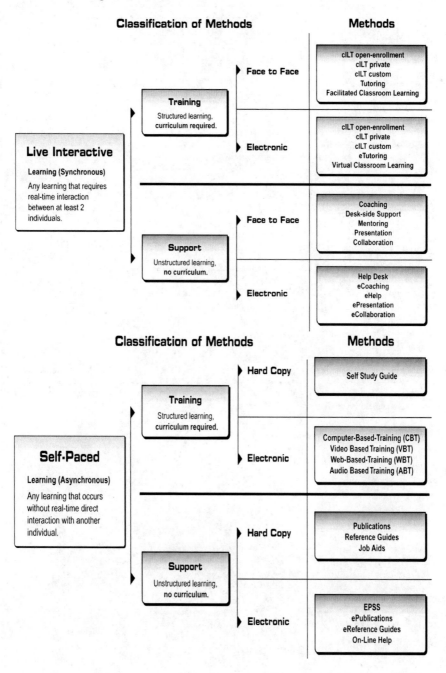

Exhibit 11-2 ADDIE Methodology

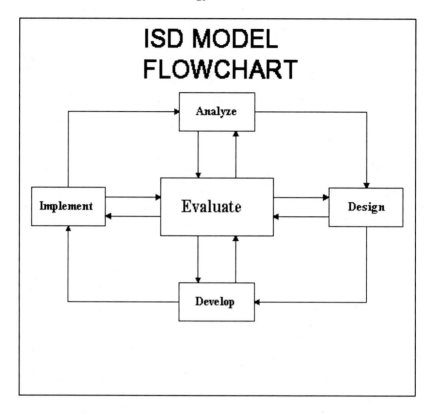

Chapter Twelve: Building a Knowledge Management System

In 1999 Chrysler built cars using virtual and physical networks of Knowledge. In 1997 Skandia, a Swedish insurance and savings company created a future-focused center or think tank of knowledge workers. In 1996 Monsanto developed a "knowledge management architecture" aimed at increasing intellectual capital. In 1997 Case Corporation built the Case Knowledge Base, a fact-based decision-making tool. In 2001 Tufts University earned a Enterprise Value Award because it developed a knowledge management system that changed the way students and professors interact and learn including digital libraries accessible online.

Are you getting the picture yet?

The organizations above were developing knowledge management solutions years ago. They recognized the importance that knowledge has on the organization. So what exactly is knowledge management? Although most people think it is information technology, knowledge management is the collective knowledge of an organization and includes knowledge that resides both internally and externally.

Knowledge itself may range from better ways to improve a process to saving costs. In fact, organizations like Chevron refer to managing knowledge as a way to reduce operating costs by more than $2 billion a year. Unipart, a logistics and distribution organization buckets business intelligence, collaboration, knowledge transfer, knowledge discovery and mapping, and expertise location into its domain of knowledge management.

In fact, performance indicators have suggested that better knowledge management has improved the quality of work and the capabilities of employees. 3M for example has had a knowledge sharing culture for years and that intensity in its innovation results in more than 40 percent of its revenues being derived from products less than 5 years old.

At the dawn of the new millennium, you will be hard pressed to find any organization that does not perceive its employees' collective knowledge to be critical in its success. Because of this, organizations are striving to foster, support, and reward employee collaboration and then work on ways to harness these efforts for competitive advantage.

In 2001, International Data Corporation (IDC) conducted a survey on the state of knowledge management. The study found that organizations understand the value of knowledge management and place a high priority on its success. IDC predicted that the average budget for knowledge management initiatives would increase to over $1million in 2002.

A few keys to successful knowledge management are 1) to build your knowledge management approach to fit your company's culture rather than trying to use knowledge management to change your culture, and 2) measure the value of knowledge management. To further address point 2, look at Capital One who gauges its intense knowledge management efforts by including them on employee surveys.

Continuous improvement would fail at its efforts to be continuous without sustainability. As workers come and go, including you as a manager, it is important to leave the knowledge behind so it can continue to grow and flourish. That is why it is important to be thinking about knowledge management and how it fits into your continuous improvement process.

Organizational knowledge is the useful, actionable, and meaningful information retained in a system, despite the comings and goings of individuals who contribute to the system.

Managing your organization's knowledge is essential because:

- Collective knowledge is more powerful than individual knowledge, even your own
- Knowledge management acts as a hedge against employee turnover
- Effective knowledge management can lead to more effective training programs, increased employee productivity, competitive advantage, and more satisfied customers

Creating a knowledge management system can be complex or simple. For example, you might have a very sophisticated corporate intranet that all employees can log onto to share information, collaborate on ideas or extract the knowledge of their coworkers to apply to their job.

Conversely, you can accomplish the same goals by having a simple set of file folders set up on your local area network so that if you are a small company all employees in the office can have some dedicated space to share presentations, communications and other work products.

The key is to encourage and facilitate the formal collection, packaging, and dissemination of information. Doing so will lessen your risk of lost knowledge as employees leave your department or organization.

So how can you go about creating a knowledge management system? I will discuss some basic principles and then we can clarify it by example.

The basic pieces of a knowledge management system might include the creation of a knowledge map and knowledge objects followed by the appropriate content to populate the objects. A knowledge map is the organized schema through which users navigate to find or contribute relevant content. Knowledge objects are the subdirectories of topics within a particular area on the knowledge map. The objects are best exploited when they are consistent across the knowledge map as it makes the map easier to search and more user friendly as you navigate throughout the map.

Let's put these concepts into perspective with an example. We'll start by creating a knowledge map. If your organization has no current map begin with something generic. This may be the market segments you serve, the industries you operate within, your product lines, or business units.

I like to start with business processes. Some core processes common to any business may very well include the following:

Sales and Marketing
Supply Chain
Finance Function
Information Technology
Human Resources

Next it would be a good idea to define the sub-processes within each of these functions. That way you can complete your knowledge map with a good layer of detail.

For example here are some sub-processes for the core processes listed above:

Human Resources
Compensation Design and Administration
Benefits Design and Administration
Employee Relations
Labor Relations
Training
Performance Management
Recruiting
Staffing
Managing Change
Managing Diversity
Compliance (EEO etc.)
HRIS/File Management
Strategic Planning/Organizational Design
Organizational Development/Management Development

Finance Function
Payroll
Travel and Entertainment Accounting
Accounts Payable
Billing
Accounts Receivable Credit and Collections
Close the Books/Financial Reporting
Financial Budgeting
Fixed Asset Accounting
Internal Audit
Tax
Treasury Risk Management
Cost Management
Cash Management

Sales and Marketing
Market segmentation
Marketing and advertising
Sales Forecasting
Pricing Policies
Channel management

Supply Chain
Procurement
Production planning and scheduling
Warehouse management
Order fulfillment
Logistics

Information Technology
Applications development
Technical and user support
Networking services
IT policy/administration

Next you should define the knowledge objects that will be standardized and consistent across all of these processes and sub-processes. Recall that knowledge objects are the subdirectories of topics within a particular area on the knowledge map.

Some common knowledge objects I might suggest if you are creating knowledge management systems include the following:

<u>Subject Specialists</u> this is an area where the internal and external experts are listed and users of the system can contact or look to as a reference source for first hand knowledge on this area of the knowledge map.

<u>Books and Links</u> this is an area where you can list the best websites, books, articles and reference sources to help users of the knowledge management system find quality research

<u>Cases</u> this is an area where those who contribute to the knowledge management system can describe their war stories through colorful examples of their experiences in working in the topic

<u>Best practices</u> this is an area where users can go to find the success factors that have worked with others both within the organization and outside of it

<u>Benchmarks</u> this is an area where key performance metrics are stored to help manage by measurement; the benchmarks can be internal or external

The key is to create templates for each of the above objects that way as users contribute to the system they do so in a consistent manner and in a way that guides and facilitates users contributions to the system.

Lastly, you populate the above knowledge objects for every aspect of your knowledge map. You don't have to populate all areas all at once. It could be done over time.

Knowledge Management Fundamentals:

Knowledge management has been studied for several years. But, in 1995 Knowledge Management was put on the map by the American Productivity and Quality Center and Arthur Andersen, when they sponsored a Knowledge Imperative Symposium. It introduced a model to measure knowledge known as the Organizational Knowledge Management Model.

The model is illustrated in Exhibit 12-1. It describes five enablers to knowledge management, Leadership, Culture, Technology, Measurement and Process. These enablers foster the development of organizational knowledge through the knowledge management process. Below is a description of each of the key enablers that comprise the Organizational Knowledge Management Model.

Leadership: Leadership focuses on ensuring that senior management champions and supports the identification, sharing, and leveraging of individual knowledge into organizational knowledge. Key elements of the leadership enabler include:

- Visible support by top leaders for knowledge management
- Understand how leveraged knowledge can have revenue-generating potential
- Commitment to employee development and training

- Hire, compensate and evaluate employees for knowledge sharing contributions

Motorola, known for its commitment to employee education, established a formal connection with Northwestern University's Kellogg School of Business. Together, they designed a manufacturing course. It also licensed local community colleges to teach Motorola courses. Motorola entered these collaborations in an effort to increase the number of potential company employees possessing the knowledge and skills it considers important.

At Pfizer, the pharmaceutical company, models were put in place for judging the performance of managers in the Treasury Department. The models were based on the notion that the company's finance and business managers must develop new attitudes based on trust, teamwork, integration, and contribution in order to participate in corporate development.

Harley-Davidson Inc. had a goal to more than double production by the year 2003, the company's 100th anniversary. The company used participation, learning, inclusion, and cooperation to facilitate the achievement of this goal. A new operating agreement with two major labor unions focused on making Harley-Davidson a "high-performance workplace." The company stressed education, offering employees 80 hours of training each year. In addition, it emphasized that workers possessed what it calls its three competencies: interaction competencies for communication and team skills; execution competencies for solving problems and making decisions; and technical competencies for task operation and commitment. Dealers and customers were also part of the arrangement. A three-day training program offered by Harley Davidson University taught dealers how to handle the increased supply of other goods, such as clothing and collectibles. The course in turn helped Harley strengthen its relationships with this critical distribution channel for its products.

Culture: Culture focuses on creating a working environment that supports sharing of knowledge. Open door policies and contributing versus hoarding of knowledge is rewarded not discouraged. Key elements of the leadership enabler include:

- A climate that trusts its employees and empowers their sharing of information responsibly
- Employees encouraged to be innovative and take responsible risks
- Empowered employees with accountability for their professional development

Rubbermaid, a manufacturer of consumer rubber and plastic goods, is known as a great innovator. The company's business teams were engineered to allow Rubbermaid to match their smallest competitors in terms of agility, and to surpass them in terms of their access to corporate resources. It is the team's job to know all market trends in a given product category and to do its own planning. If one team needs assistance from another, it simply asks, so a great deal of expertise is available to anyone at any time. Teams at Rubbermaid are permanent and run like autonomous business units. Individuals remain members from three to five years. Teams submit new product plans based on anticipated ROAE (Return on Assets Employed). The company sponsors product fairs to spotlight the top product development people. Presentations are given on the top 50 ideas. Teams with winning new product are taken on field trips to trade shows so they can look at the competition. One notable result of team activity at Rubbermaid is that 33 percent of sales volume comes from products developed during the previous five years.

3M is well known for fostering a climate of innovation and entrepreneurship. The company's decentralized organizational structure facilitates the upward flow of ideas. Status does not hinder entrepreneurial activity. Mistakes are accepted as a normal cost of doing business, and individuals are free to pursue their own ideas. In fact, 3M researchers can spend up to 15 percent of their time--about a day a week--working on their special projects, projects which are frequently cooperative efforts. Access to company resources--within and outside employees' particular divisions--is routine, and funding can be made available to foster employee initiatives. Few things are considered sacred at 3M, but the development of new product ideas is one of them. Each division must comply with the corporate requirement that at least 25 percent of sales come from products that did not exist five years ago. A new product development project can be stopped, but so much faith is placed in the innovator that the burden of proof in any decision to halt a project rests with the whistle-blower.

Technology: Technology focuses on the use of computers and automation to streamline and encourage the knowledge sharing process. Leveraging intranets, internets and groupware to share information efficiently and effectively drive the technology enablers. Other key elements of the technology enabler include:

- Using technology to connect people within the organization that are geographically dispersed.
- Using technology as the information storage and retrieval hub of collected knowledge.
- Technology that needs to be 'user-friendly' to facilitate knowledge sharing.
- Technology that continuously upgrades and improves with advancements and changes.
- Technology that 'pushes' information and knowledge to users in a proactive manner.

Intranets, which serve as both knowledge repositories and as a way for members of the organization to share and contribute ideas, are commonplace in many organizations. But only the best leverage them for knowledge sharing.

At John Deere, photographs of all its products are online. When employees need to make a presentation with pictures, they can immediately download the pictures to their computers. This has saved countless hours of picture taking, developing, and scanning.

IBM has posted most of its human resource forms, such as performance reviews and job changes, on its intranet. Managers directly access the forms they need. This "self-service mode" helped cut administrative expenses, and time spent searching for most recent versions.

Xerox also has put its forms on an intranet, saving the same type of costs. It also puts updates, revisions to manuals, and the company objectives there, where all employees easily can find the information or form they need.

DHL Systems used its intranet to distribute a new enterprise software license to all its sites globally. Before, the company would have had to send it electronically to more than 200 countries, plus other centers around the world.

All the organizations can point to tangible savings that more than cover the cost of installing an intranet, usually after the first year.

Measurement: Measurement is the end result of most improvement initiatives. Boldly, measurement of knowledge attempts to link it to cost, quality, time, and productivity metrics. It hopes to quantify the results. Key elements of the measurement enabler include:

- Measure the linkage of knowledge management efforts to bottom line performance
- Creation of a small set of well balanced indicators measuring customers, suppliers, physical, financial, and human resources and the effects of these due to knowledge sharing.
- The allocation of resources to measure knowledge. Documenting the tangible and intangible ways knowledge management continuously improves the company.

Buckman Laboratories spent 2.5 percent of revenues on knowledge management. To measure the ROI on this expense it measured its knowledge management activities carefully. It operated on the principle of "anecdote management," using examples to tell the story of its knowledge management success. Often, these examples related to a new contract or new customer that was won because of effective knowledge sharing among those involved in the sales process. These stories and related figures were collected for use at budget time, when they prove to be potent weapons for justifying the investment in knowledge for the following year.

The finance department of Skandia, a federation of savings institutions headquartered in Sweden, worked with each of the organization's companies to develop a set of performance measures for measuring knowledge. All companies developed measures in five areas: financial, customer, human, process, and renewal and development. The set of measures was termed a "Navigator," and companies used it to monitor how well they were managing the critical attributes of intellectual capital. In an article mentioning Skandia, the director of intellectual capital listed the following types of non-financial measures that helped the company determine direction and predict success in creating and managing intellectual capital:

- the number of ideas customers bring to the company and how they are developed
- the number of software packages compared to the number of employees
- the number of people tied into the Internet system
- the amount of networking done between customers and employees
- the number of good ideas produced
- the level of education or training for company employees
- the number of good ideas exchanged between two key departments
- turnover and retention figures
- the number of patents granted or articles published

Process: Processes are fundamental to most organizational changes. They involve collecting the right inputs, activities, and outputs and organizing them in a meaningful manner via policy and procedure to ensure success in knowledge management capabilities. The key elements of this process enabler include:

- Systematic identification, collection, storage, retrieval, and dissemination tools for knowledge management
- Ethical knowledge gathering mechanisms
- A process for capturing the 'best practices' and 'lessons learned' from past knowledge management experiences

Merck, a pharmaceutical company, funded basic genetic research. To discover more about DNA Merck openly published its research results. This practice was highly unusual in a very competitive industry where most new knowledge in basic research is considered proprietary and confidential. The company expected that by sharing ideas and new knowledge with others in the industry, it would accelerate its own research process. Merck has discovered that this "open policy" increased the value of their research database while competitors' DNA research banks, which were kept confidential, dropped in value.

British Petroleum (BP) believes in the value of capturing tacit knowledge. The company, which is organizationally very flat for its size encourages employees to exchange information on an informal basis. It has also created a record of all the people in the firm who have specific kinds of knowledge, making it easier to locate experts on an as-needed basis.

In 1980, the U.S. Army founded its National Training Center. Here Army personnel could fight realistic "battles," with one group of soldiers being the "enemy." A clear learning from these battles was the need for quick and decisive after-action reviews and the speedy distribution of the lessons learned that result from these reviews. One outgrowth was the establishment of the Center for Army Lessons Learned (CALL). CALL collects, codifies, and disseminates lessons and makes sure the lessons are applied promptly. For example, in the Gulf War it was discovered that problems of "friendly fire" casualties had been recognized over two years before but had been disregarded. Since then, the Army has focused on the application of lessons learned. This attitude has proved useful: after the 1994 invasion of Haiti, CALL interviewed the soldiers about their experiences during this action. CALL produced scenarios that units might encounter in the future, and in the six months following, troops did encounter almost all of those scenarios. The Army's attention to lessons-learned policies paid off tremendously when U.S. forces were sent to Bosnia in 1995. Lessons learned in the field were continually sent to CALL, which organized and studied them, and e-mailed them back to the field. Every 72 hours, CALL sent new lessons, such as, "Be careful of snow-covered roads that have no tracks because they may be mined." This system has saved many lives.

Exhibit 12-1 – Organizational Knowledge Management Model
Source: Arthur Andersen and the American Productivity and Quality Center

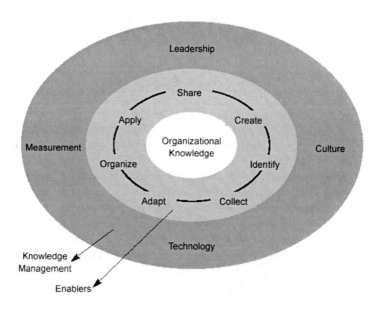

Chapter Thirteen: Communicating Results

So once all the analysis has been done, you've mapped your own process and you've compared to the best companies, you've prepared action plans so what next?   The key is to communicate results.   Although touched upon when explaining the performance improvement methodology, this chapter discusses the finer points of communicating results.

Constant communications ensures that information is flowing so adjustments can be made and so all stakeholders are aware of what has been done and what needs to be done.

Below are five key reasons why you should communicate the results of your performance improvement initiative:

1. ***Performance improvement action plans and suggestions are pointless without communication.***
    Communication is the catalyst to enable upstream and downstream feedback so that the next step, implementation can take place expeditiously. Communication at a minimum creates a sense of awareness and urgency. It creates closure to a period of intense resource allocation where physical, financial and human resources were exerted to understand a process, pinpoint deficiencies and root them out. So failure to communicate that properly lessens the impact of the performance improvement project and is a wasteful use of the organizations resources.

2. ***Communication is essential to implementation.***
    The quality and timeliness of communication is critical to enabling performance improvement to move from the drawing board to the shop floor.   Many performance improvement projects end up as expensive binders, collecting dust, in a manager's office.   They are the result of a flavor of the month initiative that goes nowhere.

    A major reason why communication is so important is because it is during these communications that implementation resources are rounded up to move the improvement initiative forward.

3. ***Communication explains resource allocation.***
    If resources were allocated to a performance improvement initiative, communication explains what was done with those resources. Communication allows the project team to explain the contributions they have made. The goal should be to make sure the stakeholders understand the extent of the team's contributions and explain any ambiguous or complex issues in the process.

4. ***Communication is sensitive.***
   Be sensitive when communicating results. People, politics, ego's and jobs may be at stake. Be objective when communicating results. Be independent when communicating results. Avoid any flip remarks or remarks that pass judgment on others.

5. ***Communication requires knowing your audience.***
   If you are communicating your results to senior managers the method and type of information you disseminate may be quite different than when you are communicating results to staff. Planning and effort are necessary to make sure the audience receives the information it needs, in the proper format, and at the proper time. Details related to scope and media will differ dramatically from one group to another. Be sure to understand your target audience prior to communicating results.

Regardless of the audience, message or medium, some general principles should guide your communication. These are as follows:

- Timely communication

  In performance improvement initiatives it is always better to over communicate than under communicate. To the extent your project plans can build in communication checkpoints the better. When your project reaches a critical milestone, that is a communication opportunity. When your project takes an unplanned turn of events, that is a communication opportunity. Understand the circumstances that dictate communication. Think about whether or not the audience should have knowledge of a certain chain of events, if they should, you should communicate it.

- Targeted communication

  The most effective presentations are tailored to a specific group. Customize the communication to the interests, needs, and expectations of the target audience. For high level managers, executive summaries, more concise overviews, and brief action plan statements with a focus on next steps is desirable. With more tactical folks, getting into the details is important. Drilling down into the findings and the specifics of the action steps and implementation resources is desired.

- Communication delivery

  Different media are desirable for different circumstances. The table below, mentioned earlier in the book is a good way to understand the varying delivery approaches for different audiences.

Type of strategy	When to use this strategy	What should be accomplished
Workshop	-intent to immediately implement the change -participants are motivated and bought into the concept of change	-present proposed changes and resulting benefits -decide on next steps (goals, timelines, and accountable roles)
Focus Group	-implementation not immediate -motivation and buy-in are needed	-present proposed changes and resulting benefits -discuss and consider the results and ramifications of change -determine next steps (move forward with implementation or not)
Formal Presentation	-implementation not immediate -motivation and buy-in needed -a later date for focus group or workshop	-debrief project accomplishments -present proposed changes and resulting benefits - determine next steps (move forward with implementation or not)
Internal Communication	-finding documentation of findings and conclusions	-to create awareness that this phase of the project has concluded

- Objective, unbiased communication

When communicating results it is vital to credibility to maintain objectivity and independence. Separate fact from fiction. It is when opinions and unsupported beliefs are presented that controversy arises. Don't get sidetracked with debates about opinions. Report the facts. Report observable, verifiable, quantifiable facts that will carry more weight than statements of sensationalism.

- Consistent communication

If you set a schedule for timely communication, keep the media, format, and method of communication consistent. For example, if you have been doing weekly updates don't just stop without any notification. Also, if you communicate weekly via a conference call, try and keep it that way versus switching to a newsletter mid way through. Finally, if you have been reporting both positive and negative (and I hope you do to be honest and objective) continue to do that so stakeholders are not misled.

- Communicate specific examples

To the extent you can be specific in your communication with examples, case studies, testimonials, quotes or specific data points your points will elevate in credibility. If you can reference specific examples, bring in an expert, or refer to hard data to support your observations you will have a smoother time with communications and find they are less likely to be questioned.

To ensure the above principles are followed, use a formal checklist to ensure communication is systematic, timely, and well-planned. Below is an outline for the major steps in your communication checklist:

1. Analyze need for communication.
2. Plan the communication.
3. Select the audience.
4. Develop information.
5. Select media.
6. Present information.
7. Analyze reactions.

Step 1 – Analyze the need for communication

This is an important step. This is where you outline the reasons for the communication. Below is a list of major reasons why communication may be necessary.

- To secure approval and buy-in for the recommendations and action plan.
- To obtain financial, physical, and human resources to implement the recommendations and action plan.
- To gain support from key stakeholders for recommendations and findings.
- To secure agreement on the issues, solutions and resources.
- To build credibility for the project outcomes and suggestions.
- To reinforce the methodology and processes used in the performance improvement project.
- To create a sense of urgency for change in the process under investigation in the performance improvement initiative.
- To prepare those affected by the change for the action steps that will need to be implemented.
- To enhance results throughout the project so that future feedback as the project progresses is improved.
- To show a complete set of results and outcomes from the project. This is typically your final presentation that is a culmination of the entire project and all of the minor communications along the way.
- To underscore the importance of the objectives of the project.
- To explain the techniques and tools used to execute the project.
- To stimulate desire in participants to get involved and stay involved in the project.
- To market future performance improvement initiatives.
- To communicate the completion of a major milestone during the project.
- To communicate an unexpected change in the project.

Step 2 – Plan the communication

If you fail to plan, you plan to fail. This step ensures you are thinking about a successful communication. Key questions that need to be planned for are the following:

- What will be communicated? Are you communicating a summary of the entire project, an event milestone, an emergency deviation from the project plan? Regardless, think through what is communicated and have an agenda for the major points for the communication.
- When will the communication occur? Timeliness is essential. As stated, having regular communications can prevent having to organize an emergency meeting every time something slightly off target occurs.
- How will the information be communicated? Written documents, face-to-face meetings, collaborative focus groups? Each has its right moment. Determine which you will use.
- Where will the communication take place? Think about convenience and perception. If it is important to be at the stakeholders place of business go there. If it is more convenient and less costly to do a virtual meeting do that.
- Who will communicate the information? Whether it is a team member, the process champion or the project manager, the person must be credible and knowledgeable of the issues.
- Who is the target audience? Determine which audience gets regular communications and which will get a communication only when appropriate.
- What are the resulting actions of the communication? Identify what the next steps are as a result of the communication. If it is simply an update there may not be specific actions but it is important to think through what you want from the communication.

Step 3 – Select the Audience

For each communication, ask yourself the following questions about the audience:

- Are they interested in the project?
- Do they really want to receive a communication on the project?
- What has already been promised to them in regard to the communication?
- What is the appropriate timing of the communication?
- Is the audience familiar to the audience?
- What is the preference as to how this audience would like to receive communication?
- Do they know the project team very well?

- Do you think they will find the results threatening?

Your customer or client is the most important target audience. This may be the internal group that championed or commissioned the performance improvement initiative or an external organization hiring you as a consultant. With this audience, the best advice is to be prepared and be organized. Credibility is very important with this audience.

Another audience that is important are department managers. These folks may be personally impacted by changes. With this audience, you want to get support and buy in and try and bring to your side champions of the project that can help when it comes to implementation.

The staff folks directly affected by the changes cannot be overlooked either. Throughout the performance improvement initiative, the team should have involved these employees along the way. This will help when it comes to any significant communications. With this audience, you don't want to surprise them or threaten them in any way. You want their support and assistance in helping with implementation details.

Step 4 – Develop Information

This is the point in which you consolidate your findings in an articulate, concise manner. This requires skill because you may have been collecting information for several weeks or even months and trying to pull out the most important points can be challenging.

Because our methodology for continuous improvement had defined steps and phases, it is advisable to arrange a formal communication around those phases so as to ensure you have completeness in your communication. Wrapped around the methodology may be an executive summary, background information, objectives, overview of the methodology, conclusion, and next steps.

Below is a brief outline with explanations for each area.

Executive Summary

This is a brief overview of the entire report explaining the purpose of the project, the methods to research, the issues, and significant conclusions and recommendations. This section is designed for individuals who do not need the details but just the finer points of the project.

Background Information

This section presents a general description of the project. It is a mini historical timeline of events that led to the culmination of the performance improvement project itself. Information detailing problems or deficiencies and how those were uncovered are presented here. Also a good description of the process under study and the problem itself are documented here.

Objectives

This section documents the objectives of the performance improvement project. It answers the question as to why the project was initiated. For example, if the objective of a project is to cut the cycle time to close the books in the accounting department from 2 weeks to 1 week than that should be clearly articulated here.

Overview of the Methodology

The methodology you chose is up to you. Whether it is the one presented in this book, or Six Sigma or a hybrid model you developed explain it here. A brief paragraph or two on the methodology, its origins, its usage and its acceptability in the marketplace are a way to build credibility in your work.

Methodology Steps

Regardless of the methodology you use to conduct your performance improvement project, explain it here. In this book we presented a methodology that had 6 major steps. Let's review those again.

1. Identify the need. Explain how you selected this process, what the composition of the project team was, key milestones and project management guidelines.

2. Map the process. Explain the steps that were undertaken to document your understanding of the existing process. Identify the tools you used, the personnel you spoke to, and summarize the data you gathered.

3. Research alternative solutions. Explain the internal and external sources you used to analyze best practices. Include a rationale for choosing these benchmark partners or research sources. Summarize the major findings and creative insights that this research brought to bear on the problem at hand.

4. Document gaps. Explain the significant variances between the current process and best practices. Organize the gaps in a meaningful manner.

For example, gaps could be organized by priority or risk sensitivity, by cost to implement, or by ease of implementation.

5. Adapt action steps. Explain the action plans. Each action plan should be separately numbered with its own unique set of talking points. Be sure to explain any barriers or enablers necessary to make the action plan feasible. Organize them in a similar manner to the gap documentation.

6. Measure and monitor. Explain the manner in which you intend to monitor this process going forward. Document the performance measures you will put in place to ensure the process stays on track in the future.

Conclusions

This section presents conclusions based on results. It is another way to summarize the recommendations and action steps. It is more bullet point in design and uses more concise statements and terminology.

Next Steps

This section communicates what you want to take place as a result of presenting this report. If the next step is to have a meeting on the implementation of your findings then state that is the next step. Perhaps the next step is a resource allocation discussion on the funding of the action steps. Think about what you want to happen from the creation of a document like this. Articulate that in this section.

Step 5 – Select Media

In addition to a formal report, several options are available to present your findings. Below are some creative ideas regarding media.

Staff meetings: These are great for progress reviews and updates. These are good forums to discuss ideas before presenting to higher-level people. This group makes a good sounding board.

Manager meetings: These are updates of higher-level issues. Specific discussion about certain findings or action steps that have or will affect their department is the focal point.

Focus groups: This is another way to get open feedback about ideas on the table for discussion. You just want to avoid individuals monopolizing the discussion or too much diversity in the ranks in the room as it may be more difficult to be frank and honest.

Best practice meetings: These are updates to communicate success. Examples, cases, testimonials are presented here to add credibility to your project and keep the momentum strong.

Newsletters: The project team may prepare a brief newsletter to document their progress. It could be disseminated via email. A typical newsletter for a performance improvement project may have an update on the project plan, any significant or interesting findings, any lessons learned, any quick wins, and any examples, cases or testimonials. Finally, a look forward at work that is upcoming regarding the project is appreciated.

Case Studies: These are written accounts of the testimonials from others of what they did, how they did it, and the results they achieved. A formal write-up in the form of a case study provided to you from internal and external sources can lend credibility to your project. See examples of many case studies in the back of this book.

Step 6 – Present Information

The biggest challenge is in the delivery of the information. Once it is prepared and the media chosen, you still have to present it. Below are some tips for successful presentation, based on the work of Peter Block in his book *Flawless Consulting.*

- Communicate quickly. Good or bad, get news out as soon as possible.
- Simplify the data. Condense the detail into manageable knowledge chunks your audience will absorb easier.
- Examine roles in the feedback situation. Understand who is giving feedback and why.
- Use negative data constructively. Don't use condescending or patronizing remarks to present negative data. For example, instead of saying "the sales group is a poor performer when it comes to forecasting," say something like "the sales group has an opportunity for improvement in the forecasting area."
- Use positive data with conservatism. Try not to get overly optimistic or extrapolate a positive finding. For example, if your research showed that your organization was performing well compared to other world-class companies, you should definitely state that as an objective finding but not embellish or extrapolate that to the entire process or the organization as a whole.
- Choose language carefully. Concise, simple, straightforward. Be focused and descriptive but not judgmental, complex or lengthy.
- Ask for reactions. If you are not getting any questions or comments ask for them.

- Ask for suggestions. If no one suggests any ideas as a result of your presentation, throw a few of your own out and get reaction. Or directly ask your audience for ideas.
- Secure agreement and buy in. Use the forum as a way to get support and champions for your cause.
- Keep feedback short. Don't let a person's comment or question sidetrack the meeting. Others may tune out. Never feel afraid to take it offline if it gets too detailed for everyone else.
- If you don't know, be honest. You may have a question asked you just don't know the answer to. That's okay. The best answer is "I don't know the answer to that without all of my notes in front of me. Please allow me to go back and review my notes and I will get back to you shortly."

Step 7- Analyze Reactions

At times reaction to a communication can be very easy to interpret. You will or won't get buy in and support. However, at times the audiences reaction is harder to gauge. Try and have project team members attending such meetings to pay attention to the audience. Monitor nonverbal gestures, oral remarks, written comments, or indirect actions that reveal how the communication was received.

Always ask for questions and comments. Try and record and tabulate the positive and negative reactions for later review.

If you are significantly concerned about the reaction and cannot gauge it indirectly, conduct a quick survey of the audience by disseminating a brief questionnaire to determine how well the audience understood what was presented, how practical they felt the suggestions were, and how supportive they are of the changes you propose.

Hopefully, with proper analysis, future communications can be improved and the current project can be better positioned.

Summary

We have spent considerable time on the communications process. Communication is critical to the success of the performance improvement initiative. It requires significantly more thought than most people realize. If done properly, the project team can truly educate and win over champions for their cause. If improperly done, the project team can have their project move in the wrong direction or cut short altogether.

Chapter Fourteen: Measuring Results

It is not uncommon for management to want to know if the benefits of a performance improvement initiative outweighed its costs. By this I am suggesting you be prepared to demonstrate an ROI on your improvement initiative.

The business case for ROI is that it is a formula for measuring results against the costs that were expended in pursuit of those results. To management, ROI is a bottom line indicator that can prove or disprove the value of a performance improvement project.

In finance, for example, measuring strategic investments is quite common. ROI analysis, along with other financial models such as Economic Value Added (EVA) or the Gordon Growth Model help the organization determine if the resource allocation was appropriate. Table 14-1 illustrates these methods in slightly more detail.

If management knocking on your door for an ROI is not enough, below are some common reasons why it is beneficial to compute an ROI on your performance improvement project.

- Customer demands. The question, "How do I know this will pay off?" is commonly asked by internal or external customers of performance improvement projects. Being able to add a credible way of answering this question is important.
- Resource allocation. As you compete within your organization for scarce financial, physical, and human resources, it is advantageous to show the actual contribution of an initiative in monetary terms. This will increase your likelihood of obtaining additional resources for future projects.
- Benchmarking. If you have done more than one performance improvement initiative, an ROI comparison analysis can help you determine the extent to which these projects were successful.
- Demonstrate value. More often than not, you are on the hook to prove yourself. It is no longer just acceptable to improve a process, rather, you are often asked to demonstrate the improvement in quantifiable, monetary terms. This exercise puts the performance improvement team on the hook for demonstrating value. An ROI exercise may help address this need.
- The spirit of improvement. Process improvements are undertaken with the overriding goal of always getting better at what you do. The quest to be world class, or at least better than you have been is important in a performance improvement initiative. Rounding that

out with an exercise such as ROI, to conclude your project is keeping with the mantra of continuous improvement.

It is important to note, that ROI is not the only way to measure the worth of your performance improvement initiative. Yes, if done correctly, it can be a credible approach, but it can sometimes be complex and time consuming. Below are some ways you can measure the value of your performance initiative.

- Qualitative feedback. This can be formally or informally documented. Essentially you talk to others and ask them how the process has changed and made their lives better. Document their reactions to the changes and the benefits that have resulted. It is also important to document the challenges they have faced as well.
- Case studies, quotes, examples. These are salient, credible ways of 'marketing' the outcomes of your project. A solid set of formally prepared documents that are easy to read helps you sell your business case easier.
- Quantitative improvements. Positive trends that can be isolated directly to the work you have done are also ways to prove the value of your project. In this instance, you are less concerned with the cost and more so with the benefit or business results that drove your performance improvement initiative. For example, if your goal was to reduce the cycle time to close the books in your accounting department from 2 weeks to 1 week, a clear reference to this achievement is a viable way of summing up your projects success.
- Best practices. Put together a matrix that address the 'best practices' you have implemented to improve the process. If presented appropriately, you can show your progression to world-class performance via the best practices you have adapted into your process.
- Cultural change. Sometimes, a performance improvement project results in a cultural shift that is more important than the process change itself. For example, if your department becomes more cohesive as a team, more passionate about their work, and more sensitive to business risk as a result of the project, that in and of itself is a valuable example of why the project is successful and should be duly noted.
- Process change. The clear point of a performance improvement project is to improve a process that was deemed problematic. Demonstration of a side by side prior vs. present process is a great way to show the areas where you made specific improvements. Highlighting the rationale and benefits further reinforces your case.
- Low hanging fruit. Often larger, more long-term action items like implementation of a new technology platform don't provide much immediate demonstration of value. Because of this it is often

helpful to document the small process changes that have already been done that caused quick wins. For example, a controller at a health care organization was able to reduce his payment cycle time by simply re-routing some of the documentation between facilities. His office got the paperwork quicker so he could pay bills on time. As simple as it sounds, that resulted in less late payments, happier vendors, and better cash flow management at the company. The more you can document your quick wins helps you keep momentum alive and support strong for the longer term action steps.

- Project management. Demonstration of value also comes in the form of how you manage the project itself. Believe it or not, project management is a process in and onto itself. If you are able to demonstrate that you utilized resources effectively and efficiently to accomplish your objectives that demonstrates your ability to be trusted with additional resource allocations.

The ROI Process - Background

In the event you are asked to compute the return on investment from your performance improvement project, you'll need to understand ROI and develop a rationale approach to calculating your ROI.

One standard that has become accepted in many circles, particularly in the human capital space is the ROI Process Model by Jack J. Phillips, Ph.D. The ROI Process is a comprehensive way to plan for an ROI calculation, collect data, analyze the data, and report credible ROI calculations to management. The ROI Process created by Phillips has been applied in many environments from training and development to consulting and project management. It has been recognized as a credible, exhaustive approach to validating the benefits of initiatives relative to their costs.

This section will take a high level look at Phillips ROI Process. Please see Table 14-2 for additional books by Dr. Jack J. Phillips on this process.

The first step in thinking about calculating a return on your performance improvement project is to understand what you're getting into. Phillips describes ten essential criteria for an effective ROI process. Let's look at each of these below:

1. Simplicity. The ROI process cannot have complex formulas and complicated steps. Not only does this increase the cost and time to conduct an ROI exercise, it confuses your audience.
2. Economical. The process should become an extension to every performance improvement project you do. It should not add significant

dollars and time to your existing performance improvement project budget and project plan.

3. Credibility. The methods you use to compute an ROI must be logical, objective, and reasonable. You will use these to create the business case to your stakeholders that your project added value. As a result, credibility is essential.

4. Theoretically sound. The steps you use must be based on generally accepted practices. Because this process has been used by a wide variety of practitioners, it has proven itself as theoretically sound.

5. Isolate benefits. The process must be able to pinpoint how the performance improvement initiative added value when compared to other influencing factors. For example, if sales increase by 10%, was it a result of the changes you implemented from your performance improvement initiative or was it external factors such as a competitor going out of business and your company being the lucky benefactor?

6. Broad applicability. The process must be able to have a broad application so that as you do more and more performance improvement initiatives, they can be benchmarked and compared against each other using a common approach to measuring success. For example if you calculate an ROI of 85% on a project designed to reduce suppliers in the supplier base, is that good or bad? Without a relative benchmark of other performance improvement projects you cannot be certain. Thus it is important to deploy a process that can be applied broadly.

7. Flexibility. The process must have the ability to be applied on both a historic, post-project basis as well as a forecasting, future oriented basis. Sometimes, you may want to forecast what a possible ROI would be prior to undertaking the performance improvement initiative or as an input to determining how much funds and other resources you need.

8. Data compatible. The process must be applicable with all types of data. The performance improvement methodology we have discussed in this book collects both quantitative and qualitative data. The process of calculating an ROI must consider both.

9. Cost inclusive. One half of the ROI equation is the cost factors. The ROI process you use must be able to organize the costs of the performance improvement project in a manner that is logical and reasonable.

10. Successful. You must use a model that has a proven history of success. Often models are dreamed up in classrooms but not applied. An effective ROI process that managers will find credible is one that gets the results expected.

A few definitions that should be taken into account will help frame your basic understanding of ROI. Four common outputs result from the ROI Process we will describe. They are all variation on each other but depict your return from different vantage points. Below is a high level definition of each.

Benefit to Cost Ratio

Formula: Project Benefits / Project Costs

This is simply the ratio of benefits that accrue from the changes you have made and action steps you have implemented relative to the costs incurred to make those changes. For example, if, as a result of a performance improvement project, you were able to save costs in the accounts payable department specific to your suggested action steps to the tune of $25,000, and the resources expended on the project were $5,000, benefit to cost ratio would be 5 to 1. This implies that the benefits were 5 times the cost.

ROI Dollars

Formula: Project Benefits – Project Cost

This is merely the net benefits. It is what you have left over in value above and beyond the cost incurred to achieve that value. In the accounts payable example above where your benefits are $25,000 and your costs are $5,000, the ROI is $20,000. This implies that the net gain from the project was a benefit to the organization of $20,000 that would not have been realized had you not done the project.

ROI Percentage

Formula: {(Project Benefits – Project Costs)/ Project Costs} x100

This is simply the ROI expressed as a percentage. The ROI percentage in our accounts payable example using the same $25,000 benefit and $5,000 cost is 300%. This implies that the benefits of the project exceeded the costs by 300%, a positive investment in the project.

Payback Period

Formula: Project Cost / Project Benefits

This is a time-based way of expressing the ROI. It is the number of years and months to recover the initial investment. In our example above, if the costs were $5,000 and the benefits $25,000 than the payback period would be .20 meaning it would take 2.4 months to payback the costs of the project with breakeven break even benefits.

In addition to the definitions, it is important to understand the benefits and challenges to conducting an ROI study on your performance improvement project. Below is a helpful short list of each.

Benefits to an ROI study
- Demonstrate value. It is a quantifiable way of demonstrating the contributions the project improvement team has made to a process and to the organization as a whole.
- Benchmark comparisons. Projects are often hard to compare because of their diversity and differences in implementation. A consistent ROI process will help understand which projects or types of improvements returned a greater benefit to the organization versus others. It's like analyzing returns on stocks for investment purposes. It is common practice to compare one stock to another rather than look at each in isolation.
- Forecasting tool. A preliminary ROI can help you forecast resource requirements for the project or decide if this project as opposed to other priorities is the best allocation of firm resources.
- Fulfills a need. Currently there is a gap between what the project team delivers and management expectations. Quite often, management expects not only to have a successful project but quantifiable proof of that success. An ROI will help close this gap.

Challenges to an ROI study
- Resources. Financial, physical and human resources must by expended to produce a credible ROI. Hopefully it is not more than the project itself! Typically, an ROI process not add more than 5% to the overall project budget.
- Competency. Computing an ROI is not unlike executing your performance improvement project. It requires skill and knowledge. If the project team members lack such skill and knowledge this exercise can be a frustrating experience and you increase the risk of an error in calculation of the ROI. Training and books are available that dive deep into this area and are highly recommended for personnel who frequently do performance improvement projects.
- Negative ROI's. Nobody likes to compute an ROI only to find out that the costs exceeded the benefits. But, that is a reality. Because of this performance improvement practitioners are sometimes skeptical about an ROI.
- Skepticism. The belief that an ROI on a project is a fruitless venture is a hard hurdle to overcome. Management and project teams may both feel an ROI would not be meaningful and is a non-value added activity. However, if you apply a methodology that is credible you can overcome this obstacle.

The ROI Process – Methodology

Now that I have explained the basics of the ROI Process, let's take a closer look at it. Recall that we will provide a high level overview but you may obtain additional resources that dive deeper. Table 14-2 is available as a starting point for those additional resources.

Exhibit 14-1 showcases the ROI Process Methodology by Jack J. Phillips. The model is a step-by-step approach to tackle the ROI question. Each step is briefly described below.

Evaluation Purposes:

The initial step of computing an ROI on a performance improvement project is to collect some data. This is typically done through evaluations. The purpose of the evaluation is to do the following:

- Validate if the changes made to the process worked.
- Formally document the cost and benefits associated with the process improvements.
- To gather the necessary qualitative and quantitative information to prove value.
- To establish the benchmarking baselines that can be used to compare other projects against and to set performance goals and hurdle rates for future projects.

Evaluation Instruments:

Just as you use performance improvement tools to collect data to map a process or gather best practices, you can use similar tools to gather information about the outcomes of the performance improvement projects. Below are a few of the more popular tools to use pre and/or post project to help in calculating the ROI.

- Surveys/questionnaires
  Advantages:
  -quick way to get quantitative data
  -obtain structured responses

  Disadvantages:
  -self-reported data
  -cannot gather the greatest qualitative feedback
  -not good for sensitive issues

- Interviews
  Advantages:
  -great way to obtain anecdotal information, quotes, and examples
  -good for more sensitive matters

  Disadvantages:
  -very time consuming and resource intensive

-cannot gather hard, quantitative information

- Focus groups
  Advantages:
  -good for gathering consensus
  -good for networking, sharing, formulating best practices

  Disadvantages:
  -hard to coordinate
  -groupthink can ruin its intended purpose
  -a few can monopolize the conversation

- Observation
  Advantages:
  -first hand verification
  -used to reinforce other data (interview, survey)

  Disadvantages:
  -time consuming and resource intensive
  -behavior often different if being observed

- Pre and Post performance measurement
  Advantages:
  -quantifiable, comparable data
  -excellent tool to validate change

  Disadvantages:
  -tainted data can ruin comparability
  -often difficult to gather or collect

Evaluation Levels

In the training chapter we learned about the Five Levels of Training Evaluation. If appropriate to your ROI business case that you are building, you can use them to structure a balanced scorecard within your analysis. Let's review the Five Levels once more:

Level One: Measuring Results and Identifying Planned Actions
In this case, you might be able to point out the elements during the course of the project that resulted in:
- Satisfaction with the project team
- Satisfaction with the deliverables/results
- Satisfaction with the methods used to reach results

Level Two: Measuring Learning

In this case, you might want to point out how the project increased the knowledge and skill set of the affected employees. If the employees learned new information that will help them be more effective on their jobs that is a value added component of the project.

Level Three: Assessing Application of the Program on the Job

In this case, you would want to point out specific areas where the process has been changed as a result of the performance improvement action steps and ideas. For example, if the project resulted in a manual task that is now automated, or a new internal control put in place to significantly reduce risk, these are items that can be pinpointed as value added contributions from the project.

Level Four: Identifying Business Results from the Program

In this case, you would provide evidence of the pre project and post project performance measures that have changed as a result of the performance improvement initiative. If prior to the project inventory turnover was 5 turns a year and subsequent to changes your team made, the turns are now at 8 per year that is a valuable piece of information to point out to senior management.

Level Five: Calculating Return on Investment

In this case you are taking it all the way. You are monetizing the benefits and comparing against the costs. This is the ultimate way to showcase value and it is the answer to a common gap between how management wants to evaluate the project and how the project team has historically evaluated the project.

Evaluation Timing

Timing is important. As a part of most performance improvement projects you collect data to understand the process and then measure again after implementation of action plans. If you can identify what aspects of your project might be used to prove value after the project or for the purpose of an ROI calculation you can build that into the project itself so it becomes more seamless and integrated.

In addition, you should be cognizant of the short term and long term measurements that must be taken to prove value. For example, if you have improved the process of developing leaders in your organization, short term effects could be measured by an identification of the right future leaders in the organization versus long term effects could be a measurement of these employees effectively demonstrating leadership skills such as coaching, mentoring, communications, and team building. Just be aware that not all outcomes of a performance improvement initiative can be felt immediately.

Collecting Data

As discussed earlier, there are a variety of ways to collect data, each have advantages and disadvantages. If you can consider how you will use data you collect during the performance improvement initiative to later prove its value you can kill two birds with one stone. For the most part, you will find that the data you are collecting serves a dual purpose: first it helps you on your project by understanding the existing process or a benchmark partners process and secondly it can be used to support the value that was added as a result of the initiative.

Below are some examples.

Surveys/Questionnaires:
While preparing a survey to disseminate to other organization's accounts payable process for benchmarking purposes, you ask for data on specific performance measures such as cost to process an invoice, voucher processing error rates, and percent of three way matches. These figures not only help you compare your AP process to the benchmark partners, but for ROI purposes, if you can later monetize the benefit of improving these measures and making yours more in alignment with a world-class organization, it sets the stage for the ROI.

Interviews:
While conducting an interview with the payroll manager during a project to improve the payroll processing function you determine that a prior management cost savings initiative helped cut costs in the department but in doing so increased business risk. You implement internal controls to mitigate that business risk significantly reducing the threat of a potentially costly set of errors valued in the millions. When preparing your ROI analysis, you can use this information to compare against the small cost of conducting the payroll analysis.

Observation:
While working on a project to improve customer service you listen to customer service representatives field live calls in the call center. You realize that numerous calls are being received regarding vague and misleading contract terms and conditions that place the representatives on the defensive with each call. Upon further investigation you realize improvements need to be made not within the customer service area but within the contract and customer sign up process. Post project measurements reveal a drop in calls related to this issue and an increase in customer satisfaction. When demonstrating ROI, be sure and document this improved business result as an outcome of your project.

Focus Groups:
A focus group was held to brainstorm about potential improvement opportunities that could be made to increase employee retention. Several ideas are mentioned such as performance based pay incentives, flextime, and childcare assistance. You do a cost/benefit analysis of these ideas and realize that if implemented the company could increase retention by implementing a few of the suggestions at a manageable cost. These become part of your action plans but also a component of your value proposition when measuring results and outcomes of your project.

Pre and Post Measurement:
You are attempting to increase sales over the prior years as sales had been slowing. You implement performance improvement initiatives as a result of a continuous improvement project. There is an aggressive training program to teach the sales team how to be more consultative in their sales approach. You give them new contact management systems and create a mentoring program so younger sales professionals can work closer with the seasoned experts. You collect data on sales before the changes were made and after. Sales have increased and you have isolated the reasons for this increase in large part due to your sales training program. If you tally the costs of the performance improvement initiative against the increased sales you have a decent ROI on the project to share with management.

Isolating the effects:

This is an essential step in computing an ROI or proving value from your performance improvement initiative. If you have not taken the time to factor out of your analysis those business drivers that changed the process other than the changes your team implemented, you cannot accurately attribute change (positive or negative) to your contributions with any degree of certainty.

Let's use an example to illustrate the importance of isolation. Let's say our project was designed to investigate the effectiveness of the existing sales force. Upon doing so we implement process changes such as product training, consultative selling protocols, and an advanced contact management system. We measure sales prior to our changes and they are at $5 million. We then measure sales subsequent to the completion of these changes and they are now at $6 million. If an isolation exercise is not done, you might conclude that your performance improvement project can be credited with a $1 million dollar sales increase. By the way, it can work in the reverse direction as well had the sales decreased.

Let's say that upon further investigation, you find that a big competitor of yours has pulled out of selling in certain sales territories. By default, your organization was the only logical supplier to customers in those territories and gained that business with relative ease. You estimate that the value from that event happening was an increase in sales of approximately $750,000. Thus, you know from this simple bit of research that at a minimum, $750,000 of the new revenue cannot be credited to your improvement initiative.

So, how does one go about isolating the effects of business results back to the performance improvement initiative? The following strategies have been utilized by organizations to assist in this process.

- Control group. Compare a group that had the changes implemented to one that did not. For example, if you made changes to your employee recruitment program, you might implement the changes first using a pilot. Pilots are a way to crawl then walk then run when it comes to the roll out of action plans. The pilot group is also the perfect opportunity to set up an analysis versus the control group. Measure the effects of the recruitment efforts of those in the pilot group versus those still operating as usual. If properly implemented, this is an effective way to isolate the effects of the performance improvements.
- Estimates. Although not scientific it is often a reasonable and rationale approach. Using estimation, those affected by the changes, their supervisors, or senior management are asked to determine what factors contributed the most to the outcomes of those changes. In the example of the sales force increase in sales, we could have asked the sales force professionals and the director of sales to complete an isolation matrix. The matrix would list several factors that can lead to a change in sales. Each respondent then provides feedback as to the percent of impact they felt each factor had and their confidence in their estimate. This data is then aggregated or weighted to arrive at an estimated isolation. See Table 14-3 for an example of an isolation matrix for the sales increase. In the example, the performance improvement team specifically implemented the contact management system, product training, and consultative sales procedures.
- Experts. Allow an independent expert to come in and estimate the impact the project had on the results it supposedly produced. This is more difficult to do if the person does not have good familiarity with the specific situation.

Converting Data to Monetary Value

An ROI, based on the formulas we discussed, requires a monetized benefit to offset the costs. To do this we need to convert the isolated impact we calculated in the prior step to a monetary value. Like isolation, several strategies can be deployed to convert benefits to monetary terms.

- Output data. Convert this data to profit contribution or cost savings. This is done based on the output data's contribution to profit or cost reduction.
- Wage data. For productivity gains, wages and benefits are used as a proxy or estimator. For example, if productivity improved due to an automation tactic put in place, use the wages and benefits as the monetization factor for the time employees no longer spend manually doing the tasks now automated.
- Historical costs. Cost data can be used to establish specific value for an improvement.
- Internal and external experts. Experts can be used to estimate the value in monetary terms. This is a model often used in the legal field where expert testimony is used to place a value on litigation claims.
- External databases. Research, government and industry databases usually provide information for certain data elements. For example, you can find research on the cost to recruit, hire and retain a new employee from external databases.
- Participants. Let those affected by the change estimate its value. In this case you need specific definitions and instructions for the participants so it is done consistently.
- Supervisors and senior managers. Let these individuals or groups estimate the value. Like participant estimations, you will need definitions and instructions.

Converting data to monetary terms is often an art more than a science. You need to use reasonable assumptions to make your conversion credible. Table 14-4 provides examples of converting different data types into monetary terms.

Tabulate costs of the project

The other essential element of an ROI is the cost. Cost tabulation should be conservative and include fully loaded costs where possible. You are attempting to cost out all of the items that went into the cost of doing the performance improvement project. You need to think through what costs would not have been incurred had you not done the project at all.

Items that should be included in the costs should be divided into 1) project costs and 2) implementation costs. Project costs are the costs to conduct the original performance improvement initiative where the result is a list of action steps you recommend to improve the process. A second set of costs can then be calculated at a deeper level for the implementation of each specific action step. Your ROI can be broken out into an ROI on the performance improvement project or on each specific action item that is implemented. In either case the same types of costs should be collected.

Note that these costs are not unlike the costs of a process you are analyzing but now you are pointing it at the project!

- Fully loaded wages and benefits of the performance improvement project team or implementation team for the time they spent on the project.
- Operating expenses. Include the costs of any supplies, training, and any other locally controllable expenses that might have been incurred during or in preparation for the performance improvement project or implementation.
- Contract services. Any outside assistance (consultants, experts) or vendors utilized and their associated costs.
- Administrative and overhead costs allocated in a reasonable manner.
- Costs of travel and miscellaneous expenses incurred during the project or implementation. For example, if you traveled to a benchmark partner for a site visit that travel is included.
- Costs of any office space (rental value) the project team may have used during the course of the project or implementation.
- Fully loaded wages and benefits of employees, supervisors or senior managers who were away from normal work while participating in the project. For example, if 5 employees and 1 supervisor attended a 1-day focus group, their fully loaded wages and benefits for a day of missed work is included in the cost.

Calculate the ROI

The Return on Investment is calculated using the formulas previously outlined. Below are those formulas:

Benefit to Cost Ratio

Formula: Project Benefits / Project Costs

ROI Dollars

Formula: Project Benefits – Project Cost

ROI Percentage

Formula: {(Project Benefits – Project Costs)/ Project Costs} x100

Payback Period

Formula: Project Cost / Project Benefits

Identifying Intangible Benefits

As discussed, in addition to tangible, quantifiable measures of value derived from the project, anecdotal, softer, qualitative information is also very powerful. You should make every attempt possible to quantify benefits and compute an ROI, but recognize where it is not feasible to do so. Information that cannot be quantified should be placed into a case study, quote list, or example section of your report to ensure it receives adequate mention. This may include the following types of items that are often more challenging to convert to a quantifiable value.

- More effective teamwork
- Improved job satisfaction
- Increased customer service
- Less conflict in the workplace or with value chain partners
- Improved organizational culture
- Increased passion and commitment to process excellence

<u>Measurement Wrap Up</u>

It is important to ensure you can value your performance improvement project. The methodology explained above is a generally accepted one that has worked well at varying organizations. Other analysis does exist that is worth considering. For example, the concept of Enterprise Value Creation is a five-step framework that uses financial performance and enterprise ROI to identify and prioritize IT projects that will have the greatest impact on shareholder value. It can serve as creative insight for non-IT projects as well.

Other ROI methodologies may rely on deeper statistical analysis such as one created by Professor Don E. Schultz of Northwestern University. Specifically it is targeted to measure the ROI of advertising on sales. It uses exponential smoothing and regression analysis among other factors to compute an ROI. Although not specific to a performance improvement project it is a methodology that might be insightful.

At the end of the day, it is important to recognize that with each dollar spent on something it could have been spent on something else. When times are tight management and shareholders need to know that resource allocation is appropriate. Ken Harris, CIO of Gap Inc., summed his impressions of ROI up the best when he said "Every project has objectives; the challenge is to find ways to quantify and get commitment to the benefits that flow from achieving those objectives."

Table 14-1 Financial Models – ROI, EVA, Gordon Growth

Model	Definitions
Traditional ROI = Program Benefits / Program Costs	Incorporates traditional comparisons between all cost and benefits (direct and indirect) over a 1—year period
Economic value add	Incorporates traditional comparisons between all cost of capital and benefits (direct and indirect) over a 3-year period using discounted cash flows
Gordon Growth Model Price = Dividend / (Required return – Dividend growth)	Incorporates traditional comparisons between the expected return against the expected risk of investments over a period of time using discounted cash flows

Table 14-2 Books on the ROI Process

The Human Resources Scorecard, Jack J. Phillips, Patricia Pullium Phillips, and Ron D. Stone
The Project Management Scorecard, Jack J. Phillips, G. Lynne Snead, and Timothy W. Bothell
Return on Investment in Training and Performance Improvement Programs, Jack J. Phillips
The Consultants Scorecard, Jack J. Phillips

Table 14-3 Sales Isolation Matrix

Isolation Factor	Your Estimate (0 to 100)	Your confidence in your estimate (0 to 100)	Adjusted Estimate (Estimate x Confidence level)
Economic/industry/competitive factors	20%	60%	12%
New products or services	10%	80%	8%
Contact management system	5%	40%	2%
Product training	15%	50%	7.5%
Consultative selling procedures	20%	50%	10%
Other technology (excluding the contact management system)	0%	5%	0%
New marketing material	5%	50%	2.5%
Special promotional offers	10%	80%	8%
Change in pricing schedule	15%	30%	4.5%
Other	0%	0%	0%
Total	**100%**		

Table 14-4 Monetary Conversion Examples

Factor	Conversion Example
Revenue	50 million currently 10% desired change of 5M for a total of 55,000,000 monetized value
Cost	25 million currently in costs 5% desired change of 1.25M for a total of 23.75M monetized value
Employee Retention	This is based on turnover rates. Current turnover is 15% (assume 38 of 250 employees) and desired turnover is 10% (assume 25 of 1000) Cost for retention is based on the cost to hire a new employee. Assume cost to hire a new employee is $350 Total cost for hiring 38 employees is 13,300
Productivity	Current output is 1000 widgets a day. Desire to have 1100 a day (10% increase). If labor intensive base on annual employee compensation. If machine intensive base on annual depreciation in the machine Assume based on labor-intensive methods: Total Payroll for company is: 10,000,000 A 10% increase in productivity is a 10% benefit in work – 1,000,000
Customer Satisfaction	Percent of favorable ratings currently is 70%. Goal is to have 85% favorable ratings. Assume that the percentage is positively correlated to the customer retention rate. Thus a 15% increase in customer sat means that you retain 15% more of your customers than before. If the cost to acquire a customer is $220 for example, than a 15% increase is a savings or benefit to your organization. (benefit of that percent retained by good service) If there are currently 300 customers, then a 15% retention rate means we keep 45 customers. Use the cost per new customer (advertising or marketing costs) as a dollar proxy $220 (45) = 9,900 benefit from 15% increased customer satisfaction
Quality	Desire a 10% increase in quality. This is measured by number of defects, number of complaints, number of returns or allowances, warranty costs etc. If our example is a widget example, and we manufacture widgets, the 10% increase in quality is actually a proxy for a 10% decrease in product returned damaged or defective. If the current returns are 4% of sales, and sales are 55,000,000, then the returns are 2,200,000. This is the proxy for quality. If the goal is to decrease the returns by 10% then that is a dollar value of $220,000 less then before, that is what we are desiring to achieve.

Exhibit 14-1 The ROI Process by Jack J. Phillips

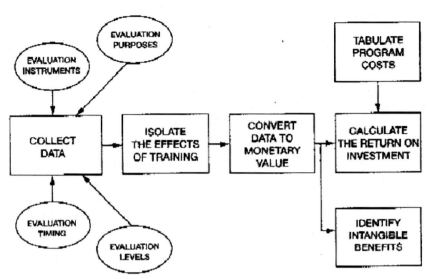

Source: Return on Investment in Training and Performance Improvement Programs, Jack J. Phillips, Gulf Publishing Company, Houston Texas, 1997, p. 25

Chapter Fifteen: Project Management

We have now discussed many tools and techniques to help you with your performance management projects.   However, without proper project management principles in place even the projects with the best of intentions can fail. This chapter focuses on some best practices in managing projects.

What is project management?

According to the Project Management Institute "a project is a temporary endeavor undertaken to achieve a particular aim. Every project has a definite beginning and a definite end. While projects are similar to operations in that both are performed by people, both are generally constrained by limited resources, and both are planned, executed and controlled, projects differ from operations in that operations are ongoing and repetitive while projects are temporary and unique."

Also, per the Project Management Institute, "according to *A Guide to the Project Management Body of Knowledge* —2000 Edition, [Project Management Institute (PMI®) December 2000], project management is the application of knowledge, skills, tools and techniques to a broad range of activities in order to meet the requirements of the particular project.

Why deploy project management practices?

Project management is used to keep focus and control over multiple tasks taking place in a compressed time period. The following are some major reasons why having a solid set of project management practices makes sense:

- **Keep things on track.** It is often challenging to manage multiple resources doing multiple tasks all at once. A solid project plan maintains order where chaos might otherwise prevail.
- **Communication tool.** When senior management, process champions and other key stakeholders check in on your project, it is often wise to show where you are at in the project plan. To this point, the project management communicates to those not involved in the trenches what is going on. To those more intimately involved it tracks their progress over time.
- **Documentation trail.** Project management results in a better documentation trail. If detailed enough, the project plan is an excellent trail of decisions that were made along the way regarding specific steps to be taken to do various tasks.
- **Prevents scope creep.** A well-run project will have a defined scope and as such scope creep is significantly less likely to occur. Often you will hear a project team member say "if it is not in the project plan it's

not in the scope of the project." The result is a focused project that does not get off track.

- **Properly defines roles and responsibilities.** Proper project management ensures that everyone knows what he or she are doing and their area of accountability.
- **Achieves commitment and buy-in.** Project management cements the project and unites the project team with a common goal through common tasks.

Tips to ensure effective project management:

Performance improvement projects can get overwhelming and that's as good of reason as any to deploy effective project management steps. The risks are just too great if a high profile project gets out of control with cost overruns, late deliverables, or fails to meet expectations. Below are some high level tips you can follow to ensure your approach to managing this project is safe and sound.

- **Diagnose the problem/assess the need.** It is at this point that you may find yourself in the position of the newly named project manager to a project you know little about. Or, you could be very close to the problem. Still, you really need to define the problem and understand the needs you are trying to reach before formally beginning to plan the tasks. We discussed the use of high-level diagnostic tools, which can be helpful if you cannot wrap your arms around the problem. Otherwise, ask high level questions about the "as is" state and what the vision is for a "should be" state. This will help you understand what the expectations of your stakeholders are for the results of this project.

- **Outline the approach to tackle the problem.** This is a way of restating the problem and the needs to ensure you understood them. But in addition to that, it is your way of putting your spin to the issue by proposing approaches to solve the problem. For example, say your boss tells you that they need to reduce cycle time to order a particular raw material essential for production. Once you understand and confirm this need, you should restate it back to your boss to confirm it, but also propose an approach to solving it. You might conclude that an evaluation of vendors that ultimately lead to the selection of a few preferred vendors that can meet your demands is the approach. You might suggest performing interviews and do a survey then benchmark results. You might also suggest analyzing historical data for past performance trends. By outlining the approach and getting buy-in on it, you have a better frame of reference to set the scope, budget, timeline and team to execute the project.

- **Set the project scope.** This is where you place finite boundaries around the process and activities you will review in your improvement project. For example, if we are trying to improve the process of collections, does it involve all customer types at all locations? The key is to try and avoid scope creep by defining the boundaries of the process early on. What activities, business units, locations, time periods, and stakeholders are to be covered in this project? Understand this before preparing a budget and timeline.

- **Prepare a project plan.** The plan explodes the scope out into tasks and subtasks. For example, on a performance improvement project you can break down the tasks into our methodology. You have already done some upfront work to Select the Process but you probably want to do some more assessment there, then follow through with the other steps. Document the 'As Is' is the next step, an activity beneath it may be to map the process, or interview the key stakeholders. Next is to determine the 'Should Be' , key steps here may include identifying benchmark partners, reviewing an industry study that was conducted, or talking with subject matter experts. Then comes your 'Gap' that is the difference between the 'As Is' and the 'Should Be'. Steps here might be to have staff team members identify the gap, then prioritize them. Following gap analysis is the adaptation of best practices. In this step, the sub-steps may be the creation of action plans, the preparation of the final presentation, issues around change management. Although my example is simple, hopefully you will see that a project plan can easily be mapped to the Performance Improvement Methodology. In a sense, it maps the methodology steps and sub steps in a formal manner and assigns those activities to team members and places a time frame around each activity.

- **Prepare a project budget.** The tip here is to be conservative. Estimate a budget for your project taking into account all the costs you can think of. For example the following costs are quite routine to include in a project budget:
  - Salaries and benefits of team members
  - Fees paid to consultants or contract labor
  - Supplies purchased for use on the project
  - Research fees to acquire access to online databases or purchase a study or periodical used in research
  - Costs associated with the purchase of analytical tools like a statistical software package, a project management software package, etc.
  - Rental or depreciation on office space and equipment
  - Training costs to arm the team with knowledge and skills to carry out the project
  - Travel costs associated with team members
  - Miscellaneous costs

- General & Admin costs. Support services costs such as duplication fees, graphic design fees, mail charges, secretarial support, etc.

- **Prepare a project timeline.** We have discussed the use of Gantt charts on the project during our chapter on performance improvement tools. In addition to a visual aide to map out the project, it is also helpful to estimate time in two ways: actual time and elapsed time. Actual time is the number of actual hours, days, weeks or months that will need to be allocated to the task. Elapsed time is the time period or duration in which the task will be accomplished. For example, for the task of interviewing key executives during the 'As Is' process you estimate it will take 2 hours to prepare interview questions, and 1 hour per executive to conduct the interview, and 2 hours to summarize the results of the interview. You will accomplish this task during the second week of the project. In this example, your actual time is 9 hours (2 in preparation, 5 in interviewing and 2 in analysis). Your elapsed time is 1 week the time period allotted to begin and complete the task. It is critical to estimate time in this manner because time periods can have multiple tasks going on at once and there may be breaks in time periods (holidays, vacation etc.) and simply showing actual time may be misleading. On the other hand just showing elapsed time is also misleading. Communicating it will take 3 months to do something without stating that it is really 80 hours (or 2 weeks) of actual time may otherwise give the impression that 100% of time is being allocated to the task for 3 solid months.

- **Construct the project team.** We have already discussed the creation of the performance improvement team when we described the performance improvement methodology. Nonetheless, the right team is an important part of project management so it is mentioned again here. Recall there is a project sponsor who initiates the project and champions the project. There is also a process owner who runs the group that is most impacted by the project scope. A facilitator is the team leader, the project manager who will carry out the tasks of the project. Finally team members are typically staff who help with the tactical aspects of the project.

Choosing the right team is important. So the below checklist of desirable skills will help you pick the write personnel for your team:

- knowledgeable in the subject area
- solid problem solving/analytical skills
- passionate and motivated about the project
- time to devote to the project
- works well in a team environment

- **Establish internal review points**. As the project manager it is important that you balance your work effort between the 'doing' and the 'reviewing.' A project manager that is doubling as a team member will ultimately put one of those roles at risk. An effective project manager delegates and empowers through appropriate coaching, mentoring and leadership. They will establish regular and formal review points with each team member upon the completion of each project step. Further, they will create an open door policy allowing for regular, informal communication when surprises might occur.

- **Create formal external communication points.** The project manager is often the representative to the external party for whom the project is being conducted. This external party could be an internal coworker or a true external, fee-paying customer. The project manager needs to always keep the client informed as to the progress of the project. Holding regular updates is advisable. You can do this through face-to-face meetings, conference calls, or published memo's or updates to the project plan. Typically the most effective approach is the regular conference call or meeting that might last half an hour or an hour just to keep the client 'in the loop.'

- **Hold-debrief sessions.** Part of improving as a project manager is to learn from your deficiencies. Holding debriefs with staff and stakeholders about performance relative to expectations can provide an invaluable source of feedback to help you improve not only on the existing project but also for future projects. Debriefs don't have to happen at the conclusion of the project. In fact, I suggest holding the 'how am I doing' conversation after the completion of significant milestones during the project.

Who is the Project Manager?

By now you see the importance of project management. So it really goes without saying that the project manager is critical to the success of your performance improvement project. The project manager must exhibit a diverse set of skills and competencies in order to be effective. Below is a brief list of critical skills that the project manager should possess:

- Coordinate schedules of multiple stakeholders
- Manage multiple items at a single time
- Discipline to follow processes, steps, and tasks to accomplish objectives
- Respected by staff and management
- Follows appropriate channels and protocols of the organization
- Anticipates problems and reacts to change

- Understands functional and technical issues
- Can 'translate' functional into technical and vice versa
- Discerns the difference between realistic versus 'perfect world' scenarios
- Effective communicator (verbal and written)
- Thinks before acting
- Leads by example, mentoring and coaching
- Fosters a climate of respect, empowerment and passion amongst the team
- Excellent negotiation skills
- Effective conflict resolution skills
- Ability to influence others without threat or coercion
- Manages time effectively
- Manages costs effectively
- Pays attention to quality in work
- Solicits feedback from others
- Gives constructive feedback to others in a timely manner
- Understands the organization and how things get done within it

The project manager wears multiple hats. They have a challenging job. They may be the babysitter, salesperson, teacher and friend in a single day. The key is to find this talented individual and give them the resources and motivation to lead a team to success!

Part II: Case Studies

The next chapters of this book will articulate a series of case studies. The case studies will help you understand how the performance improvement methodology and all of its surrounding tools and principles were used in practice.

Because I realize that many of the readers of this book come from multiple functional areas, I have selected case studies that any reader should find a positive example of creative insight. Nonetheless, they are specific to five functional areas to illustrate the use of the methodology in practice. Each case is preceded by a Pre-Case Background that discusses the process represented by the case so you have a better perspective of the functional area being improved.

Chapter Sixteen: The Supply Chain Process

Pre Case Background:

Define Process Activities

Supply chain management is the process of choosing suppliers for goods and services and managing the flows of these goods and services from inputs into outputs. Supply chain management has become increasingly important as customer demands have become customized.

Successful companies will study their supply chains to pump up performance in multiple ways. For example, Quaker Oats first examined its supply chain in the early 1990's. As a result they were able to establish better performance measures that emphasized customer needs and supplier performance. Then in 1999 Quaker took another look at the supply chain to upgrade its manufacturing and distribution capacity in North America. As a result of that project, supply chain data is easier to access and use. Their process asked critical questions such as: Where are we? Where do we need to be? How are we getting there? They used self-assessment tools to help facilitate their projects.

To some, a key piece of supply chain management is in the enabling technologies such as enterprise resource planning systems (ERP's). However, try not to get caught up in the myth that technology is the pot of gold at the end of the rainbow. Ultimately, it is the people who use the technology that improve the supply chain. Technology should be implemented in an organization that has the right structure and culture. People must possess the right motivation and attitude along with solid training and education to make technology a solid return on any supply chain's investment.

When improving your supply chain also keep in mind that both internal and external forces shape an effective supply chain. External forces like cost, market, macro economical/political, and competitive require different strategies and tactics. The key is to get creative when improving the supply chain. i2 Technologies facilitated sectorial integration by adding online modules that allow Web-enabled sharing of information vital to streamlining their supply chain.

Improvement in supply chain performance can be significant if done appropriately. Companies spend between 3-7% of revenue on supply chain activities so improvement is critical. A best practice organization with an optimized supply chain can spend 50% less on materials acquisition, meet their delivery dates 17% more often and have as much as 60% fewer inventory days than companies with average supply chains.

The goal of this study break is not to summarize the complexities of the supply chain process, but rather to provide an overview of the key components of the process, some of their activities, and some performance measures you can use to monitor and manage those sub-processes.

In my class, we discuss the key processes of the supply chain as being the following:

- Sourcing (procurement and supplier management)
- Manufacturing (production and operations)
- Warehouse management (inventory management)
- Logistics (transport goods and services)
- Order fulfillment (order management)

When I analyze a process, the first item on my to do list is to understand the components of the process. Below are examples of a list (not all encompassing) for some of the processes defined above.

Procurement
- Locate and interview prospective suppliers.
- Determine approved suppliers.
- Perform efforts to optimize the supply base.
- Develop and maintain a program to select and certify suppliers.
- Evaluate and measure supplier performance.
- Create policies and procedures governing ethical supplier relations.
- Establish purchasing requirements and specifications.
- Collect and control supporting documents (purchase orders, contracts, and schedule line
  agreements).
- Prepare purchase orders and transmit to suppliers.
- Monitor open purchase order status.
- Organize, manage, and execute company-wide purchasing activities.
- Optimize centralized and decentralized procurement activities.
- Create and manage purchase programs (procurement cards, blanket purchase orders,
  automatic replenishment).

Manufacturing
- Production planning
- Production scheduling
- Machinery and equipment staging and setup
- Produce goods
- Quality management

Warehouse management

- Maintain inventory systems and technologies
- Determine inventory accuracy from both a physical and book perspective
- Execute physical-count and cycle-count programs
- Compile, consolidate, and reconcile book inventory
- Identify, value, and dispose of obsolete, damaged, and slow-moving inventory
- Determine appropriate reserves and safety stock levels
- Forecast and plan inventory requirements
- Receive, ticket, and store inventory and maintenance, repairs, and operations supplies
- Stage and load inventory for shipment
- Analyze the cost of and alternatives to warehousing
- Maintain cleanliness and upkeep of owned warehouse space
- Determine warehouse space requirements on a continual basis
- Maintain warehouse systems and technologies

Logistics

- Establish and maintain carrier relationships
- Specify appropriate and optimal shipping routes
- Monitor and track in-transit shipments
- Maintain transit routing and tracking systems
- Determine appropriate and optimal modes of transport
- Transport goods (intracompany, to and from suppliers, to and from customers)

Order fulfillment

- Pick line items on the customer order
- Pack, seal, and label the picked customer order
- Generate and execute pick lists
- Generate packing slips and insert them into customer's fulfilled order
- Generate and execute the release order for shipment documentation
- Identify undetected back orders or incomplete shipments and notify key parties
- Periodically check ("audit") fulfilled orders to ensure their completeness and accuracy
- Maintain order fulfillment technology and systems
- Enter and confirm orders
- Track orders
- Manage customer relations regarding orders (handle inquiries related to product availability, order status, order returns)

Generate Key Performance Indicators (KPIs)

As additional background in the supply chain management arena, it is also valuable to provide some key performance indicators associated with the processes that make up supply chain management. Below are some of these KPIs. They are definitely not an all inclusive list but meant to help stimulate some creative insight to help you measure and manage the processes within your supply chain.

Procurement
Purchasing cost as a percent of revenue
Cost per purchase order
Procurement span of control (staff to management ratio)
Purchase orders processed per purchasing personnel
Number of active suppliers
Days to approve suppliers
Percent of purchases from certified suppliers
Number of approvals to add a new supplier to the supplier base
Percent of purchase orders and requisitions with errors
Purchase order to requisition ratio
Average value per purchase order
Average value purchased per purchasing agent
Percent of transactions processed via Web, EDI, and Paper

Manufacturing
First pass yield rates
Average manufacturing cycle time
Average machine availability rate
Manufacturing cost as a percent of revenue
Operations Equipment Efficiency Rate (OEE)
Scrap/Rework cost as a percent of sales
In-plant defect rate
Customer reject rate
Warranty cost as a percent of sales

Warehouse management
Inventory turnover
Warehouse management cost as a percent of revenue
Warehouse management cost as a percent of total inventory value
Percent of inactive inventory
Inventory obsolescence percentage
Cycle count accuracy percentage
Inventory stock out percentage

Logistics

Logistics cost as a percent of revenue
Percent of in-transit inventory
Percent of premium freight charges to total freight charges
Number of carriers used
On-time delivery rate
Percent of damaged shipments
Backhauling percentage

Order fulfillment

Order fulfillment cost as a percent of revenue
Order to shipment lead time
Average line items per customer order
Order line items picked per hour
Order line items picked in error

Case Study: Manufacturer A's Benchmarking the Order Entry Process for Continuous Improvement

The case presented below looks at one process of the supply chain, order fulfillment and even more specifically, order entry. It is a nice example of how you can dissect a process and generate innovative suggestions to improve the process. Please keep in mind that the cases are for illustrative purposes only. They are based on real-world examples but the names have been hidden for confidentiality.

Background, Identify the Need

Manufacturer A, established in 1986, is a medium sized manufacturer of power transformers, DC power supplies, and battery chargers. Historically, Manufacturer A started as a garage shop operation and has now grown to approximately $3MM in annual sales. Today they have two manufacturing plants. Headquarters is located in one of the plant locations and have centralized office functions.

The increase of electronic commerce has posed new obstacles and opportunities for Manufacturer A. Traditional business systems relied on relationships as an element for success. Now, relationships are developed and maintained on-line. Sales, marketing, purchasing, and several other functions are now dynamically linked to the World Wide Web. If ordinary business systems are going through this incredible change, how can companies keep up; especially, smaller companies that lack technology? How does a company quantify/support the decision to become electronically enabled (e-enabled)?

Web presence has been identified as the initial step to being electronically enabled. What next? Does the company put up a personalized site? Does the company allow for real-time stock checks? Well, the next step is not only to provide content, but also reduce overall time and cost while increasing cash-to-cash cycle times and quality of service.

Specifically, the order entry process will be reviewed in this case study. The B2B electronic commerce process begins when the customer initiates the demand chain. This event creates a progression of events streaming down the enterprise. After analyzing business processes, once a web site is rolled-out, the next vital milestone is achieving transaction based cost reductions, particularly order processing. Order processing is an end-to-end vital link between front and back-end functions. This process is closely linked to financials, customer service, and production. The order entry process is measurable, thus providing clear visibility and opportunities for improvement. The continuous improvement process allows us to examine what other corporations are doing, how they are doing it, and develop a structure to meet and/or exceed best practices. Most of all, it let's us learn from others mistakes.

Map Your Process

Currently, Manufacturer A utilizes an ERP system manufactured by Computer Associates (named SBT). The purchasing, sales order, bill of materials, general ledger, manufacturing (inventory control and manufacturing), accounts payable, accounts receivable, and payroll are fully integrated within this ERP system. For the last several years, Manufacturer A has had a web presence. They have an on-line catalog for standard products. Custom sheets are available for custom requirements. Links to national distributors and representatives are also included on the web site. Traditionally, marketing has been done by referrals, trade publications, direct mail, and catalogs. Order acceptance has been limited to traditional purchase orders via facsimile. Limited credit cards are accepted and are handled using the assistance of a local distributor.

Order entry has long been a manual end-to-end process. Efficiency in this department has been limited to a high amount of paperwork, error rate, and upper management response time. The customer service team that suffered low efficiencies due to the handling of customer complaints and stock checks performs the order entry function. These reasons were the early warning indicators for Manufacturer A wanting to improve this part of the process.

Manufacturer A used flowcharting and a self-assessment between the two owners of Manufacturer A to help identify key issues in the order entry process.

❖ Process Flowchart **(Appendix 16-1)**
❖ Self assessment questionnaire **(Appendix 16-2)**

The key activities of the order entry process are summarized below.

1. Order received via email, fax, snail mail, or phone
2. Manual function in completing internal forms attached to customer hard copy
3. New part numbers are referred to engineering to be added into the ERP system (time constraint from engineering)
4. Customer service to attain the lead time from production team for the order (time constraint from production)
5. Sales order filed for management approval (time constraint from upper management)
6. Corrections will be made (if necessary)
7. Sales order entered into ERP system
8. ERP system confirms entry
9. Immediate shipments are verbally communicated to production (possible human error)

10. Blanket orders are scheduled for delivery by ERP system. Production team is responsible for seeing this schedule and planning accordingly.
11. When product is shipped, the shipping list is turned into customer service
12. Upon processing, five forms are generated
❖ Shipping
❖ Invoicing
❖ A/R
❖ Internal sales order copy
❖ Internal master log
13. Upon processing of the shipment, open orders are re-filed for later delivery and closed orders are archived.
14. ERP system tracks payment from date of invoicing (usually net 30 days)

In summary the existing process had inefficiencies as a result of manual functions needed to complete internal forms (shipping, invoicing, accounts receivable, internal sales order copy, internal master log). The manual labor has led to human errors. In addition, there was a bottleneck with upper management because they had to approve sales orders.

Research Alternative Solutions

Manufacturer A felt they had a good idea of their own process and wanted to look at what others were doing. They went about the task of identifying benchmark partners. Benchmark partners were identified based on:
❖ Availability of information
❖ Internal contacts
❖ Process of order entry (manual and/or automated)

It is important to realize that benchmark partners were selected based on the existence of the order entry process, not the nature of the company's products. The concern is the optimization of a process.

The selected organizations were:
❖ Telecom A
❖ Electronics B
❖ Electronics C
❖ Software D

This decision was driven by access to the organization and their current processes.

A process overview was used to understand the benchmark partner's processes. This was done primarily through interviews with key contacts at these organizations along with external research from articles on the companies. Below is a summary of each process overview gathered by Manufacturer A.

BENCHMARK PARTNERS PROCESS OVERVIEW (Telecom A – manual order entry)

Telecom A_is a leading telecommunications provider in 13 states and has an international presence in this industry. Currently, Telecom A's in-house engineering staff contracts large vendors to perform electronic builds within the central office and the end customer. These electronics facilitate ISP's, WAN/ LAN networks, Inter/Intra state communications and other services.

The digital transport engineer (DTE) is the project manager for any electronic installation within a predefined geographic area. Contracting services is one of the main job descriptions and order entry management (specifically vendor billing) has been chosen as the main focus of this benchmarking study. Telecom A_has a similar ERP system to that of Manufacturer A that combines all functions within service order fulfillment. The current vendor–engineer relationship using fax and snail-mail is still very embedded. The engineering department has been overloaded with a high volume of paperwork that has compounded error rate and vendor billing response time. The engineer performs the order- entry function to a large extent. Additional headcount would create extended learning curves unable to meet current workload. This function (order entry from the engineer) has suffered low volumes, due to the handling of customer complaints, higher than normal demand for installations, and expedited service orders. Furthermore, the engineer has now become the bottleneck in the general ledger process, creating the need for end of quarter budgetary "fire drills". This quarterly process in turn creates limits on the resources available to meet customer due dates and in the end possible loss of revenue.

By studying Telecom A_and incorporating the existing Telecom A_ERP system (JAM) Manufacturer A will look to expand this into instantaneous processing of vendor billing thereby reducing delays in service (lost revenue), improved cycle times from contract to accounts payable (full utilization of capital allocations), and a reduction in rework from an accounting and engineering standpoint. This will allow resources to be reallocated from manual order entry and tracking to meeting customer service requirements.

BENCHMARK PARTNERS PROCESS OVERVIEW (Electronics B – manual order entry)

1. Electronics B's order entry process starts with the customer sending a written purchase order (PO) form to the Electronics B Sales representatives.
2. The Sales rep checks the order for accuracy of models and pricing and re-writes the order on a Electronics B PO form. Both forms are faxed to the Business Operations Center (BOC) for input into the system.

3. Once an order is received, the BOC specialist reviews both order forms to make sure that everything is filled out accurately, including, ship-to address, terms of payment, model numbers and pricing match.

4. After this initial check, the order is manually entered into the ERP system and assigned a sales order number.

5. After entering the order in the system and having an ERP order number assigned, the BOC specialist checks for pricing errors in the form of discrepancies between the system and the PO forms.

6. If there is an error, the BOC specialist contacts the sales rep and requests that they send in a meet competition form. This meet comp is a legal document filled out by the rep for a specific model and specific prices from Net price down to N/N/N (prices after all discounts are taken including payment terms). Basically, this form states that a competitor has quoted the customer a price on a particular product and the customer wants similar pricing to Electronics B's product that competes with that product based on product features.

7. Once the meet comp is sent in, the corresponding Marketing Manager needs to review the meet comp and either agree to the price or reject it. If the meet comp is rejected the Marketing Manager calls the rep to inform them and the customer has the option of rewriting their PO for that model or canceling it from the order.

8. If the Marketing Manager agrees to the price, the price is entered into the system and the BOC specialist re-prices the order to bring up the new price.

9. Next the ship date is reviewed. If the order is set for immediate shipment, the order will appear on the shipping log printed up in the warehouse. The BOC specialist can also contact the warehouse to expedite the process.

10. If the ship date is in the future, the order will appear on the shipping log printed in the warehouse, but will be scheduled for shipment using normal lead times. Once the BOC specialist finishes entering the order, the hard copy is filed.

11. Once items are shipped from the warehouse, the ERP system generates both an invoice to be sent to the customer and a packing slip for each shipment.

12. Once all items have been shipped, the order from a production side is closed out. The accounts predominantly have terms of Net 30 or Net 60, once the customer submits payment to Accounts Receivable (A/R), the amount is credited to the customer's account and once all invoices have been paid for an order, that order is closed out.

BENCHMARK PARTNERS PROCESS OVERVIEW (Electronics C – automated order entry system)

Electronics C wanted to provide a simplified solution to their order placement process. There were too many imperfect orders, which resulted in customer dissatisfaction. Telephone orders from dealers had to be resolved by order entry personnel and often, if took them two to three days to get an order right. There was also a problem with the lack of in-stock product availability and poor on-time delivery performance. Harman knew they could save time and money and improve dealer satisfaction by automating this process.

Their objective was to permit dealers to view the inventory availability, pricing information and account information that resided on Electronics C's SAP R/3 system. Another goal was to allow field representatives and dealers the use of the system to enter orders directly to the R/3 system.

Electronics C chose Proxicom, a web developer, to be the general contractor and do the implementation of the online order entry application. The application communicates with R/3 via integration middleware from Haht Software, which uses SAP's Business Application Programming Interface format.

Electronics C's own order entry people, or direct/independent sales people, or the dealers themselves can enter orders. This information is then maintained in the SAP system for further integration with the back-end R/S system. Dealers can see the product description, pricing, credit history and order history.

Electronics C has greatly benefited from their online ordering system. The two major benefits are reduced workload and redeployment. Other benefits include:

- Reducing order entry time from two or three days to approximately five minutes per order.
- 20 independent reps can see order and delivery status on their dealer's sites using Harman's system.
- The new system has the added benefit of providing information to aid in making decisions regarding improvements to the supply chain.

Electronics C made a conscious design to compile suggestions for enhancements in a list of future upgrades, instead of implementing them as they came in. They also are using a knowledge transfer method by insisting that an Internet team of in-house application developers perform upgrades on an ongoing basis. They were successful in improving dealer satisfaction and now they are able to achieve a faster time-to-market with the use of an external services provider.

BENCHMARK PARTNERS PROCESS OVERVIEW (Software D -automated order entry)

Software D Corporation is the leading provider of software applications that are designed for improving the intelligence and performance of large-scale networks, predominantly the Internet. Network applications fall into Traffic Server network cache platform, content delivery, and traffic server extensions.

Portal services include search, shopping and directory services, these applications are offered to Internet portals and web site customers. The company was founded in 1996 and subsequently went public in 1998.

Order entry in the early stages of Software D was fragmented with business contracts largely non-standard and drafted on an order-by-order basis. Significant time was spent on small volume contracts and negotiation efforts. Order tracking was done within four separate databases and sixteen spreadsheets resulting in 60% of all orders being delayed. Software D had a web based order fulfillment process that attributed to approximately 5% of all orders. This labor-intensive process led to large manual intervention in order to meet specific customer commitment dates. As this companies demand for product increased the end result was a higher error rate, constant rework, lost or late shipments, and manual tracking from contract through invoice.

This corporation was plagued with the fore mentioned companies order entry process problems, in that as the volume of business expanded the profit opportunities were limited by manual order entry. Scalability of a fully automated order entry process was a necessity. The end result was a streamlined process that began with the electronic submission of a deal sheet. From this point the terms are deemed standard or non-standard with only nine process steps from the beginning deal sheet to the final terms. In contrast, previously this flow would have had an average cycle time of 18 days, with a 60% error rate. The cycle time had not been measured at the time of this implementation, but the error rate and tracking process had dropped significantly.

Document the gaps

Manufacturer A intentionally decided to analyze four different companies with different systems against their own current order entry process. Two benchmark partners, Software D and Electronics C, have achieved automated order entry systems. The other two organizations have yet to develop an automated system and currently perform manuals operations.

After analyzing the gaps and performance of each system Manufacturer A identified certain gaps that present opportunities for improvement. These points include:

- Redundancy of work
- Accuracy of invoicing
- Accuracy of order entry
- Accuracy of communication between functional departments
- Decreased cycle time of order processing, due to automated system

The above points are a high-level summary of the gap analysis evident between automated and manual organizations in the order entry process.

Inaccuracy in orders are caused by:
- Lack of product availability
- Poor on-time delivery performance
- Inconsistent or incorrect lead/transit times
- Customer deductions from paid invoices

Much of these points can be resolved by more effective internal communication. One great tool that can be used for this is the internal ERP system of Manufacturer A. Manufacturer A should exhaust their ERP system and use it to its full functionality. This will allow Manufacturer A to forecast, communicate, and plan more efficiently. Using the ERP system's full functionality will also reduce the effects of constraints, such as manual functions and waiting time for management. Real-time on-line stock checks can serve an additional benefit by reducing the redundancy of the customer service department. Much of their current time is spent in expediting and stock checks. Another overall effect of using Manufacturer A's existing ERP system and Information Technology would be to reduce processing times of orders. The case study presented by Software D and Electronics C demonstrates clear results. Please refer to appendix 16-3 for this information. Additionally, order entry accuracy will increase.

Competitive advantage for Manufacturer A lies in time savings and convenience to customers. The use of information technology (IT) to facilitate overall improvement is essential, especially since the internal structure already exists.

The reduction of cycle time is a function of essential and non-essential activities. Manufacturer A's gap analysis identifies a few non-essential activities (i.e. manual redundancy and waiting). These non-essential functions can also be called non-value added activities. The decision is that these non-essential functions can be eliminated by implementing an on-line order entry system that can facilitate internal communication, reduce order entry error, provide on-line stock checks, reduce shipment errors, and increase cash-to-cash cycle times.

Performance measurements should also be part of Manufacturer A's continuous improvement initiatives. Analyzing the benefits of implementing an automated order entry system is clearly visible with organizations that have performance measurements. In this study, they have assigned performance measurements but can only ensure credibility if it is monitored by management.

Adapt Action Steps

After analyzing the order entry process maps for Manufacturer A and then comparing it to other organization, the critical success factors were:
- High-level executive support: Management buy-in to determine the importance of this project.

- Knowledge transfer from the "as-is" to the "after" stage. This includes training programs for staff and management.
- Streamlined system capitalizing on IT infrastructure.
- Culture supporting the implemented system.
- Selling users on the benefits of the new system. This is a form of "buy-in" but used for customers, representatives, and distributors that are affected with on-line ordering processes.
- Clearly defined functional requirements and rules.

To implement these changes, Manufacturer A first did a readiness survey with existing customers to see how they might respond to major changes in the way their orders are processed. Please refer to appendix 16-4 for this information. Manufacturer A then utilized the results of the survey to help better position any changes to its customers.

In addition, Manufacturer A then prepared action plans to help them implement the best practices. These action plans are detailed as an appendix. Please refer to appendix 16-5 for this information.

In summary the major action steps were as follows:

- Start Using Performance Measurements
- Adopt Management, User, and Customer Buy-In
- Plan, Organize, and Implement Campaign for Online Order Entry
- Test the System Before Going Live
- Promote Online Ordering Campaign
- Test Online Ordering Systems with Some Users
- Go Live with Online Ordering
- Promote Additional Online Ordering
- Monitor Performance Measurements
- Monitor User and Customer Feedback to Improve System
- User Performance Metrics to Adopt Future Continuous Improvement Efforts

Measure and Monitor

In addition to creating an action plan to use performance measures to monitor the process, Manufacturer A specified the types of measures that would be helpful to ensuring the changes they make stay on track. These measures include the following:

- Ratio of change orders vs. total orders
- Time spent communicating with engineering function
- Average time to enter orders per day
- Cost of order per employee

- Percent late shipments due to order entry
- Cycle time from order entry to invoicing

Please refer to appendix 16-5 for this information as an action plan.

Conclusion

Manufacturer A feels that by implementing the above action plans and having gone through this continuous improvement process, they will recognize the following benefits:

- New partnerships between customers and suppliers
- Increased quality and decreased cost
- Reduction of work-in-process and inventory
- Increased functional integration
- Technology enablement
- Maximize return on cost

Appendix 16-1 Manufacturer A Order Entry

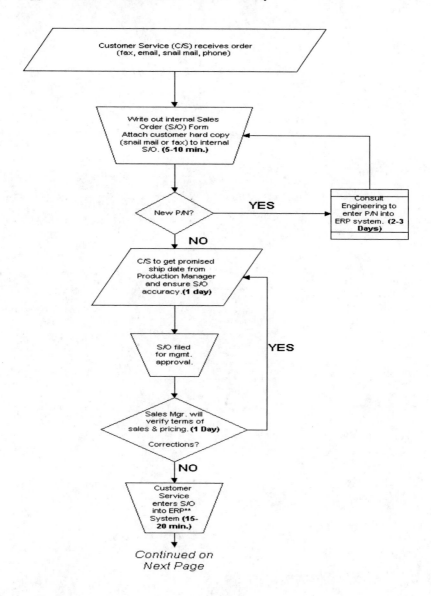

Appendix 16-1 – Manufacturer A Order Entry (cont'd)

Order Entry Process
(continued from page 1)

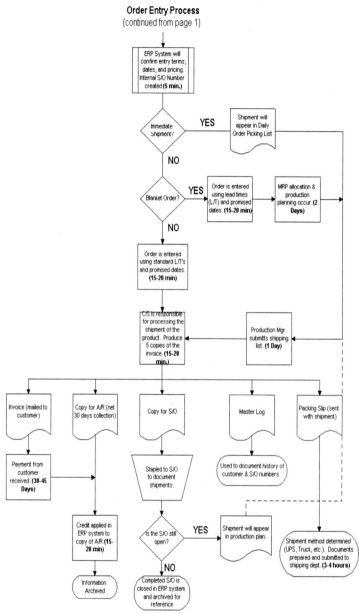

* Departments involved include Cusotmer Service, Sales, Production, and Engineering.

** ERP system used is called SBT (manufactured by Computer Associates). Plays an important role in verifying entries, stock, pricing, and communication with production.

*** **Bolded** material indicates time requirements.

Appendix 16-2 – Manufacturer A Self-Assessment
For Order Entry Process

Legend: 1= strongly agree, 2= somewhat agree, 3=don't know, 4= somewhat disagree, 5=strongly disagree

Importance Questions	Owner 1	Owner 2
1. Order entry affects revenues.	1	2
2. Electronic ordering on the sell side is important	1	2
3. Paperless environment is important to our business	2	2
4. Order entry is an important part of our business	2	2
5. An optimized order entry process is essential	2	2

Legend: 1= excellent, 2=good, 3=fair, 4=poor, 5=terrible

Performance Questions	Owner 1	Owner 2
1. Customer service due to order entry	2	2
2. Efficiency of current order entry process	3	3
3. The process of closing an order	3	4
4. Manual processes within order entry	4	4
5. Management expediting the order	3	3
6. Production managers expediting the order	4	3
7. Engineers expediting the order	3	3
8. Sales team expediting the order	2	2
9. ERP effects on the order entry function	2	2
10. Overall performance of order entry process	2	3

**Appendix 16-2 – Manufacturer A Self-Assessment
For Importance of Order Entry Process**

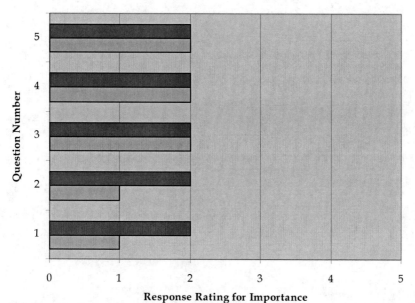

Respondent A: Upper Bar, Respondent B: Lower Bar

**Appendix 16-2 – Manufacturer A Self-Assessment
For Performance of Order Entry Process**

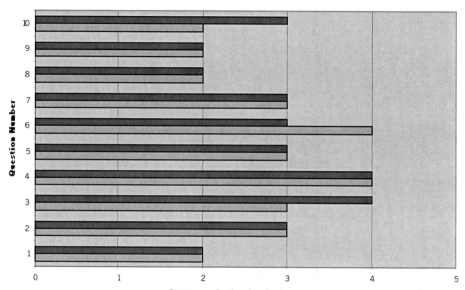

Response Rating for Performance
Respondent A: Upper Bar, Respondent B: Lower Bar

**Appendix 16-2 – Manufacturer A Self-Assessment
Matrix for the Order Entry Process**

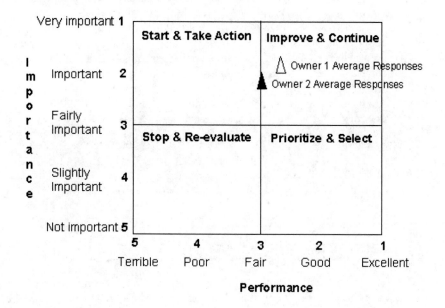

Appendix 16-3 – Performance Analysis

In this section the continuous improvement team of Manufacturer A will present some final performance data gathered and analyzed. This information was used for the gap analysis and is useful in determining goals for the order entry process. The table below has some indications of number of handoffs, degree of automation, and steps that require waiting. Furthermore, Manufacturer A then drew some statistical correlation coefficients that helped them determine the correlation between an automated system and cost reductions.

Analysis for Manufacturer A vs. Benchmark Partners

Company	Handoffs	Steps requiring waiting	Degree of automation 1=full 2=not	Invoices Generated
Mfg A	24	5	2	5
Telecom A	17	8	2	7
Electronics B	21	7	2	3
Electronics C	9	1	1	2
Software D	9	2	1	2

The information provided below is taken from the Software D and Electronics C case study, respectively. This information is useful in determining the before and after improvements that are seen after the implementation of an on-line ordering process.

Software D

Before process improvement
Order error rate
- The original order management process had 29 steps, 4 tracking systems, 3 invoice systems.
- 60% of all orders were delayed by error.

Orders per FTE
- Estimated that 1 FTE hours spent on rework and manual processing of orders.
- No other data available.

Cycle time from order entry to invoice
- Up to several weeks when vital technical data was not included on original order.
- 25% of orders and 49% of revenue occur in the last 2 weeks of quarter.

Cost measure of order entry per FTE
- Costs were 57% higher than a competing firm.

- Increased risk and revenue uncertainty – many employees circumventing processes to ensure customer satisfaction. As volumes increase so does an unprofitable error rate.

After process improvement
Order error rate
- The newly implemented order management process had at most 9 steps. 100% of all orders tracked from Deal sheet to shipment.
- Renewal rate (customer satisfaction).

Orders per FTE
- New data was to be tracked by the following Metrics
    a. Sales orders vs. invoices per FTE.
- No other data available.

Cycle time from order entry to invoice
- Standard contracts were drafted in 3-5 days.
- Cycle times tracked through comparison of:
    a. Close to create a new sales order.
    b. Create a sales order to fulfillment.
    c. Create a sales order to invoicing.

Cost measure of order entry per FTE
- FTE vs. total number of orders.
- 57% cost reduction on order processing from rework and manual order processing.
- Decreased risk and revenue uncertainty – uniform processes to ensure customer satisfaction. As volumes increase electronic order entry management can be scaled to business volume levels.

Electronics C

Quality: Error rate decreased from 20% to less than 5% with this new system
Productivity: Is now between 80%-90% per FTE
Time: In the past, it could take 2-3 days (approx 16 hours) to place 1 order Now, assuming 5minutes/order, 192 orders can be placed in 16 hours
Cost: Assuming $5 order entry per FTE.
Previously, it could cost up to $80 for one entry/FTE!
Now, it's decreased to approximately $.50 for one entry/FTE

Appendix 16-4 – Survey for Customer Readiness

The purpose of the survey if to determine readiness and feasibility of enabling electronic commerce functions between Manufacturer A and it's customers. This survey includes <u>28 questions</u> and will take approximately fifteen (30) minutes to complete; if unsure about a question feel free to leave it blank.

This survey is broken down into three sections, current status, enabling e-commerce, and demand planning. Our goal is to reduce processing, inventory, and ordering costs while increasing service levels across the entire supply chain.

Contact Information

Company _____

Name _____

Title _____

Email _____

Phone _____

Industry (i.e. distributor, OEM) _____

Purchasing structure (centralized or decentralized) _____

Current Status

1) Please indicate the total percentage of your time communicating with suppliers: _____ %

2) Please break this total time into the method of communication:

       Phone _____ % Email _____ % Other _____

       Fax _____ % On-line/Web _____ %

3) Average value of purchase orders issued to Manufacturer A:

$ _____

4) Ratio of change orders (orders modified once purchase order is submitted to vendor) to total orders:

_____

5) What is your current cost per purchase order?

$ _____

Please describe your computation and variables involved:

6) What is your current MRP/ERP system?

☐ Oracle ☐ SAP ☐ PeopleSoft ☐ i2

☐ Manugistics ☐ Other _____

7) Do you currently order materials on-line:

☐ Yes ☐ No ☐ Don't Know

8) Please indicate the percent of purchase orders processed over the web: _____ %

9) Please describe your current method of ordering products on-line (i.e. need based, via fax, ERP system is integrated with EDI):

_____

_____

_____

_____

10) How is data communicated when ordering on-line (check all that apply):

    ☐ EDI   ☐ XML ☐ Other (describe) _____

    ☐ Text Files ☐ Emails

11) Have you considered partnering with suppliers to improve the efficiency of the supply chain?

☐ Yes   ☐ No   ☐ Don't Know

12) Have you considered collaborating forecasting information with suppliers to increase the effectiveness of planning, shortening lead times, and accommodating auto-replenishment?

☐ Yes   ☐ No   ☐ Don't Know

Enabling E-commerce

13) What are your expectations of e-commerce (check all that apply)?

    ☐ Reduce lead times   ☐ Reduce purchasing costs

    ☐ Reduce customer service cost ☐ Increase service levels

    ☐ Decrease inventory cost ☐ Better inventory management
    ☐ Other

_____

_____

_____

14) How important do you feel e-commerce capability is between you and Manufacturer A (1 - not important, 3 - somewhat important, 5 - very important):

☐ 1   ☐ 2   ☐ 3   ☐ 4   ☐ 5

15) How important do you feel e-commerce capability is between you and your other suppliers (1 - not important, 3 - somewhat important, 5 - very important):

☐ 1   ☐ 2   ☐ 3   ☐ 4   ☐ 5

16) Will on-line stock checks reduce your overall cost of purchasing?

☐ Yes   ☐ No   ☐ Don't Know

17) Will on-line stock checks decrease cost of time required for purchasing?

☐ Yes   ☐ No   ☐ Don't Know

18) Will on-line stock checks increase the quality of the purchasing function?

☐ Yes   ☐ No   ☐ Don't Know

19) Will on-line stock checks reduce your overall cost of customer service?

☐ Yes   ☐ No   ☐ Don't Know

20) What is your overall cost reduction goal (percentage) by using e-commerce: _____ %

21) Indicate a supplier that currently meets your e-commerce expectations: _____

22) Describe how this supplier meets your expectations: _____

_____

23) What would you do differently: _____

_____

_____

_____

24) Would you use e-commerce functionality if it existed between you and Manufacturer A?

☐ Yes   ☐ No   ☐ Indifferent

Demand Planning

25) Are you currently collaborating any forecasting data with suppliers?

☐ Yes   ☐ No   ☐ Don't Know

26) Are you prepared to share forecasting information with Manufacturer A?

☐ Yes   ☐ No   ☐ Don't Know

27) Do you currently have an auto replenishment practice in place?

☐ Yes   ☐ No   ☐ Don't Know

If so, please describe: _____

---

28) Can you benefit from automatic replenishment with Manufacturer A products?

☐ Yes   ☐ No   ☐ Don't Know

Appendix 16-5 Action Plans

Management, Customer, Distributor, and Representative But-in

DEPARTMENT NAME: This step initiates from the top of the hierarchy. After management buy-in the next step would be to utilize the sample survey provided in this report to judge customer, distributor, and representative "readiness".

RECOMMENDATION: Weekly meetings stressing the importance of performance measurements. Demonstrate the benefits of such a system. Furthermore, utilize sample survey in this report for customer, distributor, and representative buy-in.

IDENTIFIED PROBLEMS: On-line ordering entry is a great system with proven benefits. But are we all ready for it? No market analysis has been done to determine its usefulness in this industry.

PERSON IN CHARGE: Upper management - President

ACTION STEP: Plan out execution of meetings, motivation tactics, and team that will implement this analysis step.

TIMING: This step should parallel the implementation of the performance measurement action plan.

REWARDS: This step helps the corporation assess if the idea (on-line ordering) will be used by its customers, distributors, and representatives. If not prepared, this action step will allow the corporation to reassess and plan its implementation plan while waiting for more customer to benefit from on-line ordering.

PERFORMANCE MEASURES: Monitoring of proper management and user buy-in will yield a solid result identifying the success of the recommendations.

Appendix 16-5 Action Plans

Plan, Test, and Execute the On-line Ordering System of Choice

---
DEPARTMENT NAME: Upper management, IT, Sales and Marketing Department

---
RECOMMENDATION: In this phase a platform for electronic commerce should be selected. In addition, a project plan must be laid out that includes project milestones. The structure of on-line ordering and the technology to be used must be outlined. Sales and marketing team will serve as front-end feedback from customers. A testing plan with selected customers should be designed along with a contingency plan. A plan for risk management should also be implemented.

IDENTIFIED PROBLEMS: At this time, there is no IT department existent for this. Such an implementation is a full-time responsibility. The lack of a plan will also be addressed in this phase.

PERSON IN CHARGE: Division President

ACTION STEP: A dedicated IT professional must be recruited. This professional must be capable of specifying hardware, designing front-end systems, and maintaining the system. Another alternative includes the complete outsourcing of this step.

TIMING: Shortly after management and user buy-in this plan should take initiative.

REWARDS: This is the first step technical step that will take Manufacturer A to an on-line ordering environment. Additionally, the testing phase will help streamline the process and verify data integrity.

PERFORMANCE MEASURES: Performance measures for this phase can be tracked by using a project management tool known as the Gantt Chart. Deadlines and milestones serve as motivational tools to ensure the implementation of this phase.

Appendix 16-5 Action Plans

Roll-out of system, Monitoring usage, and Performance Measures

---

DEPARTMENT NAME: IT, Sales and Marketing, Upper Management

RECOMMENDATION: This phase is the actual roll-out of the system. After roll-out there must be a system to monitor usage and success rate of the on-line ordering system. Internal performance measures must be strictly measured to observe improvements and analyze cost/benefits.

IDENTIFIED PROBLEMS: In addition to a present day lack of performance measures, Manufacturer A does not have a system of monitoring web usage and traffic. The roll-out plan is a new step that falls within the realm of the non-existent IT department.

PERSON IN CHARGE: Upper management, Sales and Marketing, IT department.

ACTION STEP: Execute the design of an IT department. Determine the necessity of outsourcing. Implement a Sales/Marketing survey or questionnaire that will be completed by users (also useful for continuous improvement). Develop list of performance metrics to monitor the usage of the on-line ordering system.

TIMING: No particular time can be specified at this time. It is a sequential process from the other action steps provided.

REWARDS: This step ensures on-line accuracy, data integrity, consumer loyalty, and usage. The continuous monitoring of this system will allow the visualization of performance improvements and cost savings. Additionally, customer satisfaction can be ranked using performance measurements.

PERFORMANCE MEASURES: Hits per day, cycle time of order entry process, cash-to-cash cycle time, questionnaires and surveys to measure customer satisfaction, order error rate, cost to enter orders, and manual handoffs or steps in the system.

Appendix 16-5 Action Plans

Promotion of New System

DEPARTMENT NAME: Sales and Marketing, IT

RECOMMENDATION: Upon the success rollout and monitoring parameters of the system, Manufacturer A should formulate a marketing campaign. As spelled out in the report, the result of this system is increased partnerships and loyalty. This is a great opportunity to boast a competitive advantage over other suppliers. It is also an opportunity to invite new business and ventures.

IDENTIFIED PROBLEMS: Manufacturer A manufactures commodity products that clearly do not demonstrate a competitive advantage over competitors. This system can open new doors to their current system.

PERSON IN CHARGE: Sales and Marketing, IT department.

ACTION STEP: Formulate an Internet marketing campaign using banner ads, emails, auto-replenishment, and boast reduced consumer costs due to on-line ordering and stock checks.

TIMING: No particular time can be specified at this time. It is a sequential process from the other action steps provided.

REWARDS: This step ensures the promotion of the newly acquired competitive advantage. The ramifications can be seen onto the bottom line and increase in customer base. Customer loyalty is also a success factor in this step.

PERFORMANCE MEASURES: Hits per day, cycle time of order entry process, cash-to-cash cycle time, questionnaires and surveys to measure customer satisfaction, rate of new customers per day, order error rate, cost to enter orders, and manual handoffs or steps in the system.

Appendix 16-5 Action Plans

Usage of Performance Measurements

DEPARTMENT NAME: Upper Management

RECOMMENDATION: The recommendation for this step is the adoption of certain performance measurements that are ideally the only way that a system can be assessed and improved.

IDENTIFIED PROBLEMS: Currently there are no performance measurements. It is simply impossible to assess a process without this.

PERSON IN CHARGE: Division President, which should enforce management buy-in to this process.

ACTION STEP: Please refer to the <u>Measure and Monitor</u> section to identify several possible measurements that may be implemented by the organization.

TIMING: This step should be done immediately upon management buy-in.

REWARDS: Visualization of improvements. Internal motivation tool. Inter-plant motivation tool.

PERFORMANCE MEASURES: The existence of these measurements with on-going monitoring will enhance the culture of continuous improvement.

Chapter Seventeen: Customer Relationship Management (CRM) Function

Pre Case Background:

Define Process Activities

Traditional Customer Relationship Management (CRM) definitions discuss diving deep into understanding the customer and leverage your knowledge of customer buying patterns and behaviors for revenue growth opportunities. CRM recognizes that keeping customers over the long-term results in profitability.

In my class, I lump a series of revenue enhancement processes into my CRM processes. All of these are sales-oriented processes. These are as follows:

Marketing
Selling
Customer Service

Each of these is important in revenue generation. In a study of the insurance industry, for example, five key sales activities were deemed responsible for sales success, these included 1) the skills and abilities of the sales force, 2) value of products and services, 3) superiority of products and services, 4) training of sales staff, and 5) resources and support provided to sales staff. These best practices are really common across all industries.

Best practice organizations that have world-class revenue enhancement processes include the likes of Charles Schwab. Schwab effectively uses technology to segment its customers. They also ensure the customer has multiple points of contact to reach a Schwab representative including Internet phone, and live sales personnel. Schwab also had a customer-obsessed culture and motivational management and training strategies to drive their success.

Other organizations like Fingerhut, the multi-billion dollar direct marketer leverages marketing expertise by segmenting markets into niches. Fingerhut uses proactive training techniques to educate its marketing staff on the use of data mining tools to help get the most out of marketing dollars.

The concept of CRM is a promising one. More and more organizations are focusing on CRM to get closer to their customers. According to Forrester Research, 48 percent of organizations believe an "integrated view of customers" is the most important element. Excel Communications Inc. a Texas-based telecommunications company used CRM software from Siebel to help them create more synergy amongst the sales force, hundreds of independent sales reps, and through them, their customers.

Each process has certain activities that it performs. It is important to understand these activities when attempting to improve the process.

Marketing:
- Establish business/marketing plans
- Establish appropriate market segmentations
- Evaluate existing and future markets for major products/services
- Evaluate market position and actions of competition
- Develop a marketing short- and long-term strategy
- Promote and create awareness for new, existing, and future products and services
- Promote the awareness and benefits of products/services
- Create marketing materials, including design and layout
- Measure results of promotional efforts
- Assist in creation of pricing strategy
- Assist in creation of packaging design
- Work on new business/concept development
- Perform general market research
- Maintain the price list

Selling:
- Create sales force structure (territories)
- Build and monitor sales forecasts
- Create sales force compensation structure
- Provide for sales force training
- Monitor sales profitability
- Create and implement sales promotions
- Work on pricing models
- Account management and maintenance
- Sales force administration (reporting, training)
- Respond to customer problems, manage returns
- Handle special requests (special pricing/discounts)
- Prepare proposals and presentations
- Travel and entertainment
- Writing, entering, processing, managing and expediting orders
- Go on sales calls and customer events

Customer Service:
- maintain and manage the customer service center/function
- solicit and collect customer feedback
- respond to customer inquiries and complaints
- maintain customer service technology and systems (such as call center technologies)

- analyze critical events (product, delivery, billing, etc) from a customer needs perspective
- evaluate and implement customer suggestions and comments
- analyze customer turnover and other key performance indicators of customer satisfaction

Generate Key Performance Indicators

Next, create the performance measures for each process. This will allow you to understand the process better by collecting base line historical data to compare against others or to trend. It also allows you to have a baseline system in place to monitor and measure the process once it is improved.

Marketing:
Marketing Department Cost as a Percentage of Revenue
Marketing Department Cost per Marketing Full-time Equivalent (FTE)
Time Assessing New Markets
Cost of Assessing New Markets
Time Developing Annual Marketing Plan
Cost of Developing Annual Marketing Plan
Market Share Percentages
Life Cycle Stages of Products
Marketing Budget as a Percentage of Revenue
Budget for Communications Media
Measuring Marketing Impact
Advertising Reach Rates
Percentage of Budget Related to Marketing New Products
Time on Pricing Issues
Time Before Adjusting Prices

Selling:
Years of experience of sales personnel
Sales quota performance
Performance to Plan Ratio
Sales force cost as a percentage of revenue
Training hours per sales professional
Percentage of Lost, Repeat, and New customers
Sales discounts as a percentage of revenues
Sales returns as a percentage of revenues
Compensation at risk (% that is commission and bonus for field and inside sales, sales mgmt)

Customer Service:
CSRs (customer service representatives) as a % of Total Employees
Span of Control (CSR FTEs per Supervisor FTE)
Customer Service Representative Absenteeism Rate

Customer Service Representative Turnover Rate
Number of Reporting Levels between the CSC Director and the CEO
Weekly Calls Handled per CSR FTE
% of Calls Resolved During First Call
Average Speed of Answer
Customer Satisfaction Evaluation Methods
Employee Satisfaction Evaluation Methods
Customer Complaint Tracking
% of Favorable Customer Satisfaction Ratings
Customer Service Center Department Cost as a % of Revenue

Case Study: Trade Association A's Marketing and Direct Sales Programs

The case below looks at the marketing element of a trade association. It is based on a real situation with names changed to protect confidentiality.

Description of the organization/ Identify the Need
Trade Association A is a non-profit organization that provides educational services to the financial services industry.

Trade Association A assists its customers through trade shows, conferences, seminars, and research studies. Trade shows are typically done three times per year. They draw around 500 attendees each and generate about $1 million in revenue. Conferences are done about 30 times a year and average between $50 and 500 thousand in revenue. Finally, seminars are smaller sessions of around 10 to 50 attendees and there are 150 of these per year. Seminars average $5 to 50 thousand in revenue each.

Trade Association A has been in business for over 75 years, employees over 100 people and has revenues in excess of $25million.

Currently, attendance at seminars has been down. The President of Trade Association A has requested that the organization cut the costs of producing these seminars. The President wants to target the marketing element of this because he does not want to cut costs at the event itself (cheaper venues etc.) at this point but feels as though if the target audience were selected better and with a better marketing message they could increase response rates while preventing the sending of marketing materials to a disinterested audience. To this end, Trade Association A began to look at how to value engineer (improve while cutting costs) in the marketing element of seminars.

Map the Process
Trade Association A mapped their process through interviews and focus groups. They also examined organizational charts and standard forms and documents to better understand what is currently done to market and sell the seminars. They did this to assess their existing needs better.

They did two levels of maps. The first was a high-level overview of the process illustrating how the organization plans and delivers seminars. The second was a much more detailed flowchart of the key steps within the marketing and selling aspects of the process.

First, a summary of Trade Association A's process of planning and delivering of seminars is as follows:

- The process involves the cross-functional interaction of 4 groups:
  - Programs Group

- o Seminar Planning Group
- o Database Marketing Group
- o Marketing Group
- The Marketing Group and Programs Group will review existing programs that Trade Association A is running. They will review attendance, profitability, and satisfaction results and compare these to historic and preset goals.
- The Database Marketing Group then runs analysis on historic programs and prepares statistics on trends.
- The Programs Group decide on the type of new programs that should be held based on analysis and input from the Associations research group.
- Database marketing runs analysis to predict attendance rates based on contacts in the database that fit the profile for attending this proposed event.
- The Programs creates the curriculum and lines up speakers for the event (assuming the database marketing group results showed it could be profitable)
- The Seminar Planning Group lines up the hotel and facility for the event.
- The Marketing Group will design, print and mail brochures to create awareness for the event
- The Database Marketing Group will run mailing lists of target attendees
- The Seminar Planning Group will ship the brochures to the targets
- The Seminar Planning Group will track sign-up statistics. If a minimum threshold is not met the event is cancelled. If met the event is held.
- The Programs Group and Seminar Planning Group will do a Post-Event review

A more detailed set of tasks was analyzed for the development and updating of the brochure, the selection of the mailing list candidates, and brochure printing and mailing. Trade Association A felt it was important to expand upon these because of the marketing and selling elements. Other instances of the high level process above were determined to be outside the scope of the project and detail was not required.

Below is a summary of the detailed tasks.

Develop and Update Brochure: Marketing Group
(see Exhibit 17-1 for flowchart)

1. The Marketing Group receives a detailed Program Description from the Program Group. It describes the nature of the

seminar, the intending audience, intended time, place, and pricing.

2. Marketing Group will review prior brochures to see if there are any that can be leveraged here. They also place this marketing project into a project tracking database.
3. 26 weeks before the event, the Programs Group will provide a formal agenda and the Seminar Planning Group will provide hotel information. The Marketing Group takes this information to begin creating the brochure.
4. 20 weeks before the event the Database Marketing Group provides a file with a list of contacts to the Marketing Group. Marketing will sort the file and pick a final set of targets from it.
5. 18 weeks before the event, the Marketing Group finishes its brochure design and spec. It is reviewed and finalized at 14 weeks before the event.
6. 10 to 14 weeks before the event the brochures are mailed to a group of targets by the Seminar Planning Group. Marketing provides a finalized mailing list that it has refined from what it received by Database Marketing.
7. 8 to 10 weeks before the event Marketing will provide two additional "merge/purge" lists to Seminar Planning to resend brochures to certain audiences.

Select Mailing List: Database Marketing Group
(see Exhibit 17-2 for flowchart)

1. The Marketing Group provides a Marketing Plan for this project to the Database Marketing Group.
2. The Database Marketing Group runs some preliminary numbers prior to preparing the list file.
3. The Marketing Group provides a more refined list based on the preliminary numbers.
4. The Database Marketing Group runs additional counts and numbers based on revisions.
5. The Marketing Group provides additional edits to the request.
6. The Database Marketing Group runs numbers again and will do so until approved by Marketing.
7. Once approved by Marketing, the Database Marketing Group will prepare a file with the target contacts.
8. Marketing will review and edit.
9. 16 to 20 weeks before the event, Database Marketing will prepare final list.
10. List is sent to Marketing.

Brochure Printing and Mailing: Seminar Planning Group
(see Exhibit 17-3 for flowchart)

1. The Seminar Planning Group receives the design and layout specs from Marketing Group.
2. The Seminar Planning Group solicits prices from Printers to produce the brochure and settles on a contract with a Printer/
3. 14 weeks before the event the Seminar Planning Group has the finalized Marketing brochure printed by the Printer.
4. 10 to 14 weeks out the Seminar Planning group receives the file provided by Database Marketing to the Marketing Group who then provides it to the Seminar Planning Group to use to mail the printed brochures.
5. 8 to 10 weeks out the Seminar Planning Group receives two more "merge/purge" lists from Marketing to send resend brochures to selected audience.

Once Trade Association A has mapped this process they have a better understanding as to what the various groups roles and responsibilities are in the marketing process. They are ready to try and make improvements.

Research alternative solutions

To understand what Trade Association A should be doing with their marketing programs, they took a 3-pronged approach:

1) They interviewed the marketing director at another Trade Association they frequently co-sponsored programs with to gain insights external to their organization
2) They used an assessment tool in a focus-group setting with key team members from Seminar Planning, Marketing, Database Marketing, Programs, and senior management that asked them what could be done to make the process better. They used the "As Is" process as the starting point to build off of
3) They interviewed customers who attended seminars and those on target lists that did not to help understand what could be done to make improvements

Trade Association A then characterized several of their "Should Be" suggestions into the following categories:
- Leadership – senior management steps that could be taken
- Technology – ways to improve the process through automation and technology
- Review – ways to improve the process through better reviews and controls
- Process – ways to improve the process through better work flow designs

Document the Gap

Once the focus group session had concluded and Trade Association A grouped its suggestions, together and compared them to their existing environment the following key points were where the biggest gaps existed:

- Communications
- Approval Process
- Marketing Materials
- Logistics

Communications

Internal communications at Trade Association A were good but could be improved. For example, Trade Association B would hold weekly meetings among all the teams when the seminar was within 12 weeks. In addition, the Program Managers were out of the process after they provided the Project Description and stated in the focus group their desire to be a part of the process.

Also, customers stated they didn't feel there was adequate communication about upcoming events. If they missed the brochure, upcoming events were not promoted prominently on the Associations web site and were not discussed at other events.

Trade Association B would provide personal phone calls to key customers and organizations they heavily frequented other events. They segmented their customer database by "Gold, Silver and Bronze" customers to help identify more personalized approaches beyond mass marketing for these folks. Trade Association A did not do this.

Approval Process

The Program Manager was not involved in the approval process. No member of senior management was involved in the process. Both the Program Manager Group and senior management felt they should have a review period to ensure they were reaching the right people with the right message.

<u>Marketing Materials</u>

Currently the brochure was where the most time and efforts were placed and it was sent to a mass distribution list along with up to two additional mailings of it for key contacts.

The focus groups revealed the need for more diverse types of communications. This was supported by Trade Association B's personalized marketing campaigns for key customers.

<u>Logistics</u>

The flow of information back and forth throughout the process was time consuming and not effective. Less handoffs and re-reviews were needed.

Adapt Action Steps

Based on the Gap's, Trade Association A developed action steps to narrow the gaps. Specifically, they planned on doing the following:

- Eliminate the handoff's between groups and begin to hold weekly meetings where all members could gather to review items and get updated on the status of the project
- Database marketing would begin segmenting the customer base into a "Gold, Silver, Bronze" status
- Marketing would develop more personalized communications for "Gold, Silver, Bronze" targets and send less of the more expensive brochures to non-target audiences
- Follow-up communications would be low-cost email blasts for non "Gold, Silver, Bronze" audiences and personalized letters for the "Gold, Silver, Bronze" folks.
- A more prominent area on the web site would be created for upcoming events
- Seminar Planning would provide brief verbal and high-level written reminders of upcoming events at existing events

Monitor and Measure

Trade Association A would use the weekly meetings and keep their debrief meetings (now expanded to include senior management and Program Management) to monitor and measure the process. Specific performance measures were not slated to be tracked at the time the project concluded.

Conclusion

Trade Association A was able to create a better process for marketing their seminars. They felt the greatest value from studying the process was the feedback they got from customers and secondly the process of mapping what they did so each group could really see what the other did.

Exhibit 17-1: Develop and Update Brochure – Marketing Group

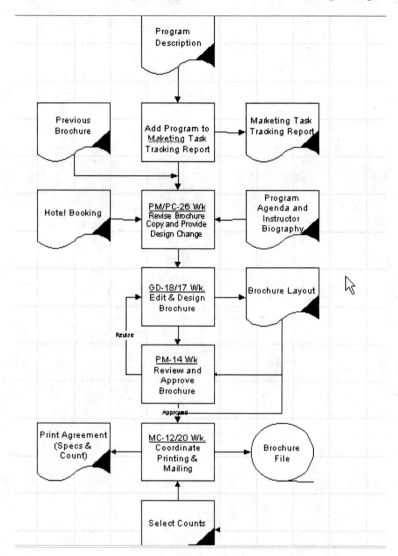

Exhibit 17-2: Select Mailing List – Database Marketing Group

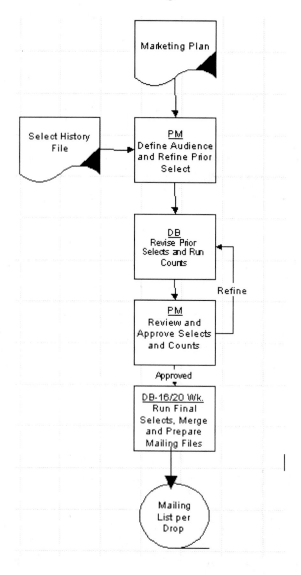

Exhibit 17-3: Brochure Printing and Mailing

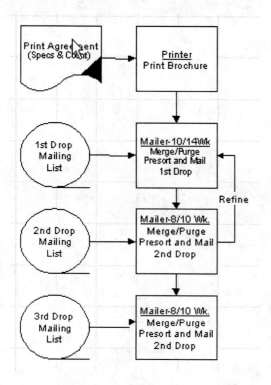

Chapter Eighteen: The Finance Function

Pre Case Background:

The modern day finance function has shifted its tasks from the intensity of transaction processing to the ability to act as a more value added business partner to management. This has been done through the leveraging of automation and technology to reduce the manual burden of transactional tasks.

CFO's of world-class organizations are continuously improving their finance functions in a variety of ways and across multiple processes that comprise their finance functions. For example, Entergy introduced the concept of natural work teams to improve their finance function. Through goal setting and the natural work teams Entergy focused on identifying defects, cycle times, and costs. They developed training to help teams focus on improving results. In addition, self-assessment surveys were used amongst managers to collect additional opinions. As a result of this total quality focus, within a year, 90% of the work teams were active. Of these, 64% developed defect, cycle time and cost based performance measures to manage their processes. Success included reducing accounts receivable 60 percent and a reduction in general ledger closing time by 88%.

Sun Microsystems leverages automation and technology to improve its finance and accounting department. It devised internal web pages to run expense reporting, management reports, budgets, check processing and financial reports. This improves efficiency and information decision-making. Sun Tea, the expense reporting system saved the company $3.6 million per year in expense report processing costs. Another tool, Saltool, a salary review processing application paid back its $300,000 in development cost within 3 months.

EDS won recognition by CFO magazine for its finance function. They reduced their billing systems from 25 to 5, centralized accounts receivable and collections into one location, reduced A/R remittance processing costs from $14.94 to $.73, reduced customer invoice processing costs from $14.29 to $3.65 and reduced their T&E transaction error rate from 20% to less than 1%. This was done through a combination of technology, process and procedural changes that leveraged best practices.

The finance function covers a broad range of processes that help the organization keep its books accounted for properly. As part of our continuous improvement regiment we will first look to define the activities of these processes and then determine the appropriate performance measures to help manage them.

As a follow-up we'll explore one example of finance managers dilemma within a nursing home operation to improve their receivables payment process.

Define Process Activities
Payroll
- setup and maintain employee payroll files
- time reporting and approval
- payroll processing
- process payroll time sheet
- distribute paychecks and registers
- process payroll accounting entries
- prepare, review, and file payroll tax returns
- resolve payroll inquiries

Travel and Entertainment Accounting
- establish and update company T&E policies
- gather and compile employee T&E data
- review and analyze T&E information for compliance and validity
- maintain general ledger system for activities associated with posting T&E information
- manage and analyze T&E applicable trends to determine financial impact to company
- process T&E adjustments for errors or omissions
- create and produce T&E reports for management review

Accounts Payable
- gather and compile A/P documentation, including company purchase orders, vendor
  invoices, receiving information, etc.
- establish new vendor accounts
- obtain verification of receipt of goods/services and obtain vendor payment approval
- maintain A/P system
- post payments to General Ledger accounts
- generate and post manual or "special" check disbursements
- generate or transmit vendor payment
- evaluate and review A/P balances, including account analysis, review of cash disbursements
- resolve vendor billing discrepancies and related inquiries
- process A/P adjustments for errors or omissions
- create and produce A/P-related reports for management or other review

Billing
- create new customer billing accounts (order entry is an input to this process, and therefore
  should not be included)
- collect and compile company invoices prior to transmitting/sending invoices to the customer
- review billing invoices for accuracy, completeness, and integrity

- transmit billing invoices to customers
- maintain billing system
- respond to customer billing inquiries and resolve billing discrepancies
- generate and issue customer credit memos
- process billing adjustments for errors or omissions
- create and produce collection-related reports for management or other review

Accounts Receivable
- receive and post customer remittances to customer accounts
- investigate and research over/under payments
- implement actions to re-bill customer or forward account to collections
- process A/R adjustments for errors or omissions, including credits/debits to accounts
- maintain A/R system
- review receivables and specific account balances to ensure timely receipt of payment
- produce A/R reports for management review
- establish and update company credit and collections policies
- compile credit information pertaining to new and existing customer accounts
- evaluate and authorize credit limits
- maintain, evaluate, and analyze credit and collections accounts and trends
- review and monitor customer payment histories to identify delinquent or late-paying accounts
- research and contact delinquent customers
- transfer and monitor delinquent customer accounts sent to outside collection agencies
- process collections adjustments

Financial Reporting
- maintenance of general ledger chart of accounts
- administration of G/L database reporting/consolidation structure
- preparation, review, and recording of journal entries
- monitoring of the closing process at unit and corporate levels
- preparation, review and analysis of accounts and trial balances at the unit level
- preparation of consolidated corporate trial balance, including eliminating and consolidating
  journal entries
- generation and distribution of monthly financial reports
- reconciliation of balance sheet accounts
- consolidation of expense type information
- maintenance of allocation pools and related rates
- development, review, and distribution of accounting and internal control policies and
  procedures manuals
- record retention/archiving
- preparation, review, and submission of financial information (financial statements, footnotes,
  and other supplementary information)

• research of GAAP and international accounting issues and briefing of new FASB/

  International Authorities pronouncements
• external and/ or parent audit coordination and related fees

Financial Budgeting

• gather and organize information necessary for designing and analyzing the budget, operating

  plan, and strategic plan
• analyze budget, operating plan, and strategic plan information
• prepare budget, operating plan, and strategic plan
• obtain budget, operating plan, and strategic plan approval
• maintain planning/forecasting system
• report and distribute budget, operating plan, and strategic plan information
• investigate and evaluate financial performance and variances between budget and actual

  figures
• prepare and distribute budget and actual variance reports
• periodically recast budget
• create and produce reports for internal management or external third party review

Fixed Asset Accounting

• establish and/or change fixed asset accounting policies, including depreciation capitalization
• gather information to evaluate fixed assets
• classify fixed assets based on asset description
• maintain fixed asset accounting system
• analyze the company's fixed asset performance (e.g., return on investment calculation, tax

  implications, etc.)
• prepare fixed asset adjustments for errors, misclassifications, or omissions
• prepare fixed asset reports for management, including fixed asset register, tax depreciation

  reports, etc.

Tax

• compile and gather relevant tax information
• monitor the adherence to company and regulatory tax guidelines
• design tax plans and programs
• prepare supporting schedules and tax forms, including all tax-based accounting
• manage tax regulatory relationships
• maintain tax general ledger system
• create and produce tax reports for management and other review

Cash Management

• Manage incoming and outgoing cash flows (including lock box, transfer consolidations)
• Manage and leverage intercompany cash flows and use of foreign currencies.
• Manage collections and payment disbursement processes.

- Coordinate and build relations with banking partners.
- Perform cash forecasting to determine the optimal liquidity needed for company growth.
- Manage short-term investment activities (marketable securities).

Generate Key Performance Indicators
Next, create the performance measures for each process. This will allow you to understand the process better by collecting base line historical data to compare against others or to trend. It also allows you to have a baseline system in place to monitor and measure the process once it is improved.

Overall finance department
Total finance department cost as a % of revenue
Total finance headcount as a % of total company headcount
Total finance staff to management ratio

Payroll
Total payroll department cost as a % of revenue
Total payroll department cost per paycheck
Average cycle time to process payroll
% of paychecks with errors

Travel & entertainment (T&E) accounting
Total T&E department cost as a % of revenue
Total T&E department cost per T&E report
Average T&E payment amount
Annual number of T&E reports processed per full time equivalent
% of T&E submissions not in compliance with T&E policy

Accounts payable
Total A/P department cost as a % of revenue
Total A/P department cost per invoice processed
Average A/P payment amount
Annual number of invoices processed per FTE
% of payables with transaction errors

Billing
Total billing department cost as a % of revenue
Total billing department cost per customer invoice
% of invoices with errors
Average elapsed time between shipment/service and billing

Accounts receivable
Total A/R department cost as a % of revenue
Credit cost per account requiring credit activity
Collections cost per account requiring collections activity
% of AR remittances with errors
Annual number of remittances per FTE
Accounts Receivable Turnover

Financial Reporting
Total financial reporting department cost as a % of revenue
Percentage of journal entries with errors

Number of days to close the books
Number of FTEs required to close the books
Financial Budgeting
Total financial budgeting department cost as a % of revenue
Total financial budgeting department cost per budget prepared
Cycle time to prepare budgets
Variance of budgeted to actual as a % of budgeted
Fixed assets accounting
Total fixed assets department cost as a % of revenue
Total cost per fixed assets transaction
Total cost per fixed asset tracked
Annual volume of fixed assets tracked per FTE
% of fixed assets that are misallocated or misclassified
Minimum capitalization value
Tax
Total tax department cost as a % of revenue
Total tax department cost per tax return filed
Penalties, fines, & interest as a % of cash income taxes paid
Cycle time to prepare an average tax return
Cash Management
Cash management cost as a percentage of revenue
Average cycle time to reconcile bank to book cash balances
Number of Bank Accounts per $1 million dollars
Length of Cash Conversion Cycle
Percentage of accounts with material bank to book discrepancies
Average rate of return on marketable securities investments

Case Study: Nursing Home A and its Medicare Billing Process

Description of the organization/Identify the Need
Nursing Home A is a healthcare facility based in the suburbs of a large Midwestern city. The home is a small to medium sized facility that is privately owned and been in operation for many years. Technology sophistication is limited and many administrative processes are labor intensive.

Nursing Home A provides a variety of healthcare services to its patients including skilled nursing care that is covered under the Medicare program. Historically reimbursement for services rendered by a skilled nursing facility like Nursing Home A can be difficult to obtain. However, with the proper training and processes in place payment can be received quickly and easily. At Nursing Home A this is not the case.

Currently, Nursing Home A is experiencing cash flow problems. Their vendors are pushing them to pay on-time although their payments are historically late. Nursing Home A would prefer to take advantage of early-pay discounts but does not have the cash flow to do this. The main reason for this is that their receivables owed from its customers are historically very late in paying bills.

Typically, residents of Nursing Home A pay via 4 sources. First is Public Aid (government assistance) , 73% of residents have some form of Public Aid but only 53% of the sales revenue is generated from Public Aid reimbursement. The next source of payment is private funds (from the patient themselves). This accounts for 15% of the residents and 14% of sales revenues. The next source is Medicare. Medicare is 9% of the residents but 26% of the sales revenues. The final source is via other miscellaneous funds. See graphs in Exhibit 18-1.

Nursing Home A recognized that a key bottleneck in cash flow was tied up in the 26% of revenue from Medicare. They determined if they could have significant improvement on Medicare receivables, there cash flow could be dramatically improved on a day-to-day basis.

Map the Process
A new assistant administrator had recently been hired within the last month. For purposes of this case we will call this person Adam Smith. Adam was asked by the owner of Nursing Home A to solve the cash flow problem by finding a way to collect Medicare payments more efficiently and effectively.

The first step for Adam was to understand the existing Medicare process. Adam went about this task by talking to key personnel first asking open-ended questions and following up with more structured inquiries. Adam was careful to manage his work carefully. Being new he did not want to step on the toes of people who had been there a long time. He also did not want to come across as accusing anyone of doing a bad job. Further, although the owner asked Adam to fix this issue, the owner was not a regular presence that openly championed Adams project increasing the difficulty of the task.

Starting small with simple questions that asked for opinions and comments and then building to more specific requests for detail Adam got buy-in and support from the staff he was working with on this project. The staff became involved in the process in a proactive manner and felt they had a lot of say in how to improve the process. This open communication, trust and support would later prove very valuable to Adam.

After several sessions and iterations, Adam finally drew out a process flow of the Medicare billing process. It is summarized in detail below.

The following are the key steps in the process:

1. The process begins with the marketing director seeking residents to come to Nursing Home A. The Director of Nursing is alerted and works with the Medicare Biller to see if the potential patient is eligible for Medicare. A decision is made to accept or not accept the patient.

2. If accepted the person is admitted to the home.

3. On the 1st to the 8th days of each month, a representative from Medicare will come to Nursing Home A to assess the Minimum Data Set or MDS. This is the federal form used to determine the level of care and subsequently payment for residents of the home on Medicare. The Medicare representative will use nurses charts, therapy notes and physician orders in her review. Upon completion, the Medicare representative will complete the MDS form and place it in the resident's chart located at the Nurses station on the floor in which they reside. The Medicare representative will then fill out a Billing Information Form with additional information to bill Medicare for approved expenses. This form is provided to the central bookkeeping office located off site at another nursing home owned and operated by the same owner of Nursing Home A. The billing information is photocopied in central bookkeeping and sent back to Nursing Home A upon the request of Nursing Home A.

4. On or after the first of every month the Director of Nursing will give the billing department a list of all Medicare residents for the previous month along with all of their diagnosis codes (numeric classification of diseases that Medicare uses in their system). This is not currently a high priority of the Director of Nursing and is often not provided after the first of the month, sometimes taking several weeks. If this is not

done promptly, it will delay the billing process because the codes are required for entering bills into Medicare's billing system.

5. Invoices from pharmacy, lab, physical therapy, occupational therapy, and medical supplies are applied to Medicare form UB92. When Nursing Home A uses vendors for these services they are invoiced by these vendors and those invoices are sent to the Director of Nursing who verifies the product or service was received and it is a valid invoice to pay. The invoices are then sent back to the off site location where central bookkeeping is located to set up as a payable and eventually pay. The billing department requires these in their approval of form UB92. Often, the billing process is delayed because billing (located at Nursing Home A's facility) is awaiting the forms to be sent back to Nursing Home A from central bookkeeping.

6. New Medicare claims are then entered into the Medicare billing system by billing, once the MDS codes, patient information and UB92 forms have been approved. However, no new Medicare claims can be entered into the system unless all past claims have been paid. Any claims that had improper approval or documentation need to be resolved and resubmitted as well. This is a problem because if there are delays in the Medicare review process or errors in the process, new bills cannot be entered into the system causing Nursing Home A to accrue a huge volume of receivables without being able to collect the cash from Medicare.

7. On a daily basis, the billing will go into the Medicare billing system and check the status of entered claims. A status code will appear and if it indicates a problem, the billing group must go back and fix errors and resubmit the claim. A code of "P" indicates that Nursing Home A's claim has been approved and will be receiving payment.

Adam not only prepared a process map but also prepared a visual timeline to show the key activities and how long a process this turned out to be. Please see Exhibit 18-2 for this timeline. In summary, Adam concluded that it takes Nursing Home A over 4 months, or 140 days to go through the process of Medicare payments for any one particular month. He quickly realized the problem the owner was talking about and knew something had to be done.

Research Alternative Solutions
Adam was familiar with the nursing care industry and had a relationship with the corporate controller of another nursing home franchise, Nursing Home B. The corporate controller, Nathan Williams had been through a very similar set of circumstances a few years previously. Now, Nursing Home B was described by a leading expert as "leading the country" in this area.

When Adam contacted Nathan, Nathan agreed to share some of his war stories with Adam. After a few conversations, Nathan agreed to match up his process flowchart and Medicare timeline to that of Adams at Nursing Home A for comparison purposes. This was ideal for Adam and Nursing Home A because Nursing Home B was very similar in terms of services, had a similar patient capacity and Medicare profile as Nursing Home A.

Please see Exhibit 18-3 for the Timeline provided by Nursing Home B.

The key features of Nursing Home B's process are as follows:

- They split the process between information gathering and compilation. They gather information during the month and then during the "crunch" billing period after month end they move into the compilation stage to prepare the required forms and approvals to enter into the Medicare system expeditiously
- The information gathering stage is done only at the nursing home itself and not by a central bookkeeping unit. Most of this information is in nurses and doctors charts and orders and is on hand at the site.
- The compilation and checking of documentation is done centrally at the bookkeeping office.
- Very strict timetables are in place at all steps of the process. For example, the UB92 must be turned into the central office by the 7th of each month
- Very proactive with vendors when it comes to receiving invoices because they are required for compilation of the UB92, they require vendors to submit an invoice of services rendered within 5 days of the service being performed and they fax the vendor a standard form to complete to make the process easier and consistent across vendors
- They gather information from the patient before they even enter the home. They find out what other benefits were exhausted and what insurance they have which creates fewer delays in the actual billing and payment process.
- All Medicare bills are entered into the Medicare system on the day the documentation is received for approval in the central office.

Because of their policies and procedures, Nursing Home B is paid for all current month Medicare bills within 36 days, 94% of which are paid within 29 days.

Document the Gap

Adam was able to see with clarity several areas that could be improved upon immediately for significant impacts. Much of this was uncovered through mapping out the process and seeing what was there. It was amplified by comparing to Nursing Home B and getting confirmation that things should be done differently. Below are some significant gaps noted by Adam.

- Nursing Home A did not have strict timelines for anything. The Director of Nursing and others who were to provide information did so at their own leisure and nobody was proactive in requesting information at all.
- Documents were shuffled back and forth and incomplete requiring rework and lost time at Nursing Home A due to lack of a solid process for compilation of information.
- A 13 day difference between Nursing Home A and B was due to waiting on vendor invoices to be received after services were rendered. Recall how Nursing Home A required them within 5 days of service with their standard form.
- Lack of formal processes and procedures for everything from compilation to timelines to data gathering created chaos.

Next Adam would need to determine what best practices to suggest for implementation.

Adapt Action Steps

Adam put together a set of key action plans to present to Nursing Home A's owner. In all 7 suggestions were made. These are as follows:

1. Measure cycle time for Medicare receivables on a regular basis to track improvement.
2. Create a new process to formalize Medicare billings.
3. Use the new process to bill the overdue claims and get current.
4. Set up a timeline that specifies key activities to take place before and after month end.
5. Create a list of key forms and documents required during the data gathering process.
6. Require all vendors to submit invoices for services rendered by the 5th of the month.
7. Establish the billing deadline to be the 8th of the month.

Monitor and Measure

The new procedures were put in place with relative ease because Adam had gotten everyone involved in the process. They all had a vested interest in improving and worked proactively to do so. Within a ten-week period, un-submitted claims had been paid by Medicare and the average time to receive payment went from 140 days to 43 days. Please see Exhibit 18-4 for the revised Medicare Billing timeline.

Adam now measures the timeliness of his Medicare process on a monthly basis as a way of monitoring performance.

Conclusion

Adam learned a lot from this exercise. First he learned that by simply mapping the process and understanding inputs, activities and outputs a lot of steps can be improved through simple process changes.

Second, he realized the value of getting people directly impacted by the change involved in the process early on as it would help when it was time to implement change.

Third, he realized the importance of a good benchmark partner. Nursing Home B really helped guide Adam in his thinking and the benchmarks really helped create a definite business case for change not only to the staff but also to the Nursing Home owner.

Exhibit 18-1

Residents % by Payer Source

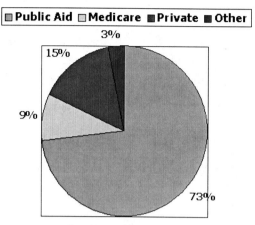

Sales % by Payer Source

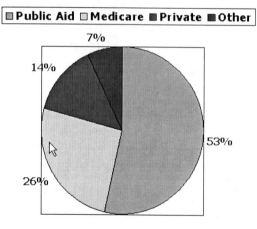

Exhibit 18-2: Timeline for the Current Medicare Billing Process

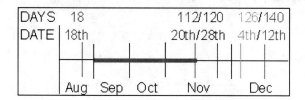

Invoices arrive	
Wasted time	
93% billed	
7% billed	
93% paid	
7% paid	

Exhibit 18-3: Nursing Home B's Medicare Billing Timeline

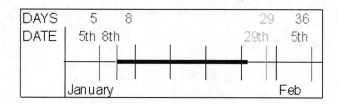

Invoices arrive	
Check claims	
100% billed	
95% paid	
4% paid	

Exhibit 18-4: Revised Medicare Billing Timeline for Nursing Home A

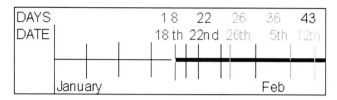

Invoices arrive	
Check claims	
60% billed	
9% billed	
12% billed	
69% paid	
12% paid	

Chapter Nineteen: The Human Resources Function

Pre Case Background:

The human resources function is a diverse set of processes that ensure an organization's human assets are properly deployed. Human resources plays the most critical role in building a workforce that can carry out the organization's strategic goals.

World class HR organizations are leveraging technology to improve their value to the organization. For example, KeyCorp implemented a human resources information system (HRIS) that supplies timely updating and database integration and manages the bank's entire HR function. At KeyCorp all employees have access to the system so it can be kept up to date. The HRIS system records, tracks, and controls almost every HR function.

Other organizations like Dell leverage their corporate intranet to allow employees to control everything from benefit enrollment to managing stock options. All together there are around 25 applications in the system for employees and managers. On any given day, over 2000 people log on to the Hr on the Net site.

Benchmarking has also played a key role in reshaping HR functions. Warner Lambert, Eli Lilly, and Allied Signal used benchmarking to yield creative insights for continuous improvement in their HR departments. For example, Warner Lambert found that 76% of HR work was administrative leading them to deploy more automation and self service to reduce the administrative burden. Allied Signal used results of its benchmarking endeavors to support the creation of 78 kiosks to be used by over 45,000 employees to help reduce the data collection, entry, and validation process formerly done by HR positions. Eli Lilly's benchmarking of the HR function created many opportunities to leverage technology to provide quicker, more accurate information.

Changes in organizational structure helped IBM improve its HR processes. In 1995 IBM consolidated all its service functions into a centralized Human Resources Service Center based in Raleigh, North Carolina. The call center helps more than 700,000 employees . The move was made to help IBM cut HR costs by 40 percent.

Measurement was the road to successful management for the Transportation Administrative Service Center (TASC) a U.S. Department of Transportation human resources office. The TASC used a balanced scorecard approach to measure their performance. Continuous measurement helps improve performance. For example, in 1999, 68% of TASC customers rated the organization's overall performance as above average, compared to only 59% one year earlier.

Let's take a look at some activities and measures for a typical HR function.

Define Process Activities

Compensation Design and Administration
•Incentive Tracking
•Salary Planning
•Job Evaluations
•Salary Surveys
•Job Analysis
•Job Descriptions
•Design Compensation Plans
•Define Incentive Programs
Benefits Design and Administration
•Design Benefits Plan
•Competitive Analysis
•Annual Enrollment Administration
•Selection And Change Administration
•Outsource Liaison
•Claims Processing
•Defined Contribution Plan
•Workers Compensation
•Medical/Dental/Equity
•Benefits Education
Employee Relations
•Policy and Procedure
•Leave of Absence
•Relocation
•Retirement
•Grievances
•Promotions
•Transfers
•Data Maintenance
Labor Relations
•Union Negotiations
•Contracting
Training
•Needs Analysis
•Training Design and Development
•Liaison to Outsourced Training
•Computer Based Training
• Distance Learning
•Training Evaluation
•Entry Level Training Programs
•Determine Training Source

Performance Management
- Performance Appraisal Development
- Performance Appraisal Tracking
- Performance Appraisal Research

Recruiting
- Interviewing
- Resume/Application Processing
- Temporary Employee Placement

Staffing
- Workforce Planning
- Assessing Human Resource needs

Managing Change
- Developing Communications for Change Management
- Counseling Employees and Executives
- Assessing and eliminating barriers to change.

Managing Diversity
- Diversity Research
- Corporate Diversity Initiatives
- Diversity Training

Compliance (EEO, ADA, FMLA, etc.)
- Compliance Testing
- Compliance Reviews

HRIS/File Management
- System Maintenance
- System Upgrades
- Updating Files

Strategic Planning/Organizational Design
- Human Resources Strategy Development
- Business Plan Development

Organization Development/ Management Development
- Succession Planning
- High Potential Employee Development
- Corporate Culture Issues

Performance Measures

Recruitment and selection

Recruiting costs per new hire

Elapsed time from job requisition to offer

Percent of offers accepted

Percentage of open positions (non-entry) filled from within

Turnover rate

Develop and train employees

Training hours per employee

Training costs as a percentage of payroll

Return on learning investment

Performance, recognition and reward

Input sources for performance measurement

Types of performance measurement systems

Compensation strategies by employee type

Benefits design and administration

Benefits administration cost per employee

Benefits cost (non-administrative) per employee

Percentage of employees contributing to a retirement plan

Contribution percentage by employee into retirement plans

Contribution percentage by organization into retirement plans

Number of sick days per employee

Number of vacation days per employee

Technology

Cost of HRIS per employee

Organizational effectiveness

Number of suggestions submitted per employee

Percentage of suggestions implemented

Case Study: Consumer Product Company A's Human Resource Department

Description of the organization/Identify the Need
Consumer Products Company A is a diversified food processor and distributor that operate in 3 business segments: dairy, specialty products, and refrigerated products. The company is a multi-billion dollar organization with over 10,000 employees and operates over 50 plants throughout the United States.

Due to intense mergers and acquisitions that fueled growth in the past ten years, the company has a very decentralized human resources function. The internal audit department was asked by senior management to review the human resource organization and determine whether or not the structure is properly positioned to add value efficiently and effectively. They also requested to know what the best practices are for human resources and where the gaps exist between their HR department and best practices. Senior management requested that the internal audit group report their results to them and to the HR department.

Map the Process
The internal audit group first decided to approach the project by agreeing to a scope with senior management. This was important because it clearly defined the project boundaries. Based on discussions with senior management and the HR group, and the time and budget to conduct this work, the following processes would be within the scope of the review:

HR planning
Staffing
Training
Performance Appraisal
Employee Relations
Compensation and benefits
HR information systems
Compliance

The audit team then determined the best tools to use to help them better understand these processes while at the same time comparing them to other organizations and best practices. The audit group decided to do the following:

1. Interview HR professionals within the organization
2. Interview 60 employees outside the HR organization regarding job satisfaction, performance reviews, recruiting and hiring practices, and training
3. Focus group with key HR professionals

The audit team collected key information and obtained relevant forms and documents. Below is a summary of this work:

- Understood existing HR strategy and how it relates to company-wide strategy
- Defined the cause and effect relationships between HR strategy and actual actions taken by HR
- Reviewed the "balanced scorecard" currently in place along with its historical data
- Reviewed and documented a management model of the HR function. It documented how the HR department planned for resource requirements, organized their department, directed training and other services, developed polices and procedures, and monitored and evaluated results.
- Understood the responsibilities of HR management vs. HR staff
- Reviewed and documented the following processes in detail defining their inputs, activities and outputs as well as the key owners of the major activities:
  - HR strategic planning process
  - Recruiting and Retaining staff process
  - Performance appraisal process
  - Employee Relations (communications) process
  - Compensation and benefits process
  - HRIS (human resources information systems) process

The audit team created visual frameworks for each of the aforementioned processes that listed the major activities and actions needed for those activities to serve as a summary of their work. These visuals were good communication pieces later on with senior management and helped them take several complex processes and summarize each on a single sheet of paper. See Exhibit 19-1 for an example of the Compensation and Benefits Framework.

After the interviews, process mapping, framework creation and the focus groups, Consumer Products Company A had a much better understanding of their own HR processes. However, they felt they could not go to senior management yet because they had no goals or improvement suggestions formulated yet.

Research Alternative Solutions
The internal audit department knew that they did not have the time nor budget to do comprehensive research and analysis. They spent the majority of their time documenting their own processes. Before the project began they knew they could rely on their external auditors to provide them with a tool to compare their HR processes with other organizations in the external auditor's database of HR benchmarks.

While this process would not allow the organization to talk with other organizations and get specific questions answered the internal audit department felt it would provide them the following benefits:

- Generate some high-level insights
- Facilitate a more meaningful discussion about their own HR department
- Provide management useful information to control and operate this function
- Provide best practices and key performance indicators (KPI's) of other organizations
- Allow an independent third party to review, analyze and compare their department to others

The benchmark group was customized as best as it could to fit that of Consumer Products Company A. Twenty-six organizations that were manufacturing or consumer-products oriented were chosen. All had revenues over 1 billion, and thousands of employees.

This database was not a set of world-class organizations. It was simply other organizations that completed the same survey that Consumer Products A would be completing. However, they felt it would give them a good baseline to compare against and do so in a cost effective and timely manner. Senior management and the HR department were also comfortable with this approach.

Consumer Products Company A completed the survey provided by the external auditor. They then compared their performance to this group along the following performance measures that they felt were aligned with the scope of this project:

Overall HR Department
- Degree of HR centralization
- HR expense as a % of revenue
- HR staff to management ratio
- HR direct labor cost per HR FTE
- Degree of outsourcing
- Cost and Time allocations by process

Recruitment and Selection
- Succession planning usage
- Recruiting cost per new hire
- Job offer acceptance rate
- Time from job requisition to offer
- Percentage of open positions
- Turnover rate
- Cost of temporary help as a % of payroll

Employee Training
- Training hours per employee
- Training cost as a % of revenue
- Training cost per employee

Performance Reward
- Sources of performance measurement
- Compensation strategies by employee type

Benefits Administration
- Benefits cost per employee
- Percent of employees covered by benefits
- Retirement plan contribution percentages
- Flexible benefits types
- Sick day and vacation day policies

Information Systems
- Number of separate HR databases
- Cost of HRIS per employee
- Integration of HRIS and payroll systems
- Type of HRIS used

Employee Relations
- Communication methods used
- Employee feedback mechanisms
- Suggestions submitted per employee
- Percent of suggestions implemented

When comparing these measures Consumer Products Company A attempted to evaluate the gap.

Please see Exhibit 19-2 for some sample charts that came out of this exercise.

Document the Gap

The internal audit group studied the benchmarks provided by their external auditors. They took into consideration what they had learned about the HR processes earlier as well. Below is a summary of their more significant gaps.

Process	Current	Future
Performance Management	Annual review performed by supervisors; spot checked and not tied to strategy	Use of 360 feedback tied to strategic objectives
Change Management	Change management is a competency that is non-existent currently but should be resident and driven by HR especially with the growth by acquisition strategy	Formal process in place and carried out with pro-active participation by management
Recruiting	Very decentralized; not coordinated and contingent upon separate supervisors who carry this out in their own manner	Formal processes and standards. Tracking of key measures like turnover. Centralized with decentralized participation
Management development	One executive program in place not widely used	A formal succession plan used by all key senior executive positions.
HR information systems	Decentralized with multiple databases not integrated with each other. No formal HRIS in place.	Centralized database with localized standards and inputs from the local business units.
Training	Very reactive. Done in a decentralized manner done in-house despite not having a core competency to do this well.	Outsource to professional vendors with expertise in creating course content.
Strategic Planning and Organizational Design	HR strategy is not currently aligned with overall company strategy	Involve the HR group in the organization's strategic planning process. Create HR strategy in conjunction with overall strategy
Employee relations	Very inconsistent across the company. No exit interviews, no supervisory training, high risk of discrimination and deteriorating employee trust	Formal employee polices that are created in a centralized area but executed at the local level. Proper training of supervisors on employee relations
Compensation Design	HR is not currently involved in setting base compensation levels, it is discretionary in the hands of the hiring manager	Use HR group to do a job analysis and external compensation surveying to objectively determine salary levels
Diversity Management	Significantly behind the benchmark group. High risk of losing credibility	Need a formal and centralized diversity policy that is administered at the local level
Benefits Design and Admin	Do this well but could do better with a centralized HRIS database	Use a centralized HR system to eliminate duplication of effort and more effectively manage
Labor Relations	Do this well but need to do more training and better contract administration	Train management on better union negotiation tactics and more centralized labor contract management

Adapt Action Steps

Consumer Products Company A delivered its report to management with key recommendations pertaining to the points in their gap analysis. Subsequent to this, senior management, the HR department and the internal audit department crafted more specific action steps that could be implemented.

The HR department rolled out a new program to help promote these new policies that would be taking place. They called the program "Business Results through People" and it would have impacts on the following HR processes:

- o Leadership capability
- o Roles and structures
- o Finding Key talent
- o Communication
- o Pay, Benefits and Rewards
- o Performance Management
- o Retention and Succession
- o Training and Development

For specific areas (particularly performance gaps) linked to these processes, the HR department created a visionary and motivational statement along with key bullets for the business strategy and HR focus. See Exhibit 19-3 for examples of a vision statements and action steps.

Monitor and Measure

The company created time lines for the implementation of several performance improvement suggestions. They then created smaller teams who were empowered and accountable to implement the changes.

As the changes were being implemented there were milestone checkpoints. Milestone checkpoints were not meant to punish the teams or the HR group for not getting tasks done on time but to merely provide a status update at a point in time.

These checkpoints listed the issues that existed as of the audit date (the date when the internal audit department issued its report), the improvements needed, and the current status. See Exhibit 13-4 for an example of these milestone checkpoints.

Conclusion

Consumer Products Company A had seen significant changes in its organization in the past decade. The neglect in the HR area was evident to senior management. This added increasing complexity to their business. As a result of this continuous improvement initiative the function has gone from a maintenance function perceived as a cost center to a value-added function with proactive leadership and support. Consumer Products Company A recognized that without appropriate guidelines to recruit, train, develop and manage human assets they were exposed to significant risks. Consumer Products Company A has a long way to go but feels they are better managing these risks.

Exhibit 19-1 – Compensation and Benefits Framework

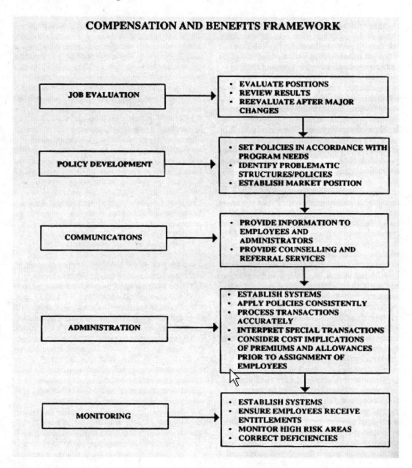

COMPENSATION AND BENEFITS FRAMEWORK

JOB EVALUATION	→	• EVALUATE POSITIONS • REVIEW RESULTS • REEVALUATE AFTER MAJOR CHANGES
POLICY DEVELOPMENT	→	• SET POLICIES IN ACCORDANCE WITH PROGRAM NEEDS • IDENTIFY PROBLEMATIC STRUCTURES/POLICIES • ESTABLISH MARKET POSITION
COMMUNICATIONS	→	• PROVIDE INFORMATION TO EMPLOYEES AND ADMINISTRATORS • PROVIDE COUNSELLING AND REFERRAL SERVICES
ADMINISTRATION	→	• ESTABLISH SYSTEMS • APPLY POLICIES CONSISTENTLY • PROCESS TRANSACTIONS ACCURATELY • INTERPRET SPECIAL TRANSACTIONS • CONSIDER COST IMPLICATIONS OF PREMIUMS AND ALLOWANCES PRIOR TO ASSIGNMENT OF EMPLOYEES
MONITORING	→	• ESTABLISH SYSTEMS • ENSURE EMPLOYEES RECEIVE ENTITLEMENTS • MONITOR HIGH RISK AREAS • CORRECT DEFICIENCIES

Exhibit 19-2- Examples of Performance Measures from benchmarking exercise

Types of employee communications methods used:

Type	Benchmark	Our Company
Written memoranda	98%	Yes
Email memoranda	85%	No
Voice mail messages	50%	No
Video presentations	45%	No
Live presentations	70%	Yes
Internet/Intranet	50%	No

Percent of job offers accepted:

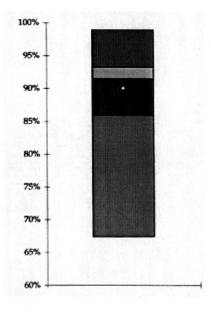

Exhibit 19-3 –Vision Statements and Action Steps

Diversity

"The success of our business will depend on growing a **diverse & inclusive** workforce that will understand the **different ways** our customers, vendors, shareholders & communities think. This will help us to meet their **changing & diverse needs**."

Business Strategies	HR Focus
◆ Drive lowest imaginable cost with optimal asset utilization	◆ Support formation of **Divisional Inclusion Councils**
◆ Deliver World Class quality and customer service	◆ Execute against Council recommendations
◆ Employer of Choice	◆ Drive **inclusion awareness training** to all field locations
	◆ Improve **diversity representation** across the Company
	◆ Develop & execute Affirmative Action Plan tool kit and training

Safety & Risk Management

"Creating and maintaining a **safe and healthy** workplace is key to increasing employee **productivity and satisfaction**."

Business Strategies	HR Focus
◆ Drive lowest imaginable cost with optimal asset utilization	◆ Support the line in **reducing accidents** and worker compensation costs
◆ Employer of Choice	◆ Develop communication vehicles to share safety "best practices"
	◆ Reporting mechanisms to communicate **workers compensation data** by sites
	◆ Participate in and manage all OSHA audits
	◆ Increase the field HR role in leading safety and workers compensation initiatives

Exhibit 19-4: Milestone Checkpoints

Employee Relations

As of Audit Date	Improvements Needed	Current Status
Inconsistent: -no exit interviews -no supervisor training -limited policy availability -risk of discrimination and deterioration in employee trust	Central guidelines/local execution	-policy written -supervisor training developed

Compensation Design & Admin

As of Audit Date	Improvements Needed	Current Status
-Needs structure and strategic linkage -currently supervisors define compensation and HR is involved in guidelines -potential to improve retention	-relative worth needs to be established from: 1) job analysis then 2) external geographic compensation survey	-Top 150 employees have been targeted for placement in common grade/range grid -New employees and promotions are reviewed against external compensation

HR Information System

As of Audit Date	Improvements Needed	Current Status
Not currently available	Central database with -local standard inputs -local discretionary inputs	Near completion, centralized payroll system as a result

Chapter Twenty: The Information Technology Function

Pre Case Background:

Lets face it, information technology has dramatically changed the way we work and live our lives. Technology has prompted organizations to change the way they do business. Technology will continue to advance and improve causing businesses to think through new processes, tools, and systems.

Just think about some of the more poignant examples of how technology has impacted business today.

- Unisys reduce the time it takes to fill open positions from 70 to 45 days by accepting thousands of resumes through its web site.
- United Parcel Service spends over $1 billion on IT annually. They leverage technology to allow their customers to check rates, verify delivery, and track any shipment online.
- Prudential Insurance Co. leverages information technology to equip it with better knowledge about its customers. Technology is leveraged to predict customer behaviors.

IT is at the epicenter of business. This is clearly seen through the billions of dollars spent on IT annually. That is why it is also important, as a manager of IT or an IT project, to track ROI on these major investments. The Gap, Inc., calculates an ROI for each IT project and ranks initiatives in importance to strategic values. Viacom Inc., uses a home grown tool called Dashboard to calculate the ROI on IT projects and prove their value to the finance managers. The Dashboard treats IT investments as a portfolio to be managed when IT outlays are made.

An obvious challenge for any manager is retaining quality employees. That is particularly true for your IT employees who are in great demand. A study done by the American Productivity and Quality Center revealed some best practices for retaining top IT talent. Among the findings include the following notable points a new manager should think about:

- Ensure there is a solid working relationship between the recruiting folks in HR and the information technology department
- Develop and maintain skill competencies on IT positions
- Use your website and web-based recruiting sites to find top notch IT talent
- Leverage apprenticeships and internships as alternative sourcing methods and roadmaps to more long term employment

- Offer employee referrals to other IT staff that recommend qualified candidates
- Provide IT employees with viable opportunities for professional development and career paths
- Offer recruits high quality new hire orientation and training programs
- Provide compensation packages that are comprehensive rather than fancy perks

In yet another American Productivity and Quality Center study, best practices were gleaned from the strategic side of IT investing. Among the more interesting findings were the following:

- the creation of shared services models to reduce costs
- the treatment of IT as a business not a cost center
- the treatment of IT as value added consultants to the business
- IT playing a major role in strategic planning
- the use of metrics to manage the IT process
- strong communications between IT and business units
- performance management reward systems in place

Now that you have a general background on the IT department, let's discuss some high level IT activities and metrics to help you really wrap your arms around a typical IT department. Then, we'll present a case that illustrates how a continuous improvement team was put in place to evaluate the migration of a university's legacy systems to more modern client-server systems.

IT Activities
Applications development
Systems, applications
database development
programming and management
maintenance of applications

Technical and user support
Internal users 'day-to-day' end-user support. e.g.. help desk

Networking services
Mainframe, LAN, WAN, telephony (voice and data), and wireless maintenance and support

IT policy/administration
Establishing IT policy (ex. security), protocol, and managing IT administrative functions

Performance Measures

IT Users per IT Full Time Equivalent (FTE)
Total IT Cost as a Percentage of Revenue or Budget
Total IT Cost per IT User
Committed Response Time
Call Resolution Time
Number of Software Applications by Functional Area
Number of Hardware Manufacturers
Number of Software Manufacturers
Hardware Average Age
Software Average Age

Case Study: College A's Financial Aide System

Description of the organization/Identify the Need

College A consists of four campuses throughout a major metropolitan area. College A is one of the premiere institutions of higher learning in the region. It is a widely recognized college with a diverse set of academic programs and a low student-to-faculty ratio.

The IT team was tasked with developing a new technical architecture to house its system for processing student financial aid transactions. Currently the system is a legacy mainframe system. The schools top administrators feel that the system is limiting because it is not well integrated with other school systems and there is a large amount of manual data entry required to populate the system. Further, as demand grows in the use of the system from a more disperse group management is concerned about its long time viability.

Map the Process

The first step the IT team did was try and get a better understanding of the functional process and functional needs for a financial aid system. They felt this was a good idea because they did not want to suggest a new technical architecture that did not meet functional needs. They already knew the existing system was falling short because they had built custom data feeds and special reports to meet customer demands that the current system could not provide.

The IT group conducted interviews with the Office of Student Financial Aid at College A and created a process flowchart to help document what happens when students apply for financial aid. See Exhibit 20-1 for this chart.

By understanding the current process, the IT group learned that over 70% of incoming freshman receive some form of financial aid. This is indicated the system was very critical to the College.

In summary the existing process works as follows:

The Office of Student Financial Aid (OSFA) at College A assists students with financial aid for a postsecondary education. Financial aid is awarded as grants, scholarships, loans and employment from various federal, state, institutional and private sources. Financial aid is available to students with financial need and those without need.

Need-based financial aid is determined from application information using a standard need analysis formula. An expected family contribution is calculated based on income, assets, family size, family members attending post-secondary education and other factors. A student's financial need is the difference between the typical cost of attending Loyola minus the expected family contribution and any veteran's educational benefits. Financial aid is "packaged" as a combination of grants, loans, and student employment to meet the financial need.

To apply for financial aid students should complete and mail a Free Application for Federal Student Aid (FAFSA) or a Renewal FAFSA to the U.S. Department of Education. An application should be completed and mailed each year as soon as possible after January 1 (preceding the academic year) listing College A as a school choice.

The U.S. Department of Education then sends the student data to the respective universities. The Financial Counselor of College A then extracts this data and verifies it. If some fields are missing, the Financial Counselor waits for more data to come from Dept. of Education. The Financial Counselor then checks the data again for completeness. After all the student data has been verified, the Financial Counselor e-mails this data to the IT Division staff.

The IT Division staff executes some programs on this data to perform certain calculations and checks for student financial aid eligibility. The result of this whole process is the Financial Aid award letter, which is printed out in Office of Student Financial Aid. The Financial Counselor forwards this letter to the Director of Financial Aid, in order to obtain his signature and them sends the letters to Mailroom. Here the Financial Aid award letters are mailed to prospective students. Financial aid awards are mailed to students beginning in early spring (preceding the academic year) after all required information is submitted.

Since College A receives the information electronically from the Department of Education, students can expect to receive an award notice within a month after the priority application date of March 1 has passed.

Research Alternative Solutions

Now that the IT group understood the complete Financial Aid Process they wanted to get a sense for what the ideal system should do. The first step the IT group did was to consider benchmarking their financial aid process against other colleges. They came up with a list of 27 colleges that were members of an academic consortium that College A was also a member. They then prepared a short survey to try and gather details from the head of the IT group about their financial aid systems. See Exhibit 20-2 for the survey example.

Unfortunately, nobody responded to the survey. Not giving up, the IT department did external research on university Financial Aid Systems to help them understand what other universities were doing in this area. See Exhibit 20-3 for the list of resources this team studied.

Finally, the IT department did find a benchmark partner. Within another separate school within College A a new grade entry system had been recently implemented that used some technologies the IT group was considering for the Financial Aid System. A different IT group had implemented it but was more than happy to discuss the process with the IT team on the Financial Aid Project.

The first thing the IT team did was understand the grade entry process to determine if it was a good benchmark fit for their process. They took a similar approach as they did with the Financial Aid Process and walked through the activities of the process and completed a flow chart of the process as well. See Exhibit 20-4 for this flowchart.

The team concluded that the systems shared a lot of synergies and because the Grade Entry System used a client-server technology for similar processing transactions it made a very good reference point for the Financial Aid Project.

Document the Gap

The IT team then compared the existing Financial Aid Process to the research they had done and the Grade Entry System as well as unmet user needs. They concluded that the following gaps existed in the current process and definitely needed to be addressed with the new system:

- System is not available 24 hours 7 days a week
- No availability for student to check real-time status of Financial Aid application
- No option to email or fax Financial Aid award letter to student
- Lengthy batch processing times
- Significant involvement of IT Division staff to run routine queries
- No possibility to distribute application to large end-user population due to mainframe structure
- Inadequate report generation tools
- Application controlled by IT Division staff rather than by Financial Aid office
- System is shared with Medical Center resources, as a result the Office of Student Financial Aid has to plan their batch processing operations well in advance
- Excessive and expensive modification lead times

Based on these gaps, the team then drew up a proposed technical architecture. It addressed all of these gaps. See Exhibit 20-5 for a schematic of this process flow. In addition, it would eliminate several steps from the original functional process flow. These are the items in gray in Exhibit 20-1.

Adapt Action Steps

To position their findings to the College Administration, they tried to position the benefits to school officials as well as provide definitions and background on the major technical suggestions. They did this because they did not want to get overly technical with non IT people as it might only confuse rather than shed light on the problem.

So, the IT team stated their recommendation to replace the existing legacy system with an integrated client/server mainframe application. They prepared a one page Action Plan template to summarize the suggestion. See Exhibit 20-6.

The key benefits the team touched upon in their presentation to management included:

- Improved operational efficiency resulting from streamlined business processes
- More timely and complete reporting capabilities

- Reduction of paper-based transactions
- Ease of coordinating maintenance and support
- Reduced cycle times of high-volume repetitive business processes
- Increased flexibility in administrative controls and security protocols
- Reduced need for specialized knowledge to operate systems
- Reduced potential for human error due to duplicate data entry

Finally, the team discussed change management issues with the college administration. During the implementation phase, the IT Division's ability to facilitate the processes of end user training and communication will be critical to the success of the project and managing change. The team felt the training efforts should be coordinated centrally by the IT Division, as education is more effective when provided just in time, as the user needs it. Equally important to the implementation process will be the Public Relations efforts, as the IT Division communicates its progress and successes to the user community. These efforts should include publishing internal newsletters and web pages highlighting successful transition activities, documenting the business value resulting from the transition and maintaining a clear, consistent vision and message about the objectives of transition.

Conclusion

The IT group was able to devise a solution for the new Financial Aid System by taking a continuous improvement approach rather than just jumping in and trying to fix what they felt was wrong. Ultimately they produced an action plan that was better positioned to meet the functional users needs.

Exhibit 20-1: Map of the current Financial Aid Process at College A

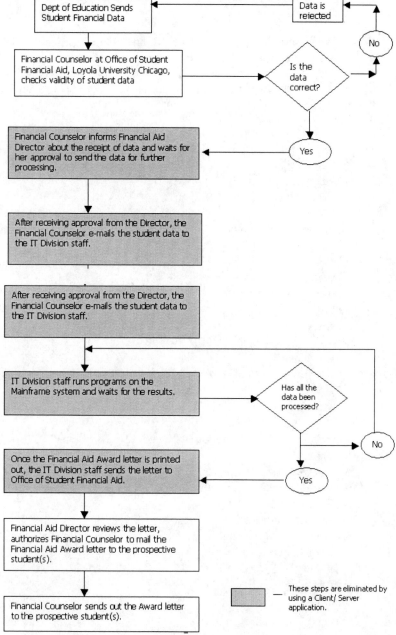

Exhibit 20-2: Example of survey sent to IT department heads

Dear Sir/Madam,

We are an IT group from College A. We are making changes to our financial aid systems. In order to do gather information from other highly reputed universities, we have prepared this short survey. This will help us make better decisions about the new system we put in place. There are only 5 questions and it will take less than 5 minutes of your time. These few minutes will greatly assist us in our research project.

1. Which system are you currently using to process student financial aid applications?
   o Legacy Mainframe System
   o Integrated Client/Server System
   o Others

2. What software are you currently using for your financial aid system?
   o PeopleSoft
   o SAP
   o Datatel
   o Oracle
   o SCT
   o Others

3. How long have you used this software product?
   o 1 – 6 Months
   o 6 Months – 1 Year
   o 1 – 3 Years
   o Over 3 Years
   o Never Used

4. Overall, how satisfied are you with this software product?
   o Not at all satisfied
   o Somewhat satisfied
   o Neutral (Neither Dissatisfied nor Satisfied)
   o Somewhat Satisfied
   o Very Satisfied

5. Would you recommend this application to other similar institutions?
   o Very Unlikely
   o Unlikely
   o Undecided
   o Likely
   o Very Likely

Exhibit 20-3: List of external resources

- *"Management Implications of Installing a Modern Financial Aid System"*, Geiger, Joseph J., Journal of Systems Management v43n3, (Mar 1992): p.6-9
- *"Princeton Taps Java to Extend its Financial Systems"*, Brown, Ted Smalley, InfoWorld v20n39, (Sep 28, 1998): p.66
- *"University of Illinois Gets Lessons in Client/Server Solutions"*, Quinlan, Tom, InfoWorld v19n1, (Jan 6, 1997): p.49
- *"Developing a Student Information System at East Texas State"*, Russell, Fred, Journal of Systems Management v43n3, (Mar 1992): p.10-11
- *"University of Iowa: Expecting More From Their Mainframes"*, Anonymous, Health Management Technology v19n1, (Jan 1998): p.20
- *"One University's Approach to the Requirements of Academic Computing"*, Lancaster, Ronald L.; Strouble, Dennis D., Journal of Systems Management v43n3, (Mar 1992): p.19-20,31
- *"University Switching from Batch to On-Line Operation with Aid of DBMS"*, Anonymous, Computerworld v16n43, (Oct 25, 1982): p. Special Report 42
- *"Towards the Design of Robust Information Systems,"* El Sawy, O. A., and Nanus, B., Journal of MIS (5:4), 1989, pp. 33-54.
- *"More Access, Easier 2000 Fix"*, Fryer, Bronwyn, Information Week n678, (Apr 1998): p.16SS-18SS
- *"The Case for ERP Systems"*, Dilip Wagle, The McKinsey Quarterly, 1998 Number 2, p. 131-138
- *"A Second Wind for ERP"*, Dorien James, Malcolm L. Wolf, , The McKinsey Quarterly, 2000 Number 2, p. 100-107
- *"The Trend Towards Client/Server Computing"*, National Electronic Commerce Resource Center v3/97 (Mar 1997): www.tda.ecrc.ctc.com
- *"Database Management Systems"*, Prof. Holowczak of Zicklin School of Business, City University of New York.
- *"Recombinations: Client/Server Computing in the 1990s"*, Patton, Peter C., University of Pennsylvania's Online Computing Magazine V8.5 (Feb 1992)

Exhibit 20-4: Flowchart of Grade Entry Process

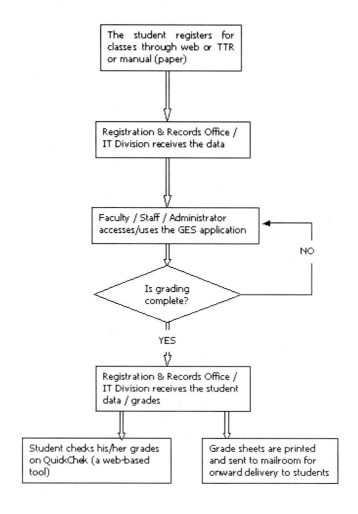

Exhibit 20-5: Schematic of proposed technical architecture

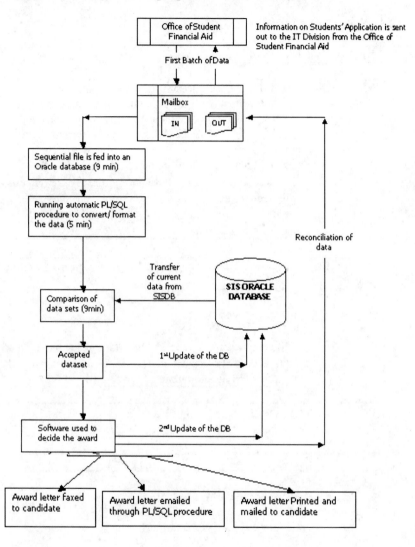

Exhibit 20-6: Action Plan

DEPARTMENT NAME: Information Technology (IT) Division

RECOMMENDATION: Replace existing legacy mainframe programs of the student Financial Aid system with an integrated client/server application. This will enable the collection, sharing, analysis, and reporting of data with greater efficiency and accuracy. Some benefits of client/server architecture over mainframe computing are:

- Reduced lead time for system enhancements
- Ad-hoc reporting tools that do not require programmer assistance
- Increased end user control of system
- Reduced cost of operation
- Graphical user interfaces

IDENTIFIED PROBLEMS: The current mainframe environment poses several problems:

- Excessive and expensive modification lead times
- High overall costs
- Inadequate report generation tools
- Application control by the IT Division, rather than by data owners
- IT Division's staff spend more time in preparing reports and less on application development

---

PERSON IN CHARGE: Mary Smith, Vice President, IT Division, and John Smith, Associate Director - Systems and Procedures, Office of Student Financial Aid

---

ACTION STEPS:
- Create a vision for the future usage of the Financial Aid system
- Gather system and end user data requirements
- Identify potential software vendors for the future client/server Financial Aid system
- Create an implementation plan and timeline for the move to an integrated, enterprise-wide business application
- Execute project plan for business application replacement
- Schedule training for IT Division staff and end users

Chapter Twenty One: Conclusion and Wrap Up

Well, we began this book hoping to help the new manager think about continuous improvement. Along the way we've learned about a methodology to help in this endeavor along with multiple tools and movements to spark creative insights.

The case studies hopefully will motivate the reader by external example, proving you can improve your processes if you take a systematic approach, and work hard.

As a manager the world changes. I remember just the other day I was at a social function and an executive of a professional services firm was talking to me. He said to me that life as an executive is so very different than a few years ago when he was simply known as "staff." Back then, he stated, "I had little worries and people told me what to do." Now, he talked of a world where senior management constantly needs updates on how he is doing and if he is working toward improving the organization. "It's an entirely different ballgame," he stated.

The best advice I can give to any manager would be to be proactive. Don't sit back in your office and revel in your being a manager. I am not trying to be negative or say you don't deserve it, but you are put into your position because you have been earmarked as a leader. Remember that.

As a leader, you're expected to always improve yourself and those you manage. Don't be complacent. Don't be on the defensive. Get out there and create change. By improving yourself and what it is you manage, you'll be helping your organization become a better one. That initiative and result is not something that goes overlooked by management.

Good Luck and go get 'em!

About the Author

Jeffrey A. Berk is Vice President of Products and Strategy for KnowledgeAdvisors, a learning measurement software company. In his current role, Berk works with clients to implement the organization's proprietary analytics software Metrics that Matter™ that helps organizations measure and value their learning investments.

Prior to joining KnowledgeAdvisors Berk worked for nine years with Andersen. While with Andersen he was the Manager of Benchmarking Services. In that role, Berk wrote the Andersen Benchmarking Methodology. He also spearheaded the development of quantitative and qualitative benchmarking tools to measure the effectiveness of client business processes.

Berk also teaches a graduate school course on performance improvement at Loyola University in Chicago and at Northwestern's Kellogg School in Evanston Illinois. He designed and developed the course curriculum.

He has participated in numerous performance improvement projects in the U.S., Europe and Australia. He has spoken on these topics and has been quoted and published in periodicals such as *Workforce Magazine, Fortune, IndustryWeek, The CPA Journal,* and *CLO Magazine.*

Berk, a CPA, began his professional career first working as an auditor before moving to consulting at Andersen. He has an MBA from the University of Chicago and degrees in business and accounting from the University of Kansas.

Performance Improvement Workshops, Training and Consulting

Jeffrey teaches a one or two day workshop version of his Performance Improvement class taught at Loyola University and Northwestern University. These workshops are excellent sources of business insight emphasizing key concepts of this book. They are wonderful training programs for newly promoted managers or any manager targeted for leadership potential or tasked with a performance improvement initiative.

Jeffrey is available to teach the workshops for corporations, universities, and the public sector. Customized workshops and training sessions are also available upon request.

Jeffrey also provides consulting services to organizations implementing performance improvement initiatives. Jeffrey and his team can provide guidance, support, and resources to bear on performance improvement gaps.

Finally, this book has been a useful guide to new managers and others tasked with leading change in business processes. If you desire to order copies of this book for a training program or for your employees please contact Jeffrey for volume discounts on book orders.

Please contact Jeffrey for more information about workshops, training or consulting. Jeffrey is available at jeffreyberk@yahoo.com.

Notes and References

Chapter One: Performance Improvement Methodology
1. C.J. Clark, The UN/CEFACT Unified Modelling Methodology, March 28, 2000, p. 2
2. National Productivity Review; Summer 1997; pp. 5-12; "Synchronized Team Thinking: The Secret to Continuous Improvement at Lucent Technologies"
3. Quality Progress; February 1999; pp. 31-32; "Quality Management and Continuous Improvement at Campbell"
4. David A. Garvin, "Building a Learning Organization," *Harvard Business Review*, July-August 1993
5. Continuous Improvement Methodology based upon "Benchmarking and Best Practices Review Methodology" Andersen, 2000.
6. Arthur Andersen Global Best Practices Knowledge Base; "Out of the Box Benchmarking Examples," 1995
7. Steven M. Hronec, Vital Signs: Using Quality, Time and Cost Performance Measures To Chart Your Company's Future ,1993
8. McAdam, Rodney, "An Integrated Business Improvement Methodology to Refocus Business Improvement Efforts," *Business Process Reengineering and Management Journal*, 63,2,no.1 1996
9. Perlmutter, Deborah F; Maleck, Margaret Richards, Helen; "The Birth of Pride," *Nursing Management*, August 2002, no. 8, pp. 566-581
10. Bisson, Barbara; Folk, Valerie Smith, Martin; "Case Study: How to do a business process improvement," *Journal for Quality and Participation,* January/February 2000, p.58-63
11. LaHay, Charles W; Noble, James S; "A framework for business system and quality management integration," *International Journal of Quality and Reliability Management*, no. 6, 1998,p. 31-32
12. Kappes, Sandy, "Putting your IDEF0 model to work," *Business Process Management Journal*, p.151 no. 2, 1997
13. Supply Chain Council, "Supply-Chain Operations Reference Model"
14. Shorey, Everett, "Process redesign," *Executive Excellence*, v10n10 Oct 1993, p16-17
15. Patching, David, "Business process re-engineering: What's in a name?" *Management Services*, v38 n11, Nov 1994, pp.8-11
16. Webster, Anne, "Continuous improvement improved," *Work Study*, 142-146, 48, no. 4, 1999
17. Gilberto, Phillip A, "The road to business process improvement – can you get there from here?" *Hospital Materiel Management Quarterly*, v17n2, Nov 1995, pp.12-20
18. Knapp, Marian L, "Applying Continuous Improvement to community health," *Quality Progress*, v31n2, February 1998, pp.43-47

19. Povey, Barry, "The development of a best practice business process improvement methodology," *Benchmarking for Quality Management & Technology*, no.1 1998, p. 27

Chapter Two: Performance Improvement Movements
1. American Society for Quality; http://www.asq.org/index.html
2. J. Gonzalez-Benito, A.R. Martinez-Lorente, B.G. Dale, "Business Process Re-engineering to Total Quality Management", *Business Process Management Journal*, Vol 5. No. 4 pp. 345-358, 1999
3. Thomas Pyzdek, "Quality Profession Must Learn to Heed Its Own Advice", *Quality Progress*, June 1999
4. http://www.iso.ch/
5. Robert, L. Desatnick, "Does QS 9000 Really Protect the Customer?", *Association For Quality & Participation*, Spring 2001
6. Binshan Lin and Kelly C. Hidalgo, "Pairing Quality Assurance And Quality Control At Frymaster Corporation," *National Productivity Review*, Summer 1999
7. http://www.quality.nist.gov/
8. Hampton Scott Tonk, "Integrating ISO 9001: 2000 And the Baldrige Criteria," *Quality Progress*, August 2000
9. http://www.isixsigma.com/
10. Lisa Connor, "Six Sigma" presentation to Loyola University on January 17, 2001
11. Murad S. Shah, "Loyola University Presentation" presented at Loyola University on September 13, 2001
12. Roderick A. Munro, "Linking Six Sigma With QS-9000," *Quality Progress*, May 2000
13. Rochelle Rucker, "Citibank Increases Customer Loyalty With Defect-Free Processes," *Association for Quality and Participation*, Fall 2000
14. Anthony C. Fletcher, "Building World-Class Performance with the Balrdrige Criteria,"*Inside Quality*, December 2000
15. John S. Ramburg, "Six Sigma: Fad or Fundamental?" *Inside Quality*, December 2000
16. Ronald D. Snee, "Dealing With the Achilles' Heel Of Six Sigma Initiatives," *Quality Progress*, March 2001
17. Hal Plotkin, "Six Sigma: What It Is and How to Use It," *Harvard Management Update*, June 1999
18. Dawne Shand, "Six Sigma," *Computerworld*, March 5, 2001
19. Tully, Chris *"Case Study: ISO at Industrial Product Company A,"* ISOM 481 Performance Improvement Class, Loyola University Chicago, October 2002
20. Rivkin, Loren *"Case Study: ISO Safety Products,"* ISOM 481 Performance Improvement Class, Loyola University Chicago, October 2002
21. Uhrich, Kristen *"Clarke American and the Malcolm Baldrige Quality Award,"* ISOM 481 Performance Improvement Class, Loyola University Chicago, October 2002

22. www.clarkeamerican.com
23. Schwartz, Stephanie *"Case Study: ISO Safety Products,"* ISOM 481 Performance Improvement Class, Loyola University Chicago, October 2002
24. Motorola, Inc. *Motorola Six Sigma Services.* Retrieved from the world wide web at http://mu.motorola.com/sigmasplash.htm. Copyright 1994-2002.
25. Pyzdek, Thomas. *Motorola's Six Sigma Program.* Quality Digest. Retrieved from the world wide web at www.qualitydigest.com/dec97/html/motsix.html. Copyright 1997.
26. Pyzdek, Thomas. *Six Sigma at Motorola.* The Complete Guide to Six Sigma, Chapter 1. Retrieved from the world wide web at www.qualityamerica.com. Copyright 1999 by Quality Publishing.
27. Sester, Dennis. Motorola: *A Tradition of Quality.* Quality: 30-34. Copyright October 2001 by Business News Publishing Company.
28. Grimaldi, Gabriel *"Motorola: Success with Six Sigma,"* ISOM 481 Performance Improvement Class, Loyola University Chicago, October 2002
29. Gabor, Andrea., "Management: Ford Embraces Six Sigma." The New York Times. June 13, 2001.
30. Garsten, Ed., "Job one: Ford says Six Sigma techniques have revived 'flatling' quality." Yahoo News. February 21, 2002.
31. "Ford Embraces Six Sigma." IsixSigma.com. June 13, 2001
32. "Ford Maximizes Six Sigma Efforts with Micrografx Solutions." The Auto Channel.com. October 2, 2000.
33. "Ford Six Sigma Busts Surface Flaws." Quality Magazine. January 1, 2002.
34. Paton, Scott M., "No Small Change: Making Quality Job 1, Again." Quality Digest. September 2001.
35. Quality Digest Sept., 2001. http://www/qualitydigest.com
36. Jiang, Meiyi, *"Six Sigma in Ford"* ISOM 481 Performance Improvement Class, Loyola University Chicago, October 2002
37. Bhovati, Pattapanee, *"Ford Motor Company and Six Sigma," "* ISOM 481 Performance Improvement Class, Loyola University Chicago, October 2002

Chapter Three: Performance Improvement Tools

1. Michael Brassard & Diane Ritter, " The Memory Jogger™ II- A Pocket Guide of Tools for Continuous Improvement and Effective Planning," GOAL/QPC 1994
2. "Affinity Diagrams," University of Vermont, Office of Audit Services, March 2001
3. Department of Industrial Engineering, Clemson University, "Continuous Quality Improvement Server – Cause and Effect Diagram"
4. "Control Chart Basics," Skymark Corporation, 2001
5. "What is Flowcharting?," Pennsylvania State Governors Office
6. Sid Sytsma and Katherine Manley, The Quality Tools Cookbook, last modified June 9, 1999
7. Flowchart symbols from Microsoft Excel 2000, Autoshape, Flowchart

8. McQuarter, R.E.; Scurr, C.H Dale, B.G. Hillman, P G, "Using Quality Tools and Techniques Successfully,"*TQM Magazine*, V7 N6, p. 37-42, 1995

9. Horai, Joann, "Tool Kit for Quality,"*Association Management*, V45 N11, p. 63-69, November 1993

10. Z. He; G. Staples; M. Ross; I. Court, "Fourteen Japanese Quality Tools in Software Process Improvement," *TQM Magazine*, 40, 8 no.4, p.40, 1996

11. Stockley, Alan, "Planning and Management Tools to Help with Provision of Effective Health Care," *International Journal of Health Care Quality Assurance*, V8, N5, p.24-29, 1995

12. Anonymous, "Seven Management and Planning Tools," *Communication of the ACM*, V36, N10, p.87, October 1993

13. Okes, Duke, "Organize Your Quality Tool Belt," *Quality Progress,* V35, N7, p.25-29, July 2002

14. Eshelman, Debra; Cooksey, Clifton, "The Quality Toolbox," *Training Supplement*, p. 19-30, April 1992

15. Carter, Carla C, "Seven Basic Quality Tools," *HR Magazine*, V37 N1, p. 81-83, January 1992

16. Hart, Marilyn K, "Quality Tools for Improvement," *Production & Inventory Management Journal*, V33 N1, p.59-63, First Quarter 1992

Chapter Four: Diagnostic Tools

1. Travis A. McCann and James T. Tashima, <u>Training Needs Assessment Tool</u>, 1994

2. "*General* Motors Does a Needs Analysis," *Training & Development*, pp. 103-104, May 1997

3. Berk, Jeffrey A, "Needs Assessments," Loyola University, 2001

4. Henbest, David A, "Analysis/Design/Approach," KnowledgeAdvisors, 2001

5. Joe Dumas, *Usability Testing Methods*, Usability Professionals' Association, 2000

6. "Education, Training and Development Prepares Ford for Future," *Corporate University Review*, May/June 1998, pp. 18-30

7. "Top of the Charts," *Industry Week Growing Companies*, June 1998, p.1, pp.30-39

8. "How the Smallest Baldrdige Award Winner Creates Big Business," *Association for Quality Participation*, January/February 2000, pp. 6-14

9. "Training Diagnostic Tool Questionnaire," KnowledgeAdvisors, 2002

10. "Training Diagnostic Tool Results Report," KnowledgeAdvisors, 2002

Chapter Five: Historic data analysis

1. Randy Kaploe, "Using Historical Data to Help Move Toward Continuous Improvement," Lecture at Loyola University November 2001

2. "Business-Critical Data Warehousing Gains Momentum in Supply Chain Management, "*Global Logistics and Supply Chain Strategies*, November/December 1999, pp.44-50

3. "Sallie Mae Links Call Center Measures to Organization Mission, Positive Results," *Measurement In Practice*, Issue 17, Third Quarter 1999, pp. 1-6
4. "Ergonomics Makes its Mark in Enhancing Human Performance," *Target*, Volume 13, No. 4, September/October 1997, pp. 12-23
5. "There's No Such Thing as a 'Lost' Customer," *Customer Support Management*, March/April 2000, pp.44-50, 99-103
6. "Digging for Data for Educators," *KM World*, November 1999, pp.12-13
7. "We've Got the Data, Now What Do We Do With It?" *1 to 1,* July 2001, pp. 3,5, 20-26
8. "Reinventing Training at Rockwell Collins," *Training*, April 2000, pp. 64-70
9. Steven M. Hronec, Vital Signs: Using Quality, Time and Cost Performance Measures To Chart Your Company's Future ,1993
10. Arthur Andersen Global Best Practices Knowledge Base; "Process 13 Manage Organization and Change," 1999
11. Garver, Michael S,"Try New Data-Mining Techniques," *Marketing News*, p.31-33, 36, no.19, September 16, 2002
12. Adams, Larry, "Mining the World of Quality Data," *Quality* p. 36-40. no.8 August 2001
13. *The Internet Glossary of Statistical Terms* written by Howard S. Hoffman, Professor Emeritus of Psychology, Bryn Mawr College and Programmed by Russell D. Hoffman, Owner and Chief Programmer, The Animated Software Company

Chapter Six: Questionnaires, Interviews and Focus Groups
1. Arthur Andersen, "Using Focus Groups to Process Map," Global Best Practices Knowledge Base
2. Dorine C. Andrews and Susan K. Stalick, Business Reengineering, The Survival Guide
3. Louis M. Rea and Richard A. Parker, Designing and Conducting Survey Research, Second Edition, 1997
4. Arlene Fink and Jacqueline Kosecoff, How to Conduct Surveys, A Step-By-Step Guide, Second Edition, 1998
5. Susan E. Gaddis, "How to Design Online Surveys," *Training and Development*, June 1998, p. 67-71
6. "ESS?" *Internal Auditor*, April 1999, p. 59-63
7. "Tapping into People," *Quality Progress*, April 2000, p. 74-79
8. "How to Create a Customer Loyalty Survey," *Customer Support Management*, September 1999, p.46-5
9. "Behavioral Interviewing at Cigna," *HR Focus*, December 1998, p.6

Chapter Seven: Checklist for Excellence in Business Processes
1. Manny Rosenfeld, "Excellent Business Processes," presented at Loyola University, January 2001
2. Cary Cohen, *Complete Company Policies and Procedures Manual,* 1992

3. Carl E. Larson and Frank M. LaFasto, <u>Teamwork : What Must Go Right/What Can Go Wrong</u>,1989
4. "Steelcase Canada Ltd.: A Smarter Way to Work," *Target*, pp. 37-40, September/October 1996
5. "Time Out!" *Inbound Logistics*, June 1997; pp.30-37
6. "TRW Canada Ltd.," *IndustryWeek,* October 19, 1998, pp. 58-60
7. Ron Webb, "Benchmarking – APQC Style," presentation to Loyola University, November 15, 2000
8. Mathew J. Ferrero, "Self-Directed Work Teams Untax the IRS," *Personnel Journal*, July 1994, pp. 66-71

Chapter Eight: Managing Business Risk
1. <u>Enterprise-wide Risk Management: Strategies for Linking Risk and Opportunity</u> by James Deloach and Nick Temple, December 2000, *Financial Times*, London, UK
2. *Managing Business Risk, An Integrated Approach*, J.W. DeLoach, 1995, Economist Intelligence Unit, New York, NY
3. Arthur Andersen Business Risk Management Knowledge Base; 1997
4. *How to Manage Risks, 2nd Edition*. LLP London, Bannister, J. 1997
5. *Risk: Analysis, Assessment and Management*, Ansell, J. & Wharton, F. (Eds., 1992)
6. *Microsoft's Universe of Risk*, CFO. March 1997, pp. 69-72, Teach, Edward
7. <u>Business Policies and Procedures System</u>, American Business Resources Inc., 1995
8. <u>Complete Policies and Procedures Manual,</u> Cary Cohen, Prentice Hall,1991

Chapter Nine: Creating Action Plans
1. Mosaics: SHRM Focuses on Workplace Diversity; Vol.3, No.2; March 1997
2. "Improving and Controlling Low-Volume, High Dollar Jobs," *Journal for Quality and Participation*, July/August 1999, p. 21-25
3. "Results First at GTE," *Training*, May 1997, p.64
4. "The Employee-Customer-Value Chain at Sears," *Harvard Business Review*, January-February 1998; p.82-97,
5. Jeffrey Berk, "Creating Action Plans," Loyola University, 2000
6. Jeffrey Berk, "Action Plan Template and Example," Loyola University, 2000

Chapter Ten: Change management principles
1. "Change Management," Jeffrey Berk Loyola University 2001
2. "Organizational Change: Managing the Human Side," American Productivity and Quality Center, 1997
3. "Commitment to Change," Training and Development, August 1996, p, 22-26
4. "Change Management 101: A Primer," Fred Nickols, 2000

5. "Basic Context for Organizational Change," Used by The Management Assictance Program for Nonprofits, Carter McNamara, PhD, 1999
6. "Mastering Change: Why Organizational Change Fails," Mark Sanborn, CSP, CPAE
7. "Making Change," Darwin Magazine, Philip Diehl, June 2000
8. "The Enduring Skills of Change Leaders," Leader to Leader, No.13 Summer 1999, Rosabeth Moss Kanter
9. "The Changing Workplace: How Flexible is Your Company?"NJSCPA, October 2000, Ellen M. Riccardi

Chapter Eleven: Training, training, training
1. Donald L. Kirkpatrick, Evaluating Training Programs: The Four Levels, 2nd Edition, Berrett-
    Koehler Publishers, Inc, San Francisco, 1998
2. Learning Taxonomy, KnowledgeAdvisors, 2001
3. Jack J. Phillips, Return on Investment in Training and Performance Improvement Programs,
    Gulf Publishing Company, Houston, Texas, 1997
4. References to ADDIE: Donald R. Clark, 1998, updated 2000
5. Arthur Andersen Global Best Practices Knowledge Base; 1998

Chapter Twelve: Building a Knowledge Management System
1. "Chrysler's New Know-Mobiles," Knowledge Management, May 1999, p.58-66
2. "How Skandia Generates Its Future Faster," Fast Company, December 1996/January 1997, p.58
3. "Planning for Knowledge Management," Quality Progress, March 2000, p. 57-62
4. "Who Knows?" CFO, December 1999, p.83-86
5. "The Knowledge Management Paradox," National Productivity Review, Winter 1999, p.59-64
6. "Strategies for Implementing Knowledge Management: Role of Human Resources Management," Journal of Knowledge Management, July 2000 p. 337-345
7. "The State of KM," Knowledge Management, May 2001, p. 31-37
8. "Managing Knowledge and Learning at Unipart," Knowledge Management Review, July 2001, p.14-17
9. "Rx for Learning: A University's Knowledge Management System is Transforming Medical Education," CIO, February 2001, p. 102-110
10. "Overcoming Cultural Barriers to Sharing Knowledge," Journal of Knowledge Management, June 2001, p. 76-85
11. "How to Measure the Value of Knowledge Management," Knowledge Management Review, March 2001, p.4, 20
12. "The Entrepreneurial Spirit at Capital One," Knowledge Management Review, Volume 3, Issue 2, May/June 2000, p.16-19

13. Arthur Andersen and The American Productivity and Quality Center, <u>The Knowledge Management Assessment Tool</u>, 1995
14. "The Knowledge Management Book," Arthur Andersen, 1998
15. "Those Who Can, Teach," *The Economist*, October 28, 1995
16. "Never Stop Learning" by Mary C. Driscoll, *CFO,* February 1995
17. "Harley Shifts Gears" by Gina Imperato, *Fast Company,* June/July 1997
18. *Industry Week,* Conference on Innovation, March 13 and 14, 1995
19. Nonaka, Hirotaka Takeuchi, *The Knowledge-Creating Company* (Oxford University Press), 1995, pp. 135-140
20. "How 3M Manages Its Global Laboratory Network" by Geoffrey C. Nicholson, *Research Technology Management,* July/August 1994
21. "Inside Four Intranets," *Financial Executive,* July/August 1997
22. Thomas H. Davenport and Laurence Prusak, *Working Knowledge*, 1997, Chapter 8, pp. 116 and 156
23. Skandia AFS Balanced Report on Intellectual Capital 1993 and1994 and Interim Report 1995
24. "Building a Learning Organization at Coopers & Lybrand" by Judith Rosenblum, and Reed Keller, *Planning Review,* September/October 1994
25. "Preparing for the Knowledge Economy" by Patricia Seybold, *Chief Executive,* January/February 1995
26. "Unleashing the Power of Learning" by Steven E. Prokesch, *Harvard Business Review,* September/October 1997
27. "Army Devises System to Decide What Does, and Does Not, Work – Corporate American Watches," *The Wall Street Journal* via Dow Jones, 5/23/97

Chapter Thirteen: Feedback and Communicating Results

1. Jack J. Phillips, Ron D. Stone, Patricia Pullium Phillips; <u>The Human Resources Scorecard, Measuring the Return on Investment</u>, Butterworth Heinemann, Woburn MA, 2001

Chapter Fourteen: Measuring Results

1. Jack J. Phillips, Ron D. Stone, Patricia Pullium Phillips; <u>The Human Resources Scorecard, Measuring the Return on Investment</u>, Butterworth Heinemann, Woburn MA, 2001
2. Jack J. Phillips; <u>Return on Investment in Training and Performance Improvement Initiatives</u>, Gulf Publishing Company, Houston, Texas, 1997
3. "Beyond ROI To Enterprise Value Creation," by Bruce D. Colbert, The E-Business Executive Daily, June 25, 2002
4. "ROI: New Brand Day," by Kris Frieswick, CFO.com, November 28, 2001
5. "ROI: Return on Information," by Justin Kestelyn, Intelligent Enterprise, February 1, 2002

Chapter Fifteen: Project Management

1. Frame, Davidson, J., *Project Management Competence: Building Key Skills for Individuals, Teams and Organizatons*, San Francisco, Josey-Bass Publishers, 1999
2. Duncan, William, R., *A Guide to the Project Management Body of Knowledge*, Upper Darby, PA, Project Management Institute, 1996
3. Heerkens, Gary, R., *Project Management*, New York, McGraw Hill, 2002

Chapter Sixteen: Case - Supply Chain Function

1. F. Ian Stuart and David M. McCutcheon, "The Manager's Guide to Supply Chain Management," *Business Horizons,* 2000
2. David Bovet and Joseph Martha, "Unlocking the Rusty Supply Chain," *Harvard Business Review*, 2000
3. "Self –Assessment: A Foundation for Supply Chain Success," *Supply Chain Management,* July/August 2000, pp. 81-87
4. "Debunking Five Supply Chain Myths,"*Supply Chain Management Review*, March/April 2000, pp.52-58
5. "Good and Getting Better: Continuous Improvement Transforms Supply Chain," *APICS-The Performance Advantage*, May 2001, pp. 5, 11, 49-51
6. "Study Shows Improving Supply Chain Can Recover Revenue," APICS, July 1997, p. 14
7. Arthur Andersen Global Best Practices Knowledge Base;2000
8. Candidate Entry Form/Questionnaire, "America's Best Plants," *Industry Week*, 1999
9. Ajay Sharma, Tom Masterson, Joe Waske, and Lisa Connor, "Benchmarking the Order Entry Process for Continuous Improvement," Loyola University ISOM 481, February 2001

Chapter Seventeen: Case - Customer Relationship Management (CRM) Function

1. Darcie Capretta, Chris Isaac, Leslie Guckert, "Process Improvement Project: Trade Association A Marketing Process," Loyola University ISOM 481, February 2001
2. "Study Identifies the Top 5 Keys to Sales Success," *National Underwriter*, September 9, 1996, p. 15-16
3. "The Traits of Great Sales Forces," *Sales and Marketing Management*, October 2000, pp. 67-72
4. "Marketing for Survival," *CIO*, April 15, 1998, pp.44-48
5. "In Your Face," *CFO*, July 2000, pp. 109-118
6. Arthur Andersen Global Best Practices Knowledge Base;2000
7. "A Crash Course in Customer Relationship Management," *Harvard Management Update*, March 2000, p. 3

Chapter Eighteen: Case- The Finance Function
1. "Walking the Talk: Here's the Real Example," *Journal for Quality and Participation*, January/February 1996, pp. 30-34
2. "Champions of Change," *CFO*, December 1997, p. 35-40
3. "Finance Tightens Belt," *InternetWeek*, September 14, 1998, p.40

4. Finance and Accounting Diagnostic Tool, Arthur Andersen Global Best Practices Knowledge Base;2000
5. Ari Shabat, Natan Weiss, "Benchmarking: A Case Study, Medicare Billing Process," Loyola University ISOM 481, February 2001

Chapter Nineteen: Case- The Human Resources Function
1. "HR Audit Presentation," presentation to Loyola University, January 2001
2. Arthur Andersen Global Best Practices Knowledge Base; 2000
3. "The Pursuit of Excellence in HR Management at the US DOT," Journal of Cost Management, January 2001, p.15
4. "Out of the Red, Into the Blue," Workforce, March 2000, p. 50-52
5. "Benchmarking Human Resources Effectiveness," Controller Magazine, March 1997, p.35-37
6. "Being Direct," Human Resources Executive, March 4, 1999, p. 44-46
7. "KeyCorp Boosts Staff Access In Automating its HR System," Bank System + Technology, January 1998, p.58

Chapter Twenty: Case - The Information Technology Function
1. "The Enterprise of the 21st Century," Knowledge Management; January 2000, pp.28-50
2. "IT Delivers for UPS," IndustryWeek, December 21, 1998, pp.58-64
3. "United Front," InformationWeek, July 20, 1998, pp. 38-44
4. "Gap Refashions IS," InformationWeek, April 13, 1998, pp.105-108
5. "Payback Time: Making Sure ROI Measures Up," Information Week, August 2001, pp. 34-42
6. APQC Consortium Benchmarking Study Best-Practice Report; "Recruiting and Retaining IT Talent; 1999
7. APQC Consortium Benchmarking Study Best-Practice Report; Aligning Information Technology with Corporate Strategy; 1999
8. Abhishek Sharma, Dimpsy Teckchandani, Gunjan Badjatya, Jyoti Mishra, Thomas Thalakottu, Yamauchi Yasutomo, "Information Systems Continuous Improvement Project," Loyola University ISOM 481, November 2001